# Knowledge and Practice:
# Representations and Identities

This Reader is one of a series of three which form part of *Curriculum, learning and society: investigating practice* (E846), a course belonging to the Open University Masters in Education programme. The series consists of the following books:

*Learning and Practice: Agency and Identities* (edited by Patricia Murphy and Kathy Hall)

*Pedagogy and Practice: Culture and Identities* (edited by Kathy Hall, Patricia Murphy and Janet Soler)

*Knowledge and Practice: Representations and Identities* (edited by Patricia Murphy and Robert McCormick)

# The Open University Masters in Education

The Open University Masters in Education is now firmly established as the most popular postgraduate degree for education professionals in Europe, with around 3000 students registered each year. It is designed particularly for those with experience of teaching, the advisory service, educational administration or allied fields. Specialist lines in leadership and management, applied linguistics and special needs/inclusive education are available within the award. Successful study on the Masters entitles students to apply for entry into the Open University Doctorate in Education programme.

Details of this and other Open University courses can be obtained from the Student Registration and Enquiry Service, The Open University, PO Box 197, Milton Keynes MK7 6BJ, United Kingdom; telephone: +44 (0) 845 300 609; e-mail: general-enquiries@open.ac.uk.

Alternatively, you may wish to visit the Open University website at http://www. open.ac.uk, where you can learn more about the wide range of courses and packs offered at all levels by The Open University.

# Knowledge and Practice: Representations and Identities

Edited by
Patricia Murphy and Robert McCormick

Los Angeles • London • New Delhi • Singapore

The Open University

The Open University
Walton Hall
Milton Keynes
MK7 6AA
United Kingdom
www.open.ac.uk

First Published in 2008

SAGE Publications Ltd
1 Oliver's Yard
55 City Road
London EC1Y 1SP

SAGE Publications Inc.
2455 Teller Road
Thousand Oaks, California 91320

SAGE Publications India Pvt Ltd
B 1/I 1 Mohan Cooperative Industrial Area
Mathura Road
New Delhi 110 044

SAGE Publications Asia-Pacific Pte Ltd
33 Pekin Street #02-01
Far East Square
Singapore 048763

**Library of Congress Control Number: 2008920075**

**British Library Cataloguing in Publication data**

A catalogue record for this book is available from the British Library

ISBN 978-1-8478-7369-9
ISBN 978-1-8478-7370-5 (pbk)

Typeset by C&M Digitals (P) Ltd, Chennai, India
Printed by The Cromwell Press Ltd, Trowbridge, Wiltshire
Printed on paper from sustainable resources

# Contents

# Acknowledgements

We would like to thank the authors who contributed their chapters, as well as colleagues within and outside The Open University who helped with the preparation of the manuscripts. Special thanks are due to the following people for their assistance in the production of this book:

Sally Jones (course secretary)
Fulden Underwood (course manager)
Professor Valentina Klenowski (external assessor)
Gordon Bloomer (critical reader)
Gill Gowans (copublishing media developer)

**Chapter 2**

From: *Educational Researcher*, 27 (3), (AERA, 1998), pp. 11–22.

**Chapter 3**

From: *Educational Researcher*, 27 (2), (AERA, 1998), pp. 4–13.

**Chapter 4**

From: *International Journal of Educational Research*, 37 (Elsevier, 2002), pp. 1–15. Reproduced with permission.

**Chapter 5**

From: *Journal of Curriculum Studies*, 38 (1), 2006, pp. 31–48. Reprinted by permission of the publisher (Taylor & Francis Ltd, http://www.informaworld.com).

**Chapter 6**

From: *Music Education Research*, 3 (2), 2001, pp. 243–253. Reprinted by permission of the publisher (Taylor & Francis Ltd, http://www.informaworld.com).

**Chapter 7**

From: *Educational Communication and Information*, 1 (1), 2000, pp. 39–57. Reprinted by permission of the publisher (Taylor & Francis Ltd, http://www.informaworld.com).

**Chapter 8**

From: *British Educational Research Journal*, 26 (5), 2000, pp. 631–648. Reprinted by permission of the publisher (Taylor & Francis Ltd, http://www.informaworld.com).

**Chapter 11**

From: Roth, W.F. & Tobin, K. (eds.) *Science, Learning, Identity: Sociocultural and Cultural-Historical Perspectives*. (Rotterdam, Netherlands: Sense Publishers, 2007). Reproduced by kind permission of the publisher.

**Chapter 12**

From: *Journal of Research in Science Teaching*, 42 (7), pp. 807–828. © 2005 Wiley Periodicals, Inc. Reprinted with permission of John Wiley & Sons, Inc.

**Chapter 13**

From: *Pedagogy, Culture and Society*, 11 (1), 2003, pp. 11–30. Reprinted by permission of the publisher (Taylor & Francis Ltd, http://www.informaworld.com).

# Introduction

*Patricia Murphy and Robert McCormick*

The book is one of three readers examining relational views of learning, knowledge and pedagogy from a sociocultural perspective. Longstanding cultural heritages about the nature of knowledge continue to dominate Western education. The book provides a rich collection of readings that challenge this tradition, posit alternatives and provide tools for innovating change and transforming practice, such that learning is recognised as an intrinsically social and collective phenomenon and accords value to different ways of knowing that embrace those that learners bring.

There is much written about learning; what it is and what it is not, but often these accounts do not problematise the ontological and epistemological interrelationship. It is as though, in spite of what we might claim about our views of mind, knowledge is somehow different. We might argue, as Sfard puts it, that individual minds are not the principle source of their own development (Sfard, 2006: 156), but in practice in what we recognise as learning, and how we support and value it, we nevertheless deny the social nature of learning, assuming that learning processes are invariable and tasks are stable across diverse situations, contexts and learners. We have only to consider assessment at all levels to recognise that we give credence to assumptions that it tells us something generalisable and pre-existing about our learners. We do so without consideration of learners' cultural and historical lives and the consequence of this for what they learn and how they interact with tasks. In so doing, we continue to treat knowledge as if 'in the head'; a property of an individual. As Lave and Wenger (1991: 112) note, it 'engenders a fundamental conflict between learning to know and learning to display knowledge'. This demarcation between knowledge production and reproduction has major implications for how we understand both learning and pedagogy and importantly how we position learners. As Lave (2008) in this book, notes, ironically, by *not* making knowledge problematic in its relationship to how we understand mind, we reduce much of learning to a purely epistemological problem. To learn becomes understood as a movement away from the ignorance of the everyday to the specialised knowledge made available by experts. In so doing, we revitalise in our practice as educators, often unintentionally, the image of the learner as the empty vessel and knowledge as external and objective, that is, brought into the mind without recourse to a process of meaning-making.

Between those who theorise and research learning and knowledge production, and those who practise in the communities that feature in this research, there has over the last three decades emerged a consensus that meaning-making is an essential aspect of being in the world, and therefore that it is central to learning and knowing. What remains contentious is how the relationship between the individual and society, the collective, is understood in this process of meaning-making and therefore the nature of that meaning or knowing. In separating knowledge reproduction and creation and treating learning as an epistemological problem, we separate the individual and society. For others, the notion of the individual and society is treated as a continuum that is moved along as individuals' active knowledge, drawing on Vygotsky's (1986) distinction between everyday spontaneous concepts and scientific concepts, is transformed into culturally given and valued knowledge. According to Lave and Wenger (1991: 48), this reduces the social character of learning to a 'small aura of socialness' that provides the input through instruction and interaction for the process of individual acquisition of the culturally given. In both cases, mind remains individual and local. If, however, individual and society are treated as duality, such that the two entities are not in opposition or different in degree, rather as Wenger (1998: 62) describes it they form a unity: 'to understand one, it is necessary to understand the other'. Then mind is not local but distributed, situated between individuals in social action in cultural settings and within cultural, historical relationships (Cobb, 1999) and resides between individuals' interactions and reactions (Elwood, 2007). In viewing mind as non-local, 'meaning exists neither in us, nor in the world, but in the dynamic relation of living in the world' (Wenger, 1998: 54).

This participationist perspective on knowledge and learning makes the claim that 'patterned collective forms of distinctly human forms of doing are developmentally prior to the activities of the individual' (Sfard, 2006: 157). This view does not deny that biological givens underlie collective forms of life but that this collective life brings about all other human characteristics including, as Sfard points out, the individualising of the collective. As McDermott (1996: 277) puts it: 'The term *learning* simply glosses that some persons have achieved a particular relationship with each other, and it is in terms of these relations that information necessary to everyone's participation gets made available in ways that give people enough time on task to get good at what they do'. Learning is therefore perceived as re-enactments of collective activities and this is one source of contention in the current debate about the nature of knowledge and our metaphors for understanding it (Paavola et al., 2004).

Understanding self as relational and learning as being both a process of becoming competent and belonging, i.e. becoming a particular type of person, makes identity and knowledge interdependent. Learning in practice is therefore negotiating an identity (Wenger, 1998). In a social practice view of learning, which is concerned with achieving particular relations with others, experiencing mutuality and sustaining mutual engagements are critical to participation. It is this aspect of participation which highlights the need to consider from a sociocultural perspective what learners bring to settings and to communities with which they choose to, or are required to, engage. Mutual engagement 'draws on what we do and what we know, as well as our ability to connect meaningfully to what we don't do and don't know – that is the contributions and knowledge of others' (Wenger, 1998: 76). Therefore, in both trying to understand what is known and what is not known and how or if learning is occurring, learners' histories of participation, their understanding and ways of knowing, and the distance between them and the representations of knowledge made available through practice in settings, have to be attended to.

In articulating a particular sociocultural view of learning and knowledge, pedagogy is no longer defined as something that goes on in schools, rather it is central to any practice that 'takes up questions of how individuals learn, how knowledge is produced and how subject positions are constructed' (Giroux, 1992: 181 cited in González, 2005: 41). Such a perspective can therefore be usefully applied to any collective learning, be it becoming a reader as a young child, becoming a science learner in school, or becoming a particular person with a particular role within a community of practice.

In the book, we have selected several readings that adopt what we term a sociocultural approach to learning and knowledge, and which span educational and workplace settings and participants.

The book begins by looking at epistemological dilemmas such as the treatment of knowledge creation as separate and distinct from the knowledge reproduction that under-lies much of educational policy and practice. Readings explore the assumptions behind this position and offer alternative perspectives to consider the extent to which views of knowledge, as a commodity to be acquired, or as creative and productive participation, are useful in accounting for learning in both educational and workplace settings. In Chapter 1, Jean Lave, in a new contribution, challenges understandings of the everyday and locates common strategies in theorising about it and the epistemological implications. In so doing she identifies specious divisions between learning and using knowledge and learning and living. In particular, she challenges whether there is a need for a metaphor of knowledge creation as it divides the production of knowledge from the reproduction of knowledge. In arguing for a view of learning as a movement deeper into and through social existence, Lave suggests that knowing is creative and reproductive participation at the same time. This challenges common interpretations that a social practice theory of learning is about the reproduction of existing knowledge, as in the process of re-enacting collective activities, individuals improvise new practice and ongoing practice evolves.

Robert Sternberg, in Chapter 2, is not arguing from a sociocultural view but neverthe-less raises a fundamental challenge to viewing abilities, and therefore the capacity to know, as pre-existing. He argues that ability tests, typically standardised tests of IQ or of cogni-tive abilities widely used in education and the workplace, are treated as though their outcomes predict what people can do. He challenges the distinctions drawn between abil-ity measures and achievement measures, instead arguing that they are constructs that rep-resent developing forms of expertise and are not different in nature. No assessment, according to Sternberg, can specify the asymptote a learner can achieve. He is not critical of ability tests per se, seeing all tests as informative and potentially complementary, argu-ing that there is no one right kind of assessment. What he does challenge is the narrow representation of valued knowledge enshrined in testing and in formal instruction. He seeks instead a much richer perspective which allows for learners' diverse styles and ways of knowing, in the same way that experts reveal diversity in their use of knowledge.

Anna Sfard's seminal piece on metaphors for learning, in Chapter 3, delineates the rela-tional views of learning and of knowledge that underpin these metaphors and the predomi-nance of usage of the acquisition metaphor. In discussing these metaphors, Sfard considers what they offer as ways of understanding learning and the nature of knowledge. She argues that in the participation metaphor, associated with a sociocultural perspective, the issue of transfer of knowledge and acquisition terms, such as concepts and knowledge itself, are under-mined and asks the question 'what would subjects become if the participation metaphor was to become the dominant interpretive framework?' Debates of this kind, about both institutional reified knowledge and workplace knowledge, are crucial if a sociocultural perspective is taken seriously to inform how we engage with and support learners. At the point of writing the chapter, Sfard was of the view that current understanding meant that both metaphors were needed, noting the limitations of theorising and the localised nature of sense-making. She also suggests the possibility that the acquisition metaphor should continue to be used but freed from ontological stipulations, rather using it as part of our narrative construal (Bruner, 1996) about the world.

If knowledge is seen as creative and productive participation, then ideas about intrinsic differences between vocational and professional knowledge, and the generalisable nature of knowledge, are challenged and the notion of transfer becomes re-conceptualised. John Stevenson, in Chapter 4, uses a sociocultural approach to address just such a challenge and through a discussion of workplace settings in the tourist industry, argues for not using the idea of 'transfer' but the 'transformation of self, practice and knowledge'.

Viewing learning as a movement into and through social existence removes the boundaries between educational and workplace settings and other lived experiences. Curriculum in this view emerges in relations among participants, the purposes they address and the cultural tools they have access to. The challenges this raises for how knowledge is understood and valued are examined in a number of respects in the second section of the book. In Chapter 5, Stephen Billett, discussing the workplace curriculum, argues that it should be conceptualised as intents directed to individuals' progression towards full and effective workplace performance. This is shaped by workplace factors and is ultimately experienced by workers as learners. So whether the intentions are realised is premised on the support (affordances) for their enactment by interests within the workplace. Workplace affordances, like those in educational institutions, emphasise the role that the norms and social practices that comprise workplaces play in regulating individuals' engagement in, and learning through, work. The degree to which these affordances invite, structure, support, and guide participation, and are likely to engage workers in the kinds of thinking, acting, and learning required for effective workplace performance, is important for developing vocational practice. The conception of an ideal curriculum directed towards full participation, Billett argues, is subject to the affordances of the interests of managers, co-workers, and factors affecting production, as well as the intentionalities of worker-learners themselves.

Curriculum, based on a view of knowledge as a commodity, is seen as stuff or skills to be acquired, and John Sloboda writing about the music curriculum, in Chapter 6, shows how this approach ignores the musical lives of learners. He describes the collapse of the consensus about what it is to be musically educated as a consequence of major cultural shifts which he identifies. In recognising that a dominant cultural ideology of music is no longer sustainable, Sloboda implicitly argues for viewing music education as developing a music identity, and that this may be at odds with the visions of such identity that teachers in schools might hold. This conflict, he argues, explains the drop-out of children from instrumental music. He posits the possibility of a new more effective music education environment within the mixed economy of out-of-school music provision, which recognises not only diverse styles and genres but creates new relationships between teachers and students. In this way, Sloboda begins to address Sfard's question about what happens to subjects in a sociocultural perspective of knowledge.

In Chapter 7, Robert McCormick and Peter Scrimshaw show how cultural tools, such as information technology and the practices associated with it, have the potential to transform the process of learning and knowledge creation. They give examples that indicate how the nature of the learning experience in art that uses information technology can change the nature of the art itself. Rather than being used to mimic existing techniques of art, technology, through techniques of filtering and image manipulation, can transform it entirely. This is a challenge to conventionally trained art teachers who, when faced with using computer technology, have to rethink what 'art knowledge' consists of, and indeed their own identity as an artist.

Jo Boaler and her colleagues (Chapter 8) exemplify the way that assessment practices and structures shape the access different learners have to forms of knowledge. They show

how ability grouping resulted in a polarised curriculum, with students in lower groups offered a restricted opportunity to learn through, moving deeper into the practice of schooled mathematics compared with those in higher groups. Not only were students in lower groups given a profoundly negative learning experience but students in all setted groups were unhappy with this arrangement.

All these readings point to ways in which teaching and assessment practices, and representations of knowledge made available through them, have to change to meet the needs of future learning communities.

The final section of the book focuses on the dilemmas that those who support learning face in trying to include the different ways of knowing and of being of their learners in the contexts of different settings (vocational, school and university) and the strategies to address these that are offered. David Boud and his colleagues in Chapter 9 argue that vocational education has been driven for too long by standards that are enacted through various assessment regimes, and which pay no attention therefore to the quality of the learning experience. Drawing on a sociocultural approach, they propose sustainable assessment that is oriented towards lifelong learning. This draws on the ideas of assessment for learning, so that learners will be able to, for example, identify for themselves the standards that will be needed in a new situation, and be able to assess whether they are able to meet them. They propose a number of features for assessment tasks with this in mind; for example, that such tasks should involve students in identifying appropriate communities of practice to assist in developing criteria for good work. This, they argue, will require vocational education to change significantly so that assessment and learning are more closely interrelated, and pedagogy becomes a more central concern.

Although the ideas on learning, knowledge and pedagogy are well articulated from a sociocultural perspective, how this is enacted in assessment is less clear. The classic work of a decade ago by Greeno, Pearson and Schoenfeld (1997) in laying out a framework for what counts as achievement that forms the basis of the assessment of literacy and mathematics, viewed from a sociocultural perspective, has hardly been developed. Central to such a perspective is the interaction between the learner and the teacher in any assessment situation, and for the need to record a learning journey in any assessment tools. In the context of early education, Marilyn Fleer and Carmel Richardson (Chapter 10) show ways of documenting how young children participate in sociocultural activity and how that participation changes. This documentation naturally includes how others are involved in this participation, including the scaffolding of teachers and interactions with peers. The change in practice from an individual orientation to a collective perspective was a significant challenge for the teachers, and the chapter charts the issues and difficulties they faced in changing perspectives.

Karen Tonso, in Chapter 11, observes how college engineers exhibit identities and how these relate to different learning. The usual image of participation in communities of practice that is projected in some sociocultural accounts of learning is of particular trades, occupations or academic discipline communities. The identity that a learner is taking on in such learning is of these communities, ignoring the identities that learners themselves may have or develop, which reflect the experience of the learning institution. Tonso maps a range of such identities that those learning to be engineers exhibit and their associated images of competency, arguing that we need a more subtle account of identity and hence a more sensitive approach to pedagogy that will respond to this. This is turn reflects the power of the sociocultural perspective on learning which, as we noted earlier, is concerned with achieving particular relations with others, experiencing mutuality and sustaining mutual engagement.

The histories of participation of these different college students, their understanding and ways of knowing, and the distance between them and the representations of knowledge that are made available in college engineering courses, call for a rethinking of pedagogy.

Teaching science in schools continues to be problematic and has given rise to many attempts to reform the curriculum to deal with different aspects of scientific knowledge, whether that be to emphasise fundamental concepts and theories of science, to bring in more contemporary concerns such as genetic engineering, or to move it to the social and ethical concerns that might be of interest and importance to non-scientists. All of these are premised on a view of science as a body of knowledge, and though each approach is motivated by a concern to relate to the lives of young people, a sociocultural approach requires a more profound concern for the learner. Rowhea Elmesky and Kenneth Tobin give an account of the most difficult of settings, that of learning science in urban schools in New York (Chapter 12). Their approach was to explore the capital that urban young people bring to school and situate them as student researchers, i.e. as active participants who exercise agency through accessing and appropriating a variety of resources. They were active members of a research team, and were both teachers and learners, curriculum developers and ethnographers. This approach, although requiring considerable resources, shows what can be done in the difficult situation of urban education.

Finally, in Chapter 13, Guida de Abreu and Tony Cline show how the personal development of the learner can be conceptualised in terms of links between social representations of mathematical practices and the development of social identities. They illustrate their approach working in multi-ethnic primary schools in England and propose how the processes of (i) 'identifying the other', (ii) 'being identified' and (iii) 'self-identification' each play a complementary role in the formation of schooled mathematical identities.

These readings offer insights into alternative ways of knowing that take account of gender and cultural knowledge, and argue the need for students to be engaged with epistemological critique and curriculum development to develop awareness of the affordances and shortcomings of different forms of knowing in a subject. Across the readings, a variety of tools is offered for changing practice to move beyond familiar knowledges, and authority relations to take account of other ways of knowing, raising further questions about valued knowledge and the purposes of education.

# References

Bruner, J. (1996) *The Culture of Education*. Cambridge, MA: Harvard University Press.

Cobb, P. (1999) 'Where is the mind?' In P. Murphy (ed.), *Learners, Learning and Assessment*, London: Sage.

Elwood, J. (2007) 'Gender issues in testing and assessment.' In C. Skelton, B. Francis and L. Smulyan (eds), *Gender and Education Handbook*, London: Sage. (Reader 1: *Learning and Practice: Agency and Identities*.)

González, N. (2005) 'Beyond culture: the hybridity of funds of knowledge.' In N. González, L.C. Moll and C. Amanti (eds), *Funds of Knowledge: Theorizing Practices in Households, Communities and Classrooms*, Mahwah, NJ: Lawrence Erlbaum Associates.

Greeno, J.G., Pearson, P.D. and Schoenfeld, A.H. (1997) 'Implications for national assessment of educational progress of research and cognition.' In R. Glaser and R. Linn (eds), *Assessment in*

*Transition: Monitoring the Nation's Educational Progress. Background Studies*, Stanford, CA: National Academy of Education, Stanford University.

Lave, J. (2008) 'Everyday life and learning.' In P. Murphy and R. McCormick (eds), *Knowledge and Practice: Representations and Identities*, London: Sage.

Lave, J. and Wenger, E. (1991) *Situated Learning: Legitimate Peripheral Participation*. Cambridge: Cambridge University Press.

McDermott, R.P. (1996) 'The acquisition of a child by a learning disability.' In S. Chaiklin and J. Lave (eds), *Understanding Practice – Perspectives on Activity and Context*, Cambridge: Cambridge University Press.

Paavola, S., Lipponen, L. and Hakkarainen, K. (2004) 'Models of innovative knowledge communities and three metaphors of learning', *Review of Educational Research* 74(4): 557–76.

Sfard, A. (2006) 'Participationist discourse on mathematics learning.' In J. Maasz and W. Schloeglmann (eds), *New Mathematics Research and Practice,* Rotterdam, Netherlands: Sense Publishers.

Vygotsky, L.S. (1986) *Thought and Language*. Cambridge, MA: MIT Press.

Wenger, E. (1998) *Communities of Practice*: *Learning, Meaning and Identity*. Cambridge: Cambridge University Press.

# Section 1

## Epistemological Dilemmas

# 1

# Everyday Life and Learning

*Jean Lave*

## Introduction

There are two points to be developed in this chapter. One is that when learning and every-day life are characterized together as about knowledge and its acquisition, the relation between them is one in which learning is supposed to involve movement away from the ordinary and the mundane knowledgeability of some 'everyday life.' Any question about 'away from the everyday *towards what?*' leads straight to the political assumptions under-lying theories of learning formulated in this way. Second, if we construct a *social* analytic approach to organizations, social relations, social practice and everyday life, but leave learning in an epistemological realm, we perpetuate incommensurate theoretical stances reflected in customary patterns of uneasy silence on the subject. It looks useful to highjack our conception of learning into the social, socially constituted world of everyday social practice.

What are theories of learning *about*? Learning is generally assumed to be entirely an epistemological problem – it has long been assigned to the conceptual-mental rather than the social-material side of human being. Just as we would expect (given that we grew up going to school), theories of learning are about individuals' psychological processes, lead-ing to knowledge acquisition. They are typically framed as (1) transmission (training, teaching, inculcation) that leads to (2) input, storage in memory, internalization of what's transmitted, followed by (3) retrieval and transfer to 'problem solving in new situations.' This is a curious characterization of everyday life, one that merits critical examination. But what seems more startling is the narrow, pervasive history of philosophical and psycholog-ical treatments of 'learning' as wholly an epistemological problem – it is all about know-ing, acquiring knowledge, beliefs, skills, changing the mind, moving from intuitions to rules, or the reverse, and that is all. It might seem that a separation between learning and social life is precisely a division between epistemological concerns with regard to learn-ing and social concerns about the world in which learning takes place or which it is about. A history of philosophy, social theory, anthropology and Western cultural practices might be taken up almost anywhere and furnish arguments, mostly in favor, for the proposition that social life is socially constituted while learning happens in the head. But 'everyday life' has also been highjacked across the divide and turned into an epistemological prob-lem. There is a preoccupation in theorizing about learning with a conception of social life conceived in epistemological terms every bit as strongly as conceptions of learning. This conception of social life brings learning and a version of social existence together, on the epistemological side of the analytic divide, and so separates learning from everyday life in *epistemological* terms. This means that neither common intuitions about learning *nor* about everyday life are likely tools for approaching the problem of incorporating analysis of learning into socio-logical research.

# Everyday life

'The everyday' is an odd concept. Its recent history and field of meanings matter, because the term often substitutes for situated, social practice without analysis in the discourse of social practice theorists. It also plays a key, different, but equally unexamined role in a binary politics of changing practice. Like 'cognition' used freely or 'learning' used freely in all sorts of venues in which education is at issue, 'the everyday' is widely taken to be one of those 'natural' terms for a thing without a compelling history. Not so.

'The everyday' has a variety of common meanings: (1) life experience that is mundane, prosaic, humdrum, boring; (2) that which reoccurs, the routine, the unchanging, the ordinary and expected, the perhaps inescapable round of daily existence; (3) it is sometimes equated with culture, the customary, the commonplace; sometimes with the fabric of belief, value and lived experience, the everywhere of our lives that is nowhere in particular; or (4) the site of praxis, pragmatics, and social practice. If anything, these meanings sustain the vague and open sense of the term. We might expect, then, that the problem with 'the everyday' would turn out to be its lack of specific meaning in fields of endeavor in which its pivotal role should recommend a more searching acquaintance. But in fact the problem is just the opposite: 'the everyday' has a longer history and a more broadly shared, more narrowly constrained meaning than many users of the term are aware. The Critical Theory Program at UC Davis held a conference entitled 'The Problematics of Daily Life in the Human Sciences' some years ago. Speakers began in similar ways, with a disclaimer: none of the authors felt that they had any idea of what a conference on the everyday might be about; then they went on to discuss a surprisingly closely related set of issues. All of them claimed dissatisfaction with some well-known ways of conceiving of the everyday. All of them took the matter at hand to be a question of how and what people *know* under ordinary circumstances. Given that everyday life is a key conception in a variety of theoretical arenas, and that it has a history of which its friendly users seem unaware, it is worth exploring further.

There are three common strategies for assigning 'location' to different conceptions of the everyday, each amply represented in classical accounts on the subject. Each of these strategies specifies how everyday life is *separated* (or not) from other aspects of social existence. They may be placed along a continuum from asocial construal of a strictly epistemological 'everyday,' to a partially social view of everyday life in which different zones of social life have different epistemological characteristics, polarized between the ordinary and the special or privileged, and finally, a view of everyday life as the fabric of social existence (see Figure 1.1). The 'everyday' as either logical operator or as a zone of social life

| The everyday | The everyday | The everyday |
|:---:|:---:|:---:|
| ——as—— | ——as—— | ——as—— |
| residual category vis-à-vis philosophy, high culture, science, in some sense merely a logical operator. | banal, but a form of existence with special times, places and characteristics, e.g. as private, domestic sphere. | social practice, as all of social living; culture as praxis. |

**Figure 1.1   Different conceptions of the everyday**

implies that there are other aspects of life that aren't everyday. The everyday (whether as logical operator or as zone of social life limited to certain kinds of activities by certain kinds of persons) preserves a dualism between the ordinary and the exceptional, however these may be conceived. It is evidently asymmetrical and polarized. The epistemological everyday is a residual category vis-à-vis high culture, the latter indicating idealized endpoints of learning; or the banal locus of social activity of kinds that supposedly produce a limited and private knowledge (unself-conscious, tacit, silent or what have you). The epistemological everyday is likewise the foil, the baseline in cognitive and other genres of theorizing about learning. Together they suggest that learning – 'acquiring knowledge' – involves movement away from something towards something else: from ignorance to knowledge, from empty to full, from child to adult, from the mundane to the specialized expert/science/philosophy.

# Everyday life as social practice

The third version of 'the everyday,' as the stuff of social practice, follows so simply from the drastic commitments implied in years of ethnographic fieldwork, that I have a hard time not seeing it as the defining mode of anthropology. It does not, or course, follow that all anthropologists would draw this lesson from fieldwork, but the opposite does hold: ethnographic field research is strongly indicated in this view of the everyday lived-in world. The point here is that all social existence is given in day-to-day terms – in social practice. Questions of boundaries and divisions, differences in power, in value, and the complex, conflictual relations separating the high and low components of social life, assumed and justified in those accounts of zones and logical operators, are all assumed to be made; they are processes structured and structuring in practice. By the third account of everyday life, if knowledge production is reserved in ideological and structural terms for privileged classes or institutions, it is done in political, economic and cultural relations and practices, not because daily living somehow confines some people but not others, or permits the escape of a privileged few. There is no other way to engage in knowledge production than in everyday ways. It requires political-economic and cultural analysis to explain qualitative differences in the epistemological characteristics of social living, not epistemological analysis. For me, anthropology is not grounded in the psychic unity of mankind, nor even humankind, nor is it floating in a cultural phenomenology. Rather, it is the constitutive everyday character of social existence that grounds my continued participation in the field.

There is now a formidable body of research speaking to these issues, in Science, Technology/Society (STS) studies, which since Latour and Woolgar's initial *Laboratory Life* (1979) have worked in many different settings on the proposition that 'knowledge production', at sites of the sorts of practices located at the 'high' poles in the first two versions of the epistemological everyday, is in fact a matter of day-to-day social practice. It is the political and institutional arrangements of laboratory science that make differences among practices in concrete terms, not special minds, special ethics, nor power to create knowledge independent of the *institutional* arrangements that make 'knowledge creation' an acceptable label for what goes on in laboratories and other sites of science practice. Indeed, a good deal of Latour's work is aimed at laying out the complexities of their institutional arrangements. This body of research encourages a pursuit of different understandings of the nature of learning with respect to everyday life. It immediately raises the question: if the work of science is done in everyday ways, what does that do to our conception of the everyday everyday? This raises questions about what would happen if we stopped mystifying political-economic differences and dominant ideologies of difference by assigning them to differences among minds, differences in knowledge, and differences in capacities to create knowledge. STS work encourages us to analyse scientific discovery in terms of its social production in practice. In turn, this provides a powerful argument against an exclusively epistemological reading of everyday life (and learning).

Having introduced three different common uses of 'the everyday,' let us go back to those first two conceptions of everyday life where common and academic theories of learning dwell. Given pervasive epistemological concerns about 'the everyday,' we must consider in turn how that everyday logical operator or zone functions in theorizing about learning.

# The voice of the hermit

Academic theorizing about 'learning' for the most part is very little transformed by widely shared views across the social spectrum and far beyond the academy. Much of what goes under the name 'learning' is not about learning at all, but about cultural transmission, teaching, instruction, or inculcation. Further, I have never found in academic discussions of learning any speculation on what constitutes a theory of learning.

This last point, however, is easy to remedy. Martin Packer has proposed a useful notion of what a theory of learning might be, at minimum requiring three kinds of stipulations: a telos (direction, purpose) for the changes implied in notions of learning; an assumption about the relation between subject and social world; and mechanisms by which learning is supposed to take place (1993). This is a useful analytic tool, furnishing a set of questions for interrogating anything claiming to be an example, or for that matter a theory, of learning.

Common notions about the telos of learning are quite revealing concerning the ways in which learning and life are made to separate (in both senses). 'Learning' (whether in common parlance, as elaborated in the part of the academy reserved for its direct consideration, or in socio-cultural-historical research which makes assumptions about learning too) is a process, one that moves learners in the direction of 'higher' knowledge, which also implies moving away from 'lower,' knowledge that is, whatever constitutes the lowest common denominator, the everyday knowledge of everyday folks. Separation of knowledge producers from everyday life – which implies that novice knowers must withdraw or separate themselves from everyday concerns, and that knowledge is conditional on such movement – is a major theme in learning and education literature, and in discussions of knowledge, its production and acquisition. The problem of life is to accumulate (or articulate) knowledge;

coming to know is a process of distancing oneself from the thing to be learned, via contemplation, or as a matter of representation, while everyday life is on the whole viewed as entrapping and limiting. This 'everyday' lives in an interesting limbo. It is the epistemological space you wouldn't want to inhabit were you a significant learner or a philosopher.

There is a further elusiveness about what is to follow. I have in the past anchored a critical account of common claims about learning in the social evolutionary theory of late 19th century and early 20th century proto- and early anthropologists, especially Levy-Bruhl (1910), because of his continuing influence on the present. But Tylor, Morgan, Spencer, Durkheim and Mauss, among others, were all grappling with the same issues. I am sometimes asked, 'why begin then?' and 'why then?', for which I have none but presentist answers – their influence is still felt today. Timothy Mitchell (1988) locates broad sweeps of Western thought in the technologies of colonial domination (*Colonising Egypt*). Yet, when Steven Shapin describes the strong presence of these separations and social hierarchizations in Christianity, Greek thought, and early science, it makes me uneasy about my anthropologically bound 'history' or Mitchell's complex political, economic, social and cultural history. Are they adequate historical accounts of deeply practiced beliefs about knowledge, learning, and a politics of social privilege? There is over determination in many dimensions of ideology and practice that claim to lay down a separation of knowledge production from its reception or reproduction, including the separation of designated 'knowledge producers' or, more broadly, 'high culture producers' from 'ordinary folks,' and the understanding of learning processes that result. To learn requires withdrawal from ordinary life – learning requires distance; to learn is to become specialized, non-ordinary.

Steven Shapin insists on the historical depth of very general beliefs about the direction, or movement, of what might be called the *telos* of learning (note that he does not think he is talking about learning!):

> Certain understandings and stipulations about the place of knowledge 'have' ... scarcely changed from their Greek and Roman origins, and indeed, remain fundamentally unchanged today. ... In our culture we do not have to listen hard to hear the hermit's voice. (1991: 208)

Further,

> [W]e inherit the historical legacy of so much testimony that the producers of our most valued knowledge are not in society. At the point of securing their knowledge [at the end of the learning process], they are said to be outside the society to which they mundanely belong. And when they are being most authentically intellectual agents, they are said to be most purely alone. (Shapin, 1991: 192)

He catalogues a long list of religious prophets, artists, poets, writers, painters, composers and philosophers struggling in or sitting on an assortment of hilltops, wildernesses, cells, garrets, logs in forests, islands and pond-sides, both literary inventions and real. He quotes popular poetic views such as the lines of Wordsworth on Newton: 'Voyaging through strange seas of thought, alone.' He observes that 'Descartes prefaced his *Discourse on Method* with a picture of chilling aloneness ... Descartes decided that his renewal of philosophic method depended on separating himself from society, resolving "to remove myself from all places where any acquaintance were possible, and to retire to a country such as this [the Netherlands] ... where ... I can live as solitary and retired as in deserts the most remote"' (Shapin quoting Descartes, 1991: 194). He describes separation-solitude-withdrawal in terms of retirement (1991: 202), and it applies equally to scientific discovery and moral enlightenment (p. 206). 'The solitary philosopher, like the religious isolate, might be seen as separated from the corruptions and contaminations of social life,' from publics or civic society of various kinds, or mundane life (p. 206).

The nature of that 'solitude,' as one guise for the separation of social life and learning, requires careful thought – it is only a symbolic (or ideological) solitude, as Shapin points out; in concrete social terms, it requires withdrawing *into* certain kinds of – notably privileged – social and institutional settings (the company of gentlemen or the brotherhood of monks) and often pointedly announces withdrawal from specific contaminants (e.g. the company of women and the hurly burly of 'ordinary' life. For 17th-century scientists in England, it implied refuge from participation in a dangerous political scene as well.) This is also only made possible by the scientists' access to wealth and position, and by the labor of others. 'No solitude without servitude' is the way sociologist of science Leigh Star has summed it up.

Shapin doesn't say a whole lot about *from* 'what' the scientists felt the need to withdraw, though class prejudice and misogyny both seem heavily implicated. But even without elaboration, withdrawal – indeed, the making of distinctions – seems to be a fundamental gesture of privilege, or conventional practices, including withdrawal into elite pursuits, into rational, neutral objectivity, away from dominated and common, crude persons, activities, locations, collectivity and ways of knowing.

Bourdieu (1979/1984) pursues this line of argument in his analysis of the axis of ease/necessity in *Distinction*. Cultural competence is learned, he says, under certain objective conditions of acquisition, for instance, at home or in school. These shape what is learned, but also the manner in which they are learned. The manner of learning is related to both content and circumstances: it is part of culture, it is a cultured relation with culture, and it grows out of, and helps to perpetuate, the conditions of acquisition. This thickens the notion of 'cultural competence' into a nexus of relations rather than a single operation. It insists on the situated character of cultural competence, as always acquired in relation to a particular social field (though of course the social world is not exhaustively composed of social fields).

To get to the telos of learning, we can begin with an obvious candidate for the high cultural endpoint: artists' and connoisseurs' command of 'the pure aesthetic gaze.' We can ask about the conditions of production of French cultural understanding (and practice) in the *anthropological* sense, of such cultural competence. It is notable that this high cultural competence and its acquisition depend deeply on various kinds of separation from the everyday.

> The aesthetic disposition, a generalized capacity to neutralize ordinary urgencies and to bracket off practical ends, a durable inclination and aptitude for practice without a practical function, can only be constituted within an experience of the world freed from urgency and through the practice of activities which are an end in themselves, such as scholastic exercises or the contemplation of works of art. In other words, it presupposes the distance from the world ... which is the basis of the bourgeois experience of the world. (Bourdieu, 1979/1984: 64)

The main social conditions, according to Bourdieu, are relations of different social classes to economic ease or necessity. The cultural valuation of wealth and prosperity as freedom *from* necessity, as separation from the concerns of 'ordinary' folks who must act according to their economic necessities, is characteristic of claims about cultural production in the schoolish-academic-scholarly terms that infuse and shape the broad cultural constitution of high culture. They make distance from necessity the keystone of privilege and the deeply embedded characteristic of high-cultural endeavors, including the production of knowledge and the identification of culture-heroic destinies or destinations (or the directional beacons of academic assumptions about learning). This involves movement away from the ordinary in two senses, from lower social-class positions, and from economic functional urgencies.

> Economic power is first and foremost the power to keep economic necessity at arm's length. ... This affirmation of power over a dominated necessity always implies a claim to a legitimate superiority over those who, because they cannot assert the same contempt for contingencies in gratuitous luxury and conspicuous consumption, remain dominated by ordinary interests and urgencies. ... The tastes of freedom can only assert themselves as such in relation to the tastes of necessity, which are thereby brought to the level of the aesthetic and so defined as vulgar. This claim to aristocracy is less likely to be contested than any other, because the relation of the 'pure', 'disinterested' disposition to the conditions which make it possible ... has every chance of passing unnoticed. The most 'classifying' privilege thus has the privilege of appearing to be the most natural one. (Bourdieu, 1979/1984: 55–6)

He argues that the manner of using symbolic goods [whether artistic or intellectual],

> especially those regarded as the attributes of excellence, constitutes one of the key markers of 'class' and also the ideal weapon in strategies of distinction, that is, as Proust put it, 'the infinitely varied art of marking distances'. (Bourdieu, 1979/1984: 65)

In fact, learning theory, to the extent that it implies movement away from the everyday towards something that is supposedly not, could be summed up in Proust's phrase. It isn't learning itself, surely, that generates these distinctions, distances and relations of domination. Rather, theories of learning are instruments in bringing them about.

This leads to further questions: Whose points of view shape theories of learning? Do we need to worry about whether what Bourdieu says about the pure aesthetic gaze operates in radically different ways than the cultural competence more typical of physicists, prophets, and experts in American and British discussions of learning? The question is not whether aesthetic analysis does, or could, effortlessly include the academic/rationalist stuff of the science- and expertise-directed theories of learning. The real question is where to turn for conceptions of becoming culturally competent when the term culture begins with a small c rather than a capital C. For one can only conclude, along with Bourdieu, that theorizing about the acquisition of cultural competence is being purveyed from a thoroughly bourgeois point of view, and with respect only to what is commonly accepted as high culture. The rest of learning-everyday-life goes unexamined and untheorized as well.

# Reification and the politics of telos

Though it is impossible to separate casual conceptions of learning as movement away from the everyday from conceptions of learning as movement towards a state of knowledgeable cultural privilege, each has distinct analytic implications. The claim that to learn is to move away from some putative everyday (whether merely a residual dualist category or some zone of living) is to set apart and reify learning as a process in and of itself. To stipulate general societal ends towards which learning should move is an inescapably political act. Mainstream and unintended assumptions and claims about 'learning' are not apolitical or neutral, as they might wish to claim. Rather, they have the effect of accepting and justifying the contemporary social order in culturally powerful, powerfully cultural, terms. Indeed, if Shapin (1991), Bourdieu (1979/1984) and de Certeau (1984) are right, present ways of theorizing about learning rest on political premises and have political effects that go back to ancient and/or colonial and/or assorted recent histories, closely reflected in contemporary standpoints.

The drawbacks of reifying learning, whether in the common terms of short formal stints of mentally internalizing knowledge, or less immediate terms, are quickly catalogued: as a thing in itself, 'learning' is something that must take place elsewhere than in the circumstances in which what is learned is supposed to be 'applied,' or at least it must happen before the test, or as a precondition for 'learning transfer' to occur, or in childhood as preparation for adulthood, or in transitions from school as preparing for a changing world of work. These create disturbing (and specious) divisions between learning and using knowledge, and linear relations in time between learning 'before' to use 'after.' Most seriously, they produce a division such that one may be learning *or* living but not both at once. They also tend to produce an ideology of specific institutional settings for propagating and characterizing (and studying) 'real learning', while leaving as a vague residual (everywhere and nowhere) unstudied operators or zones of life in which application of the products of learning – 'knowledge,' 'skill' – (not learning) is the order of the day. The emphasis on learning now for other times and places has in it an idea of connectedness, indeed of absolutely essential connectedness 'then and now' or 'now and later.' But what isn't clear is that any theory of learning that starts with this principle is proposing that learning is produced in a site in which 'real life' is temporarily suspended, as 'product' knowledge is to be applied in real life in which whatever people are doing is not 'learning.' This is a set of normative prescriptions for relations among communities of practice so exotic that it is difficult to see how they have come to be mistaken as universals.

Stipulation of a telos for learning of what should constitute movement towards greater knowledge or mastery is at its root a political declaration. A number of privileged directions of knowledge accumulation, cultural capital and expertise have been discussed already in Shapin's account of early science and Bourdieu's analysis of relations among French class cultures: monks and saints, artists and other producers of high culture, philosophers, scientists, and perhaps less romantically, professionals and experts.

There are two common ways of expressing the telos of learning:

1.  Given a logical operator view of the everyday as 'not philosophy,' the telos of learning involves a belief that some knowledge is more scientific, truthful, general or abstract (or transferable) than other knowledge.

There are widespread evolutionary views about the accumulation of knowledge and the conditions for acquiring it as progression in the direction of rational inquiry, science, individuality, or continual organizational learning. This assumption about telos does hardly more than invoke a conventional Whig history of science or ideas. Examples would include the two principle strands of cognitive science that recommend movement towards self-contained, computational rationality (e.g. Haugeland, 1981: 28) and professional life (Simon, 1976) or expert knowledge (Dreyfus and Dreyfus, 1986); or Piaget's (1976) developmental trajectory is that of formal operational intelligence, inspiration for his genetic epistemology coming from the mathematical foundations posited by a French mathematical group, the Burbaki. The point is that theorizing about learning is always about whom learners should stop being and who they should become, what masters they should follow and what makes those masters exemplary.

2.   Given the everyday as social zone, the telos of learning involves a belief that some social categories or cultures or locations have better knowledge than others.

It is also about which few should arrive at exemplary knowing and which should not. Contrastive social categorizations or identities are partly furnished and made vivid by the way in which they are commonly assumed to be able to know, know a lot more, or be deficient at knowing. As Bourdieu suggests, cultural competence is characterized not only by how much of what sorts of high culture is acquired, but also the manner of relating to it. A theory that posits a telos of refinement (a move away from the messiness of practical concerns, to a realm of reflection and detachment where genuine knowledge resides) embodies suppositions about unequal social categories. Inequalities of social class, ethnicity, and gender relations are fashioned, assumed, indeed learned, in terms positively and negatively valued with respect to the class, gender and ethnic hierarchies bounded at one pole by the ordinary everyday and at the other pole by a telos of mastery. Or in 'scientific' accounts of rationality, formal logic, and distanced contemplation, knowledge production, autonomy and neutral objectivity are thought to characterize the dominant category in each case. The everyday world of reproduction and maintenance, the ordinary, routine, particular and interested, are assumed to characterize the dominated category (Lave, 1988, 1996).

Whether in common 'common sense' or academic 'common sense' terms, distance from the ordinary is equated with privilege. The shape of this argument should seem familiar, and owes a debt to Bourdieu, as we have seen. His argument in *Distinction* in the end levels at Kant's project the charge that it is generated in bourgeois culture and embodies a bourgeois ideology of culture rather than a universally valid aesthetics. The same is true for theories of learning which take high cultural ends as the telos of 'normal' learning. Where is the telos of culture learning in the anthropological sense? In everyday life? In everyday social practice? There is extraordinary silence about this, or rather abstractly negative judgments. Or else, a kind of abstract assumption that whatever constitutes modes of knowledgeability in high cultural terms, the everyday learning of everyday life must have opposite characteristics.

The advantages of being privileged involve appropriating the legitimate possibility of producing knowledge. This is simply another way to speak to hegemonic power or knowledge relations, as these are reflected indirectly in assumptions about what learning is about. Bourdieu insists that in French class culture, at least, the production of culture is reserved by the haute bourgeoisie for the haute bourgeoisie. He discusses at length the ways in which the dominated fraction of the dominant class is the site of cultural production in France. Lefebvre (e.g. 1971), de Certeau, Shapin, as well as Bourdieu, among others, are notable for struggling with these issues in more subtle terms than most, rather than just assuming the distinction to start with. But pervading everyday life and social research (whether it addresses learning and everyday life directly or not), there is an absolute division between producing knowledge and reproducing knowledge, mostly without the sociological analysis Bourdieu brings to bear. The division permeates Western culture and educational assumptions in a big way. Widespread belief in academic circles underwrites distinctions between teaching and research, the equation of mental and manual labor with conception and execution, not to mention those distinctions themselves. It is elaborated in notions that teaching is a matter of reproducing knowledge, and that creativity cannot be taught, that learning is a matter of internalizing existing knowledge, and reproducing culture (produced elsewhere). Given the gulf of practiced distinctions between knowledge production and learning as concepts, we might well wonder why two terms are required rather than one. Creating knowledge certainly involves learning. Surely the reverse is also true? Not if the term 'knowledge' actually stands for something else: for official knowledge, and the social locations reserved exclusively for the production of new philosophy, science, high culture, or as Bourdieu argues, by and for the dominated fraction of the dominant class. The dual division plays out in this work, as it is accompanied by the claim that there is only one source of (high) cultural production, and that all the rest are merely class-cultural ways of taking it up or not.

## Conclusion

I have been discussing two political premises embedded in common assumptions about learning. The first premise is that learning involves movement away from the ordinary and everyday. It thus creates divisions and distinctions in degrees of privilege and mundaneness. It relegates the study of everyday social life to epistemological abstractions and ideological pronouncements. It also defines everyday life abstractly as the base, the lowest forms of living and learning, or as the site of social disorder and faulty social reproduction. It creates polarized distinctions between learning and doing, learning and living, learning and using knowledge. Second, a pervasive naturalized assumption divides the production of knowledge from the reproduction of knowledge. It draws a line between asymmetrically valued relations concerning knowledge: knowledge is either created *or* it is reproduced. There are profound political struggles involved in deciding which is which (especially given that some much more complex state of affairs characterizes all everyday lives). Both premises grow out of that profoundly disturbing claim about the nature of social order that insists on the separation of learning from everyday life.

Suppose we reconsider learning as part of social life. If social life is not construed to be an epistemological everyday realm, then what? And is a non-reified conception of learning as part of everyday life possible? Is it possible without 'disappearing' learning altogether into everyday life? It means that everyday life is partially fashioned in relations of learning – processes of apprenticeship rather than sequences of mental exercises. This brings us to a suggestion for how to begin: social existence, everyday social practice is first of all socially-historically generated. It is not constituted in and of knowledge, knowing, truth, certainty or a humanized omniscience. Most especially, the epistemological issues of social existence are social in their constitution. There are epistemological questions and whole Western traditions that derive from an assumed primacy of epistemological concerns, their central characteristics, and very being. But if they have no existence independent of the social practice of which they are a part, then epistemological issues are subsumed within the social ontology of human existence and not the other way around. Most especially, when we explore issues of learning, knowing, skill and knowledge, in social contexts we ignore these radically counter-intuitive relations at our peril. Reversing the customary relations between social ontological and epistemological inquiry is one of the most central issues in reformulating a theory of social life and learning.

What are alternative ways to look at learning as a part of everyday life and everyday life as in part a matter of learning? If learning isn't movement away from ordinary social existence, perhaps it is movement more deeply into and through social existence; if not an individual mental process, it is a social, relational, decentered process – not simple, nor narrowly univocal. If knowledge, or rather knowing, is creative and reproductive participation at the same time, subsumed within ongoing social practice (not as preparation for it), the interesting questions lie not in dual categories of elite knowledge producers and luckless consumers (a category to which all teachers are consigned except designated 'knowledge producers'; cf. Herndon, 1971), but in the nature of those relations of apprenticeship in everyday life through which practices, participants, and ways of participating change in part to be different from before and in part to be 'the same'. These are good leads into an exploration of apprenticeship and learning as social practice. My own version begins with the notion that everyday life and learning are made in the medium of participants' partial participation in ongoing, changing social practice. It is not possible to polarize knowers from novices, learners from inculcators, or knowledge production from reproduction, for polarization ceases to be possible as soon as located people lead partial, multiple-practice, interrelated lives.

# References

Bourdieu, P. (1979, trans. 1984). *Distinction: A Social Critique of the Judgement of Taste*. Cambridge, MA: Harvard University Press.

de Certeau, M. (1984). *The Practice of Everyday Life* (S. Rendall, Trans.). Berkeley: University of California Press.

Dreyfus, H. and S. Dreyfus. (1986). *Mind Over Machine: The Power of Human Intuition and Expertise in the Era of the Computer*. New York: The Free Press.

Haugeland, J. (1981). 'Semantic engines: An introduction to mind design.' In J. Haugeland (ed.), *Mind Design: Philosophy, Psychology, Artificial Intelligence* (pp. 1–34). Cambridge, MA: MIT Press.

Herndon, J. (1971). *How to Survive in Your Native Land*. New York: Simon and Schuster.

Latour, B. and S. Woolgar. (1979). *Laboratory Life: The Social Construction of Scientific Facts*. Beverly Hills, CA: Sage.

Lave, J. (1988). *Cognition in Practice: Mind, Mathematics and Culture in Everyday Life*. New York: Cambridge University Press.

Lave, J. (1996). 'The savagery of the domestic mind.' In L. Nader (ed.), *Naked Science*. New York: Routledge.

Lefebvre, H. (1971). *Everyday Life in the Modern World* (S. Rabinovitch, Trans.). London: Penguin.

Levy-Bruhl, L. (1910; reprinted 1966). *How Natives Think*. New York: Washington Square Press.

Mitchell, T. (1988). *Colonising Egypt*. Cambridge: Cambridge University Press.

Packer, M. (1993). 'Away from internalization.' In E. A. Forman, N. Minick and C. A. Stone (eds), *Contexts for Learning: Sociocultural Dynamics in Children's Development* (pp. 254–65). New York: Oxford University Press.

Piaget, J. (1976). *The Child and Reality: Problems of Genetic Epistemology* (A. Rosen, Trans.). New York: Penguin.

Shapin, S. (1991). 'The mind is its own place: science and solitude in seventeenth-century England.' In *Science in Context*, 4: 191–218.

Simon, H. A. (1976). 'Cognition and social behavior.' In J. S. Carroll and J. W. Payne (eds), *Cognition and Social Behavior*. Hillsdale, NJ: Lawrence Erlbaum.

# 2

# Abilities are Forms of Developing Expertise

*Robert J. Sternberg*

Billy has an IQ of 121 on a standardized individual intelligence test; Jimmy has an IQ of 94 on the same test. What do each of these scores, and the difference between them, mean? The goal of this chapter is to argue that the best available answer to this question is quite different from the one that is conventionally offered—that the scores and the difference between them reflect not some largely inborn, relatively fixed ability construct, but rather a construct of developing expertise. I refer to the expertise that all of these assessments measure as *developing* rather than as *developed* because expertise is typically not at an end state but is in a process of continual development.

In a sense, the point of view articulated in this article represents no major departure from some modern points of view regarding abilities. Abilities are broadly conceived and are seen as important to various kinds of success. They are seen as modifiable in some degree and as capable of being flexibly implemented at the same time that they are viewed as having interactive genetic and environmental components. What is perhaps new here is the attempt to integrate two literatures—the literature on abilities with that on expertise—and to argue that the two literatures may be talking, at some level, about the same thing rather than distinct or even, as some believe, constructs in opposition (see Ericsson,1996).

## The relation of abilities to expertise

Traditionally, abilities are typically seen either (a) as precursors to expertise (see essays in Chi, Glaser, & Farr, 1988) or (b) as opposed to expertise (Fiedler & Link, 1994) as causes of behavior. Sometimes abilities are held up (c) as causes of developing expertise in contrast to deliberate practice (see also Ericsson, Krampe, & Tesch-Romer, 1993, who argue for the importance of the latter as opposed to the former). In this chapter, abilities are seen as themselves a form of developing expertise. An important educational implication of this view is that abilities, like expertise, can be taught.

When we test for abilities, we are as much testing a form of expertise as we are when we test for accomplishments of various kinds, whether academic achievement, skill in playing chess, skill in solving physics problems, or whatever. What differs is the kind of expertise we measure and, more importantly, our conceptualizations of what measure. The

From: *Educational Researcher*, 27 (3), (AERA, 1998), pp. 11–22.

difference in conceptualization comes about in part because we happen to view one kind of accomplishment (ability-test scores) as predicting another kind of accomplishment (achievement test scores, grades in school, or other indices of accomplishment). But according to the present view, this conceptualization is one of practical convenience, not of psychological reality. Thus, for example, solving problems on a verbal-analogies test or a test of mathematical problem solving requires expertise, just as does any other kind of problem solving, and indeed, the components of information processing on many of these kinds of tasks are highly overlapping (Sternberg, 1983, 1985, Sternberg & Gardner, 1983).

According to this view, although ability tests may have temporal priority relative to various criteria in their administration (i.e., ability test are administered first, and later, criterion indices of performance, such as grades or achievement test scores, are collected), they have no psychological priority. All of the various kinds of assessments are of the same kind psychologically. What distinguishes ability tests from the other kinds of assessments is how the ability tests are used (usually predictively) rather than what they measure. There is no qualitative distinction among the various kinds of assessments.

For example, verbal-analogies tests and mathematical problem-solving tests could be, and often are, used as predictors, but they could as well be predicted by other kinds of measures, such as school performance or other measures of achievement. Indeed, the murkiness of the distinction between abilities and achievement is shown by the fact that some of the types of items that appear as ability-test items (e.g., vocabulary) on one measure appear as achievement test items on another measure. For example, the *Kaufman Assessment Battery for Children* (Kaufman & Kaufman, 1983) labels as measuring achievement verbal items that the *Stanford-Binet Intelligence Scale* (Thorndike, Hagen, & Sattler, 1986) labels as measuring abilities.

Although individual and group tests of intelligence are administered differently, they measure roughly the same skills and have underlying them the same theories of intelligence (Daniel, 1997; Gustafsson & Undheim, 1996; Sternberg, 1990). Thus, in this discussion, individual and group tests are considered jointly.

The literatures on abilities and expertise have grown up largely separately. Why? I believe there are several reasons. First, ability testing was originally done by Binet and his colleagues (Binet & Simon, 1916) on children, whereas early studies of expertise were done on adults (DeGroot, 1965). Second, Binet's work originally focused on exceptionally low levels of performance, whereas DeGroot and other expertise researchers typically have focused on exceptionally high levels of performance. Third, the assessments Binet and other ability testers devised were viewed primarily as predictors (aptitudes), whereas the measures devised by DeGroot and others were criterion measures of performance (achievement). Fourth, Binet focused on the world of school; DeGroot and other expertise researchers on the world of work. Later work by Wechsler (1958) involved the testing of adults but on tasks almost identical to those that Wechsler used for children, which in turn are very similar to those found on the Stanford-Binet for children. Fifth, ability testing grew out of a tradition emphasizing individual differences—differential psychology—whereas expertise research grew out of a tradition—that of cognitive psychology—emphasizing commonalties across individuals with differences of interest at the level of groups. Sixth, differential researchers quickly turned toward correlational methods, whereas expertise researchers turned toward mean differences and analysis-of-variance methodology. Seventh, abilities came to be viewed (although not by everyone) as largely innate and fixed, whereas expertise has typically been viewed as acquired and modifiable. In this article, I argue that these differences are of historical interest but not of psychological or educational importance.

# Models of individuals' abilities and achievements

## Alternative models of abilities

Before arguing for the developing-expertise point of view, it would be useful to review the more conventional point of view.

The traditional model of fixed individual differences holds that, as a result of genetic endowment interacting with the environment, people come at an early age to have a relatively fixed potential for achievement. They fulfill this potential in greater or lesser degree. Those who do not fulfill it are labeled *underachievers*, and those who achieve more than might have been expected may come to be labeled *overachievers*. Ironically, in the case of the latter, ability-test scores are viewed as a better indicator of what people can do (or should do!) than what they actually do. A test of verbal analogies, in this view, might actually tell us more about a person's verbal abilities than the persons' actual understanding of the reading he or she does in everyday life, or a test of mathematical problem-solving skills might be viewed as more informative than the person's actual mathematical problem solving in everyday life. In fact, though, the two kinds of mathematical skills are often not even very highly correlated (Ceci & Roazzi, 1994; Lave, 1988). Indeed, we now know that there are many different kinds of mathematical thinking skills both academic and everyday (Sternberg & Ben-Zeev, 1996).

The traditional model has led many people (e.g., Herrnstein & Murray, 1994) to observe that the more intelligent do better in school and eventually enter the educational routes that lead them to managerial, professional, or other kinds of training that in turn lead to financial and other forms of success. The less intelligent do worse in school and may drop out of school or else retain credentials reflecting perseverance as much as ability. Eventually, they enter the labor market to fill the jobs that the more intelligent people don't want to do. Let's look in greater detail at the traditional model and then consider an alternative.

A wide variety of theories of abilities have been proposed to account for individual differences in observed levels of achievement. It is impossible to review them all here, although more or less complete reviews can be found elsewhere (Brody, 1992; Gardner, 1983; Gardner, Kornhaber, & Wake, 1996; Perkins, 1995; Sternberg, 1982, 1990, 1994b). The main difference among the alternative theories is in the proposed nature and structure of abilities.

Sternberg (1990) has suggested that a series of alternative metaphors underlies these theories. For example, a geographic metaphor of intelligence as a map of the mind underlies psychometric theories, whereas a metaphor of intelligence as a computational device underlies information processing theories. By far the most widely accepted metaphor among psychologists, at least in the United States, has been the geographic or psychometric metaphor of intelligence as a map of the mind. In Europe, the epistemological metaphor of Piaget (1972) has probably gained greater acceptance.

A well-accepted contemporary psychometric theory views intelligence as hierarchical. According to this view, intelligence comprises a general, overarching ability as well as successive levels of more and more specific abilities (e.g., Carroll, 1993; Cattell, 1971; Gustafsson, 1988; Vernon, 1971). Some prefer other contemporary psychometric theories, such as ones based on Luria (1966, 1980) and implemented in tests by Kaufman & Kaufman (1983) and Naglieri & Das (1997) (see also Das, Naglieri, & Kirby, 1994).

Gustafsson and Undheim (1996), also hierarchical theorists, suggest in addition to general intelligence, crystallized ability, broad visualization, broad speediness, and broad fluency.

The model of abilities driving the present work is the triarchic theory of human abilities (Sternberg, 1985, 1988, 1996d). According to this theory, abilities take the form of various information processes operating on mental representations at varying levels of experience in order to adapt to, shape, and select environments (see Sternberg, 1985, for more details). It is important to note, however, that one could accept the model of abilities as forms of developing expertise, in general, without accepting the triarchic theory, in particular. Where does the developing-expertise model lead us, both in terms of educational opportunities and in terms of social outcomes?

One place it leads is to a view of abilities as flexible rather than fixed. There is now substantial evidence that abilities are modifiable, at least in some degree (see Feuerstein, 1980; Herrnstein, Nickerson, deSanchez, & Swets, 1986; Nickerson, 1986; Nickerson, Perkins, & Smith, 1985; Perkins, 1995; Perkins & Grotzer, 1997; Ramey, 1994; Sternberg, 1988, 1994a, 1996d; Sternberg & Spear-Swerling, 1996). If they are, then we should probably hesitate to assign any individual to a fixed group, whether it be a 'cognitive elite' or any other. The best evidence, of course, is in favor of both genetic and environmental origins of intelligence interacting in ways that are not, as yet, fully known (see Sternberg & Grigorenko, 1997).

# The developing-expertise model of abilities

There are views of abilities and their implications that diverge substantially from fixed-abilities views such as those advocated and reviewed by Herrnstein and Murray (1994). For example, Snow (1979, 1980, 1996; Snow & Lohman, 1984) has presented a much more flexible view of human abilities, according to which abilities are not limited to the cognitive domain and also overlap with aptitudes and achievements. Ceci (1996; Ceci & Roazzi, 1994; Ceci, Nightingale, & Baker, 1992) has proposed a bio-ecological model of abilities that shares some features with the view presented here, particularly regarding the relevance of domains. Perkins (1995) and Renzulli (1986) have also proposed compatible views. The model presented here perhaps extends some of these views in its emphasis on abilities as representing developing forms of expertise.

## Abilities as developing expertise

This alternative model sees scores on ability tests as measuring a form of developing expertise, much as would be represented by chess performance (Chase & Simon, 1973), physics performance (Chi, Glaser, & Rees, 1982; Larkin, McDermott, Simon, & Simon, 1980), radiology performance (Lesgold, 1984), teaching performance (Livingston & Borko, 1990; Sabers, Cushing, & Berliner, 1991; Shulman, 1987; Sternberg & Horvath, 1995), or any of a number of other kinds of expertise (Bereiter & Scardamalia, 1993). One comes to be an expert in the skills needed for success on ability tests in much the same ways one becomes an expert in doing anything else—through a combination of genetic endowment and experience.

Expertise involves the acquisition, storage, and utilization of at least two kinds of knowledge: explicit knowledge of a domain and implicit or tacit knowledge of a field (see Sternberg, Wagner, Williams, & Horvath, 1995), where *domain* refers to a knowledge base and *field* to the social organization of that knowledge base (Csikszentmihalyi, 1988,

1996). Explicit knowledge is the kind most frequently studied in the literature on expertise (see Chi, Glaser, & Farr, 1988; Ericsson & Smith, 1991). It is knowledge of the facts, formulas, principles, and major ideas of a domain of inquiry. Implict or tacit knowledge of a field is the knowledge one needs to know to attain success in a field that usually isn't talked about or even put into verbal form. For example, in psychology, Freud's theory of depression would constitute explicit knowledge, whereas how to get a grant would constitute informal or tacit knowledge.

When abilities are measured, both explicit and implicit elements are involved. A verbal-analogies test, for example, measures explicit knowledge of vocabulary and reasoning with this knowledge, but the test also measures implicit knowledge of how to take a test. For example, one has to work within certain time constraints, choose the best of what often are all imprecise options, and so on. The connection between explicit and implicit knowledge can be fluid, as shown by the fact that courses sometimes are constructed to make implicit knowledge explicit (see e.g., *The Practical Intelligence for School* program of Williams et al., 1996).

## Characteristics of expertise

The characteristics of expertise as reflected in performance on ability tests are similar to the characteristics of expertise of any kind (see Chi, Glaser, & Farr, 1988; Sternberg, 1996a). Expertise is a prototypically rather than classically defined concept (Sternberg 1994a). Operationally, by *expertise*, I refer, in a given domain, to a prototype of people's

- Having large, rich schemas (organized networks of concepts containing a great deal of declarative knowledge about a given domain, in the present case, the domains sampled by ability tests;
- Having well-organized, highly interconnected (mutually accessible) units of knowledge about test content stored in schemas;
- Spending proportionately more time determining how to represent test problems than they do in searching for and in executing a problem strategy (Larkin, McDermott, Simon, & Simon, 1980);
- Developing sophisticated representations of test problems, based on structural similarities among problems;
- Working forward from given information to implement strategies for finding unknowns in the test problems;
- Generally choosing a strategy based on elaborate schemas for problem strategies;
- Having schemas containing a great deal of procedural knowledge about problem strategies relevant in the test-taking domain;
- Having automatized many sequences of steps within problem strategies;
- Showing highly efficient problem solving; when time constraints are imposed, they solve problems more quickly than do novices;
- Accurately predicting the difficulty of solving particular test problems;
- Carefully monitoring their own problem-solving strategies and processes; and
- Showing high accuracy in reaching appropriate solutions to test problems.

Ability tests, achievement tests, school grades, and measures of job performance all reflect overlapping kinds of expertise in these kinds of skills. To do well in school or on the job requires a kind of expertise, but to do well on a test also requires a kind of expertise. Of course, part of this expertise is the kind of test wiseness that has been studied by Millman, Bishop, and Ebel (1965) and others (see Bond & Harman 1994), but there is much more to test-taking expertise than test wiseness.

Return, for a moment, to Billy and Jimmy. Billy and Jimmy test differently on an IQ test. This difference in test scores may reflect a number of factors: differential test wiseness, differential test anxiety, differential enculturation into a culture that values IQ tests, differential mood and alertness on the day of testing, differential readiness to take the test, and, most important, differential developing expertise in the skills that the test measures.

People who are more expert in taking IQ-related tests have a set of skills that is valuable not only in taking these tests, but in other aspects of Western life. Taking a test, say, of verbal or figural analogies or of mathematical problem solving typically requires skill such as

- Puzzling out what someone else (here, a test constructor) wants;
- Command of English vocabulary;
- Reading comprehension;
- Allocation of limited time;
- Sustained concentration;
- Abstract reasoning;
- Quick thinking;
- Symbol manipulation; and
- Suppression of anxiety and other emotions that can interfere with test performance, among other things.

These skills are also part of what is required for successful performance in school and in many kinds of job performance. Thus, an expert test taker is likely also to have skills that will be involved in other kinds of expertise as well, such as expertise in getting high grades in school.

It is, in my opinion, not correct to argue that the tests measure little or nothing of interest. Moreover, the tests do not all measure exactly the same constructs, although they measure related constructs. For example, the *Stanford-Binet Intelligence Scale: Fourth Edition* (Thorndike, Hagen, & Sattler, 1986) provides a composite score plus four subscores: verbal reasoning, abstract/visual reasoning, short-term memory, and quantitative reasoning. The Wechsler scales, such as the *Wechsler Intelligence Scales for Children — Third Edition* (Wechsler, 1991), yield a composite score plus verbal and performance scores. The *Kaufman Assessment Battery for Children* (Kaufman & Kaufman, 1983), based on Luria's (1966) theory, yields a composite score plus successive and simultaneous processing as well as a separate achievement score. The *Cognitive Assessment System* (Naglieri & Das, 1997) yields composite as well as successive and simultaneous processes. Clearly, these tests tap a range of cognitive abilities.

At the same time, there are many important kinds of expertise that the tests do not measure (Das, Nagileri, & Kirby, 1994; Gardner, 1983, Sternberg, 1985), for example, what Gardner (1983, 1993) would call musical, bodily kinesthetic, interpersonal, and intrapersonal intelligences and what I would call creative and practical intelligence (Sternberg, 1985, 1988, 1996d).

To the extent that the expertise required for one kind of performance overlaps with the expertise required for another kind of performance, there will be correlation between performances. The construct measured by the ability tests is not a cause of school or job expertise; it is itself an expertise that overlaps with school or job expertise. On the overlapping-expertise view, the traditional notion of test scores as somehow causal is based on a confounding of correlation with causation. Differences in test scores, academic performance, and job performance are all effects—of differential levels of expertise.

## Acquisition of expertise

The literature on the acquisition of expertise, in general, is reviewed in Ericsson (1996). Here I concentrate on this development as it relates to abilities. Individuals gain the expertise to do well on ability tests in much the same way they gain any other kind of expertise—through the interaction of whatever genetic dispositions they bring to bear with experience via the environment. I refer to tests as measuring *developing* expertise because the experiential processes are ongoing. In particular, individuals

- Receive direct instruction in how to solve test-like problems, usually through schooling;
- Engage in the actual solving of such problems, usually in academic contexts;
- Engage in role modeling (watching other, such as teachers or other students, solve test-like problems);
- Think about such problems, sometimes mentally simulating what they might do when confronting such problems; and
- Receive rewards for the successful solution of such problems, thereby reinforcing such behaviour.

## Individual differences in expertise

None of these arguments should be taken to imply that individual differences in underlying capacities do not exist. The problem, as recognized by Vygotsky (1978), as well as many others, is that we do not know how directly to measure these capacities. Measures of the zone of proximal development (e.g., Brown & Ferrara, 1985; Brown & Frensch, 1979; Feuerstein, 1979) seem to assess something other than conventional psychometric *g*, but it has yet to be shown that what it is they do measure is the difference between developing ability and latent capacity.

Individual differences in developing expertise result in much the same way they result in most kinds of learning—from (a) rate of learning (which can be caused by amount of direct instruction received, amount of problem solving done, amount of time and effort spent in thinking about problems, and so on) and from (b) asymptote of learning (which can be caused by differences in numbers of schemas, organization of schemas, efficiency in using schemas, and so on; see Atkinson, Bower, & Crothers, 1965). For example, children can learn how to solve the various kinds of mathematical problems found in tests of mathematical abilities, whether through regular schooling, a special course, or through assimilation of everyday experience. When they learn, they will learn at different rates and reach different asymptotes. Ultimately, such differences will represent a distinct genetic-environmental interaction for each individual. Sometimes, instruction will raise mean scores but leave the existence of, or even patterns of, individual differences intact (see Sternberg, 1985).

There is no evidence, to my knowledge, that individual differences can be wiped out by the kind of 'deliberate practice' studied by Ericsson and his colleagues (e.g., Ericsson & Charness, 1994; Ericsson, Krampe, & Tesch-Romer, 1993; Ericsson & Smith, 1991). Ericsson's work shows a correlation between deliberate practice and expertise; it does not show a causal relation any more than the traditional work on abilities shows causal relations between measured abilities and expertise. A correlational demonstration is an important one; it is not the same as a causal one.

The fact that experts have tended to show more deliberate practice than novices may itself reflect ability difference (Sternberg, 1996b). Meeting with success, those with more ability may practice more; meeting with lesser success, those with lesser ability may give up. Or both deliberate practice and ability may themselves be reflective of some other factor, such as parental encouragement, which could lead both to the nurturing of an ability and to deliberate practice. Indeed, deliberate practice and expertise may interact bi-directionally so that deliberate practice leads to expertise and the satisfaction brought by expertise leads to more deliberate practice. The point is that a variety of mechanisms might underlie a correlational relationship. It seems unquestionable that deliberate practice plays a role in the development of expertise. But it also seems extremely likely that its role is as a necessary rather than sufficient condition,

Deliberate practice may play a somewhat lesser role in creative performance than in other kinds of performance (Sternberg, 1996b). We might argue over whether someone who practices memorization techniques can become a mnemonist. Probably, the individual can become a mnemonist at least within certain content domains (Ericsson, Chase, & Faloon, 1980). Ericsson and his colleagues, for example, were able to work with a college student so that he attained truly impressive expertise in memorizing strings of digits, but his memorization of strings of letters was ordinary. The reason was that he could use the mnemonic of running times to memorize digits but not letters. Even such limited practice effects do not seem to apply quite so well in other domains. It seems less plausible that someone who practices composing will become a Mozart. Of course, one could always conveniently maintain that we have not proven that someone could not become a Mozart with sufficient deliberate practice. Null hypotheses do not lend themselves to proof. But in the real world, with many millions having practiced music very hard, the evidence to date appears discouraging.

Other factors seem far more important in the development of creative expertise, in whatever field. These factors include pursuing paths of inquiry that others ignore or dread, taking intellectual risks, persevering in the face of obstacles, and so (Sternberg & Lubart, 1995, 1996).

## Relations among various kinds of expertise

Although all of the various assessments considered here overlap, the overlap is far from complete. Indeed, a major problem with both ability tests and school achievement tests is that the kinds of skills measured depart in many respects from the skills that are needed for job success (see, e.g., Sternberg, Ferrari, Clinkenbeard, & Grigorenko, 1996; Sternberg, Wagner, Williams, & Horvath, 1995).

An individual can be extremely competent in test and school performance but flag on the job because of the differences in the kinds of expertise required. For example, success in memorizing a textbook may lead to a top grade in a psychology or education course but may not predict particularly well whether someone will be an expert researcher or an expert teacher. The creative and practical skills needed for these kinds of job success may be only minimally or not at all tapped in the ability-testing and school-assessment situations. Thus, it is not particularly surprising that although test scores and school grades correlate with job performance, the correlations are far form perfect.

There are various measures that correlate with IQ that do not, on their face, appear to be measures of achievement. But they are measures of forms of developing expertise. For example, the inspection-time task used by Nettelbeck (1987; Nettelbeck & Lally, 1976) to measure intelligence or the choice reaction-time task of Jensen (1982) both correlate with psychometric *g*. However, performances on both tasks reflect a form of developing expertise, in one case, of perceptual discriminations, in the other case, of quick responses to flashing lights or other stimuli. Of course, individuals may differ in the slopes and asymptotes of their acquisition functions.

The argument here is that ability tests are typically temporally prior in their administration to the administration of measurements of various kinds of achievements but that what they measure is not psychologically prior. The so-called achievement tests might just as well be used to predict scores on ability tests and sometimes are, as when school officials attempt to guess college admissions test scores on the basis of school achievement. In viewing the tests of abilities as psychologically prior, we are confounding our own typical temporal ordering of measurement with some kind of psychological ordering. But in fact, our temporal ordering implies no psychological ordering at all. The relabeling of the *SAT* as the *Scholastic Assessment Test* rather than the *Scholastic Aptitude Test* reflects the recognition that what was called an aptitude test measures more than just aptitude. Nevertheless, the *SAT* is still widely used as an ability test and the *SAT-II*, which more directly measures subject matter knowledge, as a set of achievement tests.

An examination of the content of tests of intelligence and related abilities reveals that IQ-like tests measure achievement that individuals should have accomplished several years back. Tests such as vocabulary, reading comprehension, verbal analogies, arithmetic problem solving, and the like are all, in part, tests of achievement. Even abstract-reasoning tests measure achievement in dealing with geometric symbols, skills taught in Western schools (Laboratory of Comparative Human Cognition, 1982). One might as well use academic performance to predict ability-test scores. The problem regarding the traditional model is not in its statement of a correlation between ability tests and other forms of achievement but in its proposal of a causal relation whereby the tests reflect a construct that is somehow causal of, rather than merely temporally antecedent to, later success.

Even psychobiological measures (see, e.g., Vernon, 1990) are in no sense pure ability measures because we know that just as biological processes affect cognitive processes, so do cognitive processes affect biological ones. Learning, for example, leads to synaptic growth (Kandel, 1991; Thompson, 1985). Thus, biological changes may themselves reflect, in part, developing expertise.

In sum, if we viewed tested abilities as forms of what is represented by *developing expertise,* then I would have no argument with the use of *abilities.* The problem is that this term is usually used in another way—to express a construct that is psychologically prior to other forms of expertise. Such abilities may well exist, but we can assess them only through tests that measure developing forms of expertise expressed in a cultural context.

## Contrast with other views

The developing-expertise model is quite different from the traditional, fixed-abilities model. The developing-expertise model sees the growing problems in our society as deriving, in part, from the very model on which Herrnstein and Murray (1994) base their arguments— the traditional model of relatively fixed individual differences in abilities (see Sternberg, 1995, 1996c, 1996e, for more details). In other words, the traditional mode may be a cause of rather than a potential answer to educational problems, in particular, and societal problems in general. The traditional model is part of the problem, not a basis for a solution.

Although the developing-expertise model differs from the conventional psychometric one, the new model is not an expression of the argument that conventional ability tests—because they are multiple-choice, pencil-and-paper tests—measure little or nothing of interest (e.g., Gardner, 1983). I believe that this armchair argument can be made only by ignoring thousands of criterion-validity studies (see, e.g., Dawis, 1994: Gottfredson, 1986; Hunt, 1995; Hunter, 1986; Sternberg, 1982, 1994a; Wigdor & Garner, 1982). One can argue with the use of intelligence tests on many strong grounds; the existence of some level of predictive validity is probably not one of them. These tests usually measure a part of what is needed for various kinds of success but, of course, only a part. Indeed, I view the developing-expertise model as consistent with theories such as those of Ceci (1996) and Gardner (1983), which take a flexible, multi-faceted view of abilities—conventional or otherwise—as fashioned by the interaction of genetic predispositions with cultural and other experiences.

At the same time, the developing-expertise model differs from these prior theories in one crucial regard. All of these theories view abilities as prior to expertise—as predicting expertise in a variety of domains. The developing-expertise model, in contrast, views abilities as developing forms of expertise themselves.

The argument here is also not akin to the one that the use to intelligence tests represents a history of racist and perhaps even conspiratorial psychologists seeking to benefit certain groups (usually White Americans) and suppress others (e.g., immigrants and people of color) (Gould, 1981). In fact, by contemporary standards, there probably have been any number of racist uses of the tests, and, from time to time, there may even have been conspiracies. But psychologists (or other professionals) of the past cannot sensibly be judged according to present standards. Doctors who used leeches to cure their patients' ills would not look so competent according to today's medical practice, but they did what they believed was right at the time. Whether they were competent depends on which standards—historical or contemporary—are being used in making a judgment.

In sum, the present argument differs from the conventional one in rejecting the psychological priority of abilities. Even those who believe that abilities are developing may view them as somehow prior to achievement; in the present view, both abilities and achievement are forms of developing expertise. Neither is psychologically prior in a protocol of assessment. [...]

# Implications for education and classroom practice

The model of abilities as a form of developing expertise has a number of immediate implications for education, in general, and classroom practice, in particular.

First, teachers and all who use ability and achievement tests should stop viewing them as measuring two distinct constructs. Rather, there is no clear differentiation between the two constructs.

Second, tests of any kind tell us achieved levels of developing expertise. No test of abilities or anything else can specify the asymptote a student can achieve.

Third, different kinds of assessments—multiple-choice, short-answer, performance-based, portfolio—complement each other in assessing multiple aspects of developing expertise. There is no one right kind of assessment.

Fourth, instruction should be geared not just toward imparting a knowledge base, but toward developing reflective, analytical, creative, and practical thinking with a knowledge base. Students learn better when they think to learn, even when their learning is assessed with straightforward multiple-choice memory assessments (Sternberg, Torff, & Grigorenko, 1998). They also learn better when teaching takes into account their diverse styles of learning and thinking, the same diverse styles shown by experts (Sternberg, 1997).

Finally, some theories of cognitive development (e.g., Piaget, 1972) view such development in a relatively abstract way that then needs to be translated into educational practice. The translation is often less than clear. The theory of abilities as developing expertise has an advantage in its direct application to classroom strategies and goals. The overarching goal is to develop expertise and expert learning in every subject matter area.

## Conclusion

The model proposed in this chapter is one of abilities as forms of developing expertise. Individuals are viewed as novices capable of becoming experts in a variety of domains. A model of fixed individual differences, which essentially consigns some students to fixed levels of instruction based on supposedly largely fixed abilities, can be an obstacle to the acquisition of expertise. The key to developing expertise is purposeful and meaningful engagement in a set of tasks relevant to the development of expertise, something of which any individual is capable in some degree. For various reasons (including, perhaps, genetic as well as environmentally based differences), not all individuals will equally engage or engage equally effectively, and hence, individuals will not necessarily all reach the same ultimate level of expertise. But they should all be given the opportunity to reach new levels of competence well beyond what they and, in some cases, others may have thought were possible for them. The fact that Billy and Jimmy have different IQs tells us something about differences in what they now do. It does not tell us anything fixed about what ultimately they will be able to do.

## Note

Preparation of this article was supported under the Javits Act program (Grant No. R206R50001) as administered by the Office of Educational Research and Improvement, U.S. Department of Education. The opinions expressed in this report do not reflect the positions or policies of the Office of Educational Research and Improvement or the U.S. Department of Education.

## References

Atkinson, R. C., Bower, G. H., & Crothers, E. J. (1965). *An introduction to mathematical learning theory*. New York: John Wiley & Sons.

Bereiter, C., & Scardamalia, M. (1993). *Surpassing ourselves: An inquiry into the nature and implications of expertis*e. Chicago: Open Court.

Binet, A., & Simon, T. (1916). *The development of intelligence in children* (E. S. Kite, Trans.). Baltimore: Willams & Wilkins.

Bond, L., & Harman, A. E. (1994). Test-taking strategies. In R. J. Sternberg (Ed.,), *Encyclopedia of human intelligence* (Vol. 2, pp. 1073–1077). New York: Macmillan.

Brody, N. (1992). *Intelligence.* New York: Academic Press.

Brown, A. L., & Ferrara, R. A. (1985). Diagnosing zones of proximal development. In J. V. Wertsch (Ed.), *Culture, communication, and cognition: Vygotskian perspectives* (pp. 273–305). New York: Cambridge University Press.

Brown, A. L., & Frensch, L. A. (1979). The zone of potential development; Implications for intelligence testing in the year 2000. *Intelligence, 3,* 255–277.

Carroll, J. B. (1993). *Human cognitive abilities: A survey of factor-analytic studies.* New York: Cambridge University Press.

Cattell, R. B. (1971). *Abilities: Their structure, growth, and action.* Boston, MA: Houghton Mifflin.

Ceci, S. J. (1996). *On intelligence: A bio-ecological treatise on intellectual development* (Expanded ed.). Cambridge, MA: Harvard University Press.

Ceci, S. J., Nightingale, N. N., & Baker, J. G. (1992). The ecologies of intelligence: Challenges to traditional views. In D. K. Detterman (Ed.), *Current topics in human intelligence: Vol. 2. Is mind modular or unitary?* (pp. 61–82). Norwood, NJ: Ablex.

Ceci, S. J., & Roazzi, A. (1994). The effects of context on cognition: Postcards from Brazil. In R. J. Sternberg & R. K. Wagner (Eds.), *Mind in context: Interactionist perspectives on human intelligence* (pp. 74–101). New York: Cambridge University Press.

Chase, W. G., & Simon, H. A. (1973). The mind's eye in chess. In W. G. Chase (Ed.), V*isual information processing* (pp. 215–281). New York: Academic Press.

Chi, M. T. H., Glaser, R., & Farr, M. (Eds.). (1988). *The nature of expertise.* Hillsdale, NJ: Erlbaum.

Chi, M. T. H., Glaser, R., & Rees, E. (1982). Expertise in problem solving. In R. J. Sternberg (Ed.), *Advances in the psychology of human intelligence* (Vol. 1, pp. 7–75). Hillsdale, NJ: Erlbaum.

Csikszentmihalyi, M. (1988). Society, culture, and person: A systems view of creativity. In R. J. Sternberg (Ed.), *The nature of creativity* (pp. 325–339). New York: Cambridge University Press.

Csikszentmihalyi, M. (1996). *Creativity.* New York: HarperCollins.

Daniel, M. H. (1997). Intelligence testing: Status and trends. *American Psychologist, 52,* 1038–1045.

Das, J. P., Naglieri, J. A., & Kirby, J. R. (1994). *Assessment of cognitive processes.* Needham Heights, MA: Allyn & Bacon.

Dawis, R. V. (1994). Occupations. In R. J. Sternberg (Ed.), *Encyclopedia of human intelligence* (Vol. 2, pp. 781–785). New York: Macmillian.

DeGroot, A. D. (1965). *Thought and choice in chess.* The Hague, The Netherlands: Mouton.

Ericsson, A. (Ed.). (1996). *The road to excellence.* Mahwah, NJ: Erlbaum.

Ericsson, K. A., & Charness, N. (1994). Expert performance: Its structure and acquisition. *American Psychologist, 49,* 725–747.

Ericsson, K. A., Chase, W. G., & Faloon, S. (1980). Acquisition of a memory skill. *Science, 208,* 1181–1182.

Ericsson, K. A., Krampe, R. T., & Tesch-Romer, C. (1993). The role of deliberate practice in the acquisition of expert performance. *Psychological Review, 100,* 363–406.

Ericsson, K. A., & Smith, J. (Eds.). (1991). *Toward a general theory of expertise: Prospects and limits.* New York: Cambridge University Press.

Feuerstein, R. (1979). *The learning potential assessment device.* Baltimore: University Park Press.

Feuerstein, R. (1980). *Instrumental enrichment: An intervention program for cognitive modifiability.* Baltimore: University Park Press.

Fiedler, F. E., & Link, T. G. (1994). Leader intelligence, interpersonal stress, and task performance. In R. J. Sternberg & R. K. Wagner (Eds.), *Mind in context* (pp. 152–167). New York: Cambridge University Press.

Gardner, H. (1983). *Frames of mind*. New York: Free Press.

Gardner, H. (1993). *Multiple intelligences: The theory in practice*. New York: Basic Books.

Gardner, H., Kornhaber, M. L, & Wake, W. K. (1996). *Intelligence: Multiple perspectives*. Orlando, FL: Harcourt Brace College Publishers.

Gottfredson, L. S. (Ed.). (1986). The g factor in employment [Special issue]. *Journal of Vocational Behavior*, 29.

Gould, S. J. (1981). *The mismeasure of man*. New York: Norton.

Gustafsson, J. E. (1988). Hierarchical models of individual differences. In R. J. Sternberg (Ed.), *Advances in the psychology of human intelligence* (Vol. 4, pp. 35–71). Hillsdale, NJ: Erlbaum.

Gustafsson, J. E., & Undheim, J. O. (1996). Individual differences in cognitive function. In D. C. Berliner & R. C. Calfee (Eds.). *Handbook of educational psychology* (pp. 186–242). New York: Macmillan.

Herrnstein, R. J., & Murray, C. (1994). *The bell curve*. New York: Free Press.

Herrnstein, R. J., Nickerson, R. S., deSanchez, M., & Swets, J. A. (1986). Teaching thinking skills. *American Psychologist*, 41, 1279–1289.

Hunt, E. (1995). *Will we be smart enough? A cognitive analysis of the coming workforce*. New York: Russell Sage Foundation.

Hunter, J. E. (1986). Cognitive ability, cognitive aptitudes, job knowledge, and job performance. *Journal of Vocational Behavior*, 29, 340–362.

Jensen, A. R. (1982). The chronometry of intelligence. In R. J. Sternberg (Ed.), *Advances in the psychology of human intelligence* (Vol. 1, pp. 255–310). Hillsdale, NJ: Erlbaum.

Kandel, E. (1991). Cellular mechanisms of learning and the biological basis of individuality. In E. R. Kandel, J. H. Schwartz, & T. M. Jessell (Eds.), *Principles of neural science* (3rd ed., pp. 1009–1031). New York: Elsevier.

Kaufman, A. S., & Kaufman, N. L. (1983). *Kaufman assessment battery for children: Interpretive manual*. Circle Pines, MN: American Guidance Service.

Laboratory of Comparative Human Cognition, (1982). Culture and intelligence. In R. J. Sternberg (Ed.), *Handbook of human intelligence* (pp. 642–719). New York: Cambridge University Press.

Larkin, J., McDermott, J., Simon, D. P., & Simon, H. A. (1980). Expert and novice performance in solving physics problems. *Science,* 208, 1335–1342.

Lave, J. (1988). *Cognition in practice*. New York: Cambridge University Press.

Lesgold, A. M. (1984). Acquiring expertise. In J. R. Anderson & S. M. Kosslyn (Eds.), *Tutorials in learning and memory* (pp. 31–60). New York: Freeman.

Livingston, C., & Borko, H. (1990). High school mathematics review lessons: Expert-novice distinctions. *Journal of Research in Mathematics Education,* 21, 372–387.

Luria, A. R. (1966). *The human brain and psychological processes*. New York: Harper & Row.

Luria, A. R. (1980). *Higher cortical functions in man* (Rev. and Expanded 2nd ed.). New York: Basic Books.

Millman, J., Bishop, H., & Ebel, R. (1965). An analysis of test-wiseness. *Educational and Psychological Measurement*, 25, 707–726.

Naglieri, J. A., & Das, J. P. (1997). *Cognitive assessment system*. Chicago: Riverside Publishing Company.

Nettelbeck, T. (1987). Inspection time and intelligence. In P. A. Vernon (Ed.), *Speed of information processing and intelligence* (pp. 295–346). Norwood, NJ: Ablex.

Nettelbeck, T., & Lally, M. (1976). Inspection time and measured intelligence. *British Journal of Psychology*, 67, 17–22.

Nickerson, R. S. (1986). *Reflections on reasoning.* Hillsdale, NJ: Erlbaum.

Nickerson, R. S., Perkins, D. N., & Smith, E. E. (1985). *The teaching of thinking.* Hillsdale, NJ: Erlbaum.

Perkins, D. N. (1995). *Outsmarting IQ: The emerging science of learnable intelligence.* New York: Free Press.

Perkins, D. N., & Grotzer, T. A. (1997). Teaching intelligence and teaching for intelligence. *American Psychologist*, 52, 1125–1133.

Piaget, J. (1972). *The psychology of intelligence.* Totowa, NJ: Littlefield Adams.

Ramey, C. T. (1994). Abecedarian project. In R. J. Sternberg (Ed.), *Encyclopedia of human intelligence* (Vol. 1, pp. 1–3). New York: Macmillian.

Renzulli, J. S. (1986). The three ring conception of giftedness: A developmental model for creative productivity. In R. J. Sternberg & J. E. Davidson (Eds.), *Conceptions of giftedness* (pp. 53–92). New York: Cambridge University Press.

Sabers, D. S., Cushing, K. S., & Berliner, D. C. (1991). Differences among teachers in a task characterized by simultaneity, multidimensionality, and immediacy. *American Educational Research Journal*, 28, 63–88.

Shulman, L. S. (1987). Knowledge and teaching: Foundations of the new reform. *Harvard Educational Review*, 19(2), 4–14.

Snow, R. E. (1979). Theory and method for research on aptitude processes. In R. J. Sternberg & D. K. Detterman (Eds.), *Human intelligence: Perspectives on its theory and measurement* (pp. 105–137). Norwood, NJ: Ablex.

Snow, R. E. (1980). Aptitude processes. In R. E. Snow, P.-A. Federico, & W. E. Montague (Eds.), *Aptitude, learning, and instruction: Cognitive process analyses of aptitude* (Vol.1, pp. 27–63). Hillsdale, NJ: Erlbaum.

Snow, R. E. (1996). Abilities as aptitudes and achievements in learning situations. In J. J. McArdle & R. W. Woodcock (Eds.), *Human cognitive abilities in theory and practice.* Mahwah, NJ: Erlbaum.

Snow, R. E. & Lohman, D. F. (1984). Toward a theory of cognitive aptitude for learning from instruction. *Journal of Educational Psychology*, 76, 347–376.

Sternberg, R. J. (Ed.). (1982). *Handbook of human intelligence.* New York: Cambridge University Press.

Sternberg, R. J. (1983). Components of human intelligence. *Cognition*, 15, 1–48.

Sternberg, R. J. (1985). *Beyond IQ: A triarchic theory of human intelligence.* New York: Cambridge University Press.

Sternberg, R. J. (1988). *The triarchic mind: A new theory of human intelligence.* New York: Viking-Penguin.

Sternberg, R. J. (1990). *Metaphors of mind: Conceptions of the nature of intelligence.* New York: Cambridge University Press.

Sternberg, R. J. (1994a). Cognitive conceptions of expertise. *International Journal of Expert Systems: Research and Application*, 7(1), 1–12.

Sternberg, R. J. (Ed.), (1994b). *Encyclopedia of human intelligence* (Vols. 1–2). New York: Macmillan.

Sternberg, R. J. (1995). For whom the bell curve tolls: A review of *The Bell Curve. Psychological Science*, 6(5), 257–261.

Sternberg, R. J. (1996a). *Cognitive psychology.* Orlando, FL: Harcourt Brace College Publishers.

Sternberg, R. J. (1996b). Costs of expertise. In K. A. Ericsson (Ed.), *The road to excellence* (pp. 347–354). Mahwah, NJ: Lawrence Erlbaum Associates.

Sternberg, R. J. (1996c). Myths, countermyths, and truths about intelligence. *Educational Researcher*, 25(2), 11–16.

Sternberg, R. J. (1996d). *Successful intelligence*. New York: Simon & Schuster.

Sternberg, R. J. (1996e). What should we ask about intelligence? *American Scholar*, 65, 295–217.

Sternberg, R. J. (1997). What does it mean to be smart? *Educational Leadership*, 54, 20–24.

Sternberg, R. J. & Ben-Zeev, T. (Eds.), (1996). *The nature of mathematical thinking*. Mahwah, NJ: Lawrence Erlbaum Associates.

Sternberg, R. J., Ferrari, M., Clinkenbeard, P., & Grigorenko, E. L. (1996). Identification, instruction, and assessment of gifted children: A construct validation of a triarchic model. *Gifted Child Quarterly*, 40, 129–137.

Sternberg, R. J., & Gardner, M. K. (1983). Unities in inductive reasoning. *Journal of Experimental Psychology: General,* 112, 80–116.

Sternberg, R. J., & Grigorenko, E. L. (Eds.). (1997). *Intelligence, heredity, and environment*. New York: Cambridge University Press.

Sternberg, R. J., & Horvath, J. A. (1995). A prototype view of expert teaching. *Educational Researcher*, 24(6), 9–17.

Sternberg, R. J., & Lubart, T. I. (1995). *Defying the crowd: Cultivating creativity in a culture of conformity*. New York: Free Press.

Sternberg, R. J., & Lubart, T. I. (1996). Investing in creativity. *American Psychologist*, 51, 677–688.

Sternberg, R. J., & Spear-Swerling, L. (1996). *Teaching for thinking*. Washington, DC: APA Books.

Sternberg, R. J., Torff, B., & Grigorenko, E. L. (1998). Teaching triarchically improves school achievement. *Journal of Educational Psychology,* 90(3), 374–384.

Sternberg, R. J., Wagner, R. K., Willams, W. M., & Horvath, J. (1995). Testing common sense. *American Psychologist*, 50, 912–927.

Thompson, R. F. (1985). *The brain: An introduction to neuroscience*. New York: Freeman.

Thorndike, R. L., Hagen, E. P. & Sattler, J. M. (1986). *Technical manual for the Stanford-Binet Intelligence Scale: Fourth edition*. Chicago, IL: Riverside.

Vernon, P. A. (1990). The use of biological measures to estimate behavioral intelligence. *Educational Psychologist*, 25, 293–304.

Vernon, P. E. (1971). *The structure of human abilities*. London: Methuen.

Vygotsky, L. S. (1978). *Mind in society: The development of higher psychological processes*. Cambridge, MA: Harvard University Press.

Wechsler, D. (1958). *The measurement and appraisal of adult intelligence (5th ed.)*. Baltimore: Willams & Wilkins.

Wechsler, D. (1991). *Manual for the Wechsler Intelligence Scales for Children–Third edition (WISC-III)*. San Antonio, TX: Psychological Corporation.

Wigdor, A. K., & Garner, W. R. (1982). *Ability testing: Uses, consequences, and controversies: Part1. Report of the committee*. Washington, DC: National Academy Press.

Williams, W. M., Blythe, T., White, N., Li, J., Sternberg, R. J., & Gardner, H. I. (1996). *Practical intelligence for school: A handbook for teachers of grades 5–8*. New York: HarperCollins.

# 3

# On Two Metaphors for Learning and the Dangers of Choosing Just One

*Anna Sfard*

O! this learning, what a thing it is.

—W. Shakespeare, *The Taming of the Shrew*

Theories of learning, like all scientific theories, come and go. Some innovations reach deeper than others. Occasionally, theoretical changes amount to a conceptual upheaval. This is what seems to be happening right now in the research on learning. Numerous books and articles in professional journals come up with radically new approaches, and whether one likes the innovative ideas or not, one cannot just brush them aside. The field is in a state of perturbation, with prospects of a new equilibrium not yet in sight. The recent discussion on transfer in *Educational Researcher* (Anderson, Reder, & Simon, 1996; Donmoyer, 1996; Greeno, 1997; Hiebert et al., 1996) brings the controversial nature of current theories of learning into full relief. Strenuous attempts of many authors to come to terms with the change by forging theoretical bridges between competing outlooks (Billett, 1996; Cobb, 1995; Smith, 1995; Vosniadou, 1996) complete this picture. This chapter will take a closer look at this controversy, as well as at the issue of theorizing in general. The discussion will be organized around the question of whether the struggle for a conceptual unification of research on learning is a worthwhile endeavor. The first step, however, will be to sketch a bird's-eye view of the competing trends in our present conceptualizations of learning.

To be able to embrace the whole issue at a glance, one has to reach the most fundamental, primary levels of our thinking and bring into the open the tacit assumptions and beliefs that guide us. This means digging out the metaphors that underlie both our spontaneous everyday conceptions and scientific theorizing. Indeed, metaphors are the most primitive, most elusive, and yet amazingly informative objects of analysis. Their special power stems from the fact that they often cross the borders between the spontaneous and the scientific, between the intuitive and the formal. Conveyed through language from one domain to another, they enable conceptual osmosis between everyday and scientific discourses, letting our primary intuition shape scientific ideas and the formal conceptions feed back into the intuition. Thus, by concentrating on the basic metaphors rather than on particular theories of learning, I hope to get into a position to elicit some of the fundamental assumptions underlying both our theorizing on learning and our practice as students and

From: *Educational Researcher*, 27 (2), (AERA, 1998), pp. 4–13.

as teachers. First, however, let me add a few words on the relative status of language, metaphors, and scientific theories.

It was Michael Reddy who, in the seminal paper titled "The Conduit Metaphor," alerted us to the ubiquity of metaphors and to their constitutive role (Reddy, 1978). Using as an example the notion of communication, he showed how the language we use to talk about a given concept may take us in a systematic way to another, seemingly unrelated conceptual domain. (In his example, the figurative projection was from the domain of communication to that of transport.) Since then, the systematic conceptual mappings came to be known as conceptual metaphors and became objects of a vigorous inquiry (Johnson, 1987; Lakoff, 1987, 1993; Lakoff & Johnson, 1980; Sacks, 1978). What traditionally has been regarded as a mere tool for better understanding and for more effective memorizing was now recognized as the primary source of all of our concepts.

The idea that new knowledge germinates in old knowledge has been promoted by all of the theoreticians of intellectual development, from Piaget to Vygotsky to contemporary cognitive scientists. The notion of metaphor as a conceptual transplant clearly complements this view by providing a means for explaining the processes that turn old into new. One may say, therefore, that metaphorical projection is a mechanism through which the given culture perpetuates and reproduces itself in a steadily growing system of concepts. [...]

Eliciting the metaphors that guide us in our work as learners, teachers, and researchers is the first aim of the remainder of this article. Given my professional background, I am inclined to use examples taken from mathematics education; this, however, should not diminish the generality of the argument. After identifying two leading metaphors that inform our thinking about learning, I will examine their entailments. While doing so, I will be arguing that the implications of a metaphor are a result of contextual determinants not less than of the metaphor itself. Thus, the same figurative idea may engender several greatly varying conceptual frameworks. The principal aim of the analysis that follows is to identify the ways in which one can put the different metaphors for learning to their best uses while barring undesirable entailments. In the end, I will try to show how too great a devotion to one particular metaphor and rejection of all the others can lead to theoretical distortions and to undesirable practical consequences.

# Acquisition metaphor versus participation metaphor

The upshot of the former section can be put as follows: all our concepts and beliefs have their roots in a limited number of fundamental ideas that cross disciplinary boundaries and are carried from one domain to another by the language we use. One glance at the current discourse on learning should be enough to realize that nowadays educational research is caught between two metaphors that, in this article, will be called the *acquisition metaphor* and the *participation metaphor*. Both of these metaphors are simultaneously present in most recent texts, but while the *acquisition metaphor* is likely to be more prominent in older writings, more recent studies are often dominated by the *participation metaphor*.

## Acquisition metaphor

Since the dawn of civilization, human learning has been conceived of as an acquisition of something. Indeed, the *Collins English Dictionary* defines learning as "the act of gaining knowledge." Since the time of Piaget and Vygotski, the growth of knowledge in the process of learning has been analyzed in terms of concept development. Concepts are to be understood as basic units of knowledge that can be accumulated, gradually refined, and combined to form ever richer cognitive structures. The picture is not much different when we talk about the learner as a person who constructs meaning. This approach, which today seems natural and self-evident, brings to mind the activity of accumulating material goods. The language of 'knowledge acquisition' and 'concept development' makes us think about the human mind as a container to be filled with certain materials and about the learner as becoming an owner of these materials.

Once we realize the fact that it is the metaphor of acquisition that underlies our thinking about learning mathematics, we become immediately aware of its presence in almost every common utterance on learning. Let us look at a number of titles of publications that appeared over the last two decades: "The Development of Scientific Knowledge in Elementary School Children," "Acquisition of Mathematical Concepts and Processes," "[C]oncept-Mapping in Science," "Children's Construction of Number," "Stage Theory of the Development of Alternative Conceptions," "Promoting Conceptual Change in Science," "On Having and Using Geometric Knowledge," "Conceptual Difficulties … in the Acquisition of the Concept of Function." The idea that learning means the acquisition and accumulation of some goods is evident in all of these titles. They may point to a gradual reception or to an acquisition by development or by construction, but all of them seem to imply gaining ownership over some kind of self-sustained entity.

There are many types of entities that may be acquired in the process of learning. One finds a great variety of relevant terms among the key words of the frameworks generated by the *acquisition metaphor:* knowledge, concept, conception, idea, notion, misconception, meaning, sense, schema, fact, representation, material, contents. There are as many terms that denote the action of making such entities one's own: reception, acquisition, construction, internalization, appropriation, transmission, attainment, development, accumulation, grasp. The teacher may help the student to attain his or her goal by delivering, conveying, facilitating, mediating, et cetera. Once acquired, the knowledge, like any other commodity, may now be applied, transferred (to a different context), and shared with others.

This impressively rich terminological assortment was necessary to mark dissimilarities— sometimes easy to see and sometimes quite subtle—between different schools of thought. Over the last decades, numerous suggestions have been made as to the nature of the mechanism through which mathematical concepts may be turned into the learner's private property; however, in spite of the many differences on the issue of 'how,' there has been no controversy about the essence: the idea of learning as gaining possession over some commodity has persisted in a wide spectrum of frameworks, from moderate to radical constructivism and then to interactionism and sociocultural theories. Researchers have offered a range of greatly differing mechanisms of concept development. First, they simply talked about passive reception of knowledge, then about its being actively constructed by the learner; later, they analyzed the ways in which concepts are transferred from a social to an individual plane and internalized by the student; eventually, they envisioned learning as a never-ending, self-regulating process of emergence in a continuing interaction with peers, teachers, and texts. As long as they investigated learning by focusing on the 'development of concepts' and on the 'acquisition of knowledge,' however, they implicitly agreed that this process can be conceptualized in terms of the *acquisition metaphor.*

# Participation metaphor

The *acquisition metaphor* is so strongly entrenched in our minds that we would probably never become aware of its existence if another, alternative metaphor did not start to develop. When we search through recent publications, the emergence of a new metaphor becomes immediately apparent. Among the harbingers of the change are such titles as "Reflection, Communication, and Learning Mathematics," "Democratic Competence and Reflective Knowing," "Development Through Participation in Sociocultural Activities," "Learning in the Community," "Reflective Discourse and Collective Reflection," "Mathematics As Being in the World," "Dialogue and Adult Learning," "Cooperative Learning of Mathematics," and "Fostering Communities of Inquiry." The new researcher talks about learning as a legitimate peripheral participation (Lave & Wenger, 1991) or as an apprenticeship in thinking (Rogoff, 1990).

A far-reaching change is signaled by the fact that although all of these titles and expressions refer to learning, none of them mentions either "concept" or "knowledge." The terms that imply the existence of some permanent entities have been replaced with the noun "knowing," which indicates action. This seemingly minor linguistic modification marks a remarkable foundational shift (cf. Cobb, 1995; Smith, 1995). The talk about states has been replaced with attention to activities. In the image of learning that emerges from this linguistic turn, the permanence of *having* gives way to the constant flux of *doing*. While the concept of acquisition implies that there is a clear end point to the process of learning, the new terminology leaves no room for halting signals. Moreover, the ongoing learning activities are never considered separately from the context within which they take place. The context, in its turn, is rich and multifarious, and its importance is pronounced by talk about situatedness, contextuality, cultural embeddedness, and social mediation. The set of new key words that, along with the noun "practice," prominently features the terms "discourse" and "communication" suggests that the learner should be viewed as a person interested in participation in certain kinds of activities rather than in accumulating private possessions.

To put it differently, learning a subject is now conceived of as a process of becoming a member of a certain community. This entails, above all, the ability to communicate in the language of this community and act according to its particular norms. The norms themselves are to be negotiated in the process of consolidating the community. While the learners are newcomers and potential reformers of the practice, the teachers are the preservers of its continuity. From a lone entrepreneur, the learner turns into an integral part of a team. For obvious reasons, this new view of learning can be called the *participation metaphor*. From now on, to avoid tiresome repetition, I will sometimes use the abbreviations "AM" and "PM" for *acquisition* and *participation metaphor*, respectively.

To clarify the idea of learning-as-participation, a number of explanatory remarks would be in place. First, the question may be asked, "What is metaphorical about the issue of participation?" After all, learning implies participation in instructional activities, and thus its participational nature should perhaps be treated as literal, not as figurative. To answer this, let us take a closer look at the concept of participation as such. A quest after its roots will lead us, once again, to the world of physical objects. "Participation" is almost synonymous with "taking part" and "being a part," and both of these expressions signalize that learning should be viewed as a process of becoming a part of a greater whole. It is now relatively easy to spot those beliefs about learning that may be brought by PM as its immediate entail-ments. Just as different organs combine to form a living body, so do learners contribute to the existence and functioning of a community of practitioners. While the AM stresses the individual mind and what goes "into it," the PM shifts the focus to the evolving bonds between the individual and others. While AM emphasizes the inward movement of the object known as knowledge, PM gives prominence to the aspect of mutuality characteristic of the part-whole relation. Indeed, PM makes salient the dialectic nature of the learning interaction: The whole and the parts affect and inform each other. On one hand, the very existence of the whole is fully dependent on the parts. On the other hand, whereas the AM stresses the way in which possession determines the identity of the possessor, the PM implies that the iden-tity of an individual, like an identity of a living organ, is a function of his or her being (or becoming) a part of a greater entity. Thus, talk about the "stand-alone learner" and "decon-textualized learning" becomes as pointless as the attempts to define lungs or muscles with-out a reference to the living body within which they both exist and function.

Second, one may oppose the above classification of theories of learning by saying that most conceptual frameworks cannot be regarded as either purely "acquisitional" or purely "participational." The act of acquisition is often tantamount to the act of becoming a par-ticipant, and if so, one can find it difficult to consider AM and PM separately, let alone as mutually exclusive. No claim on exclusivity of the metaphors has been made in this chap-ter, however. Later, I will argue for the inherent impossibility of freeing the discourse on learning from either of the two metaphors. Theories can be classified as acquisition-oriented or participation-oriented only if they disclose a clear preference for one metaphorical ingre-dient over the other.

Finally, the dichotomy between acquisition and participation should not be mistaken for the well-known distinction between individualist and social perspectives on learning. The examples here have shown that the former division crosses the demarcation lines estab-lished by the latter. According to the distinction proposed in this article, theories that speak about reception of knowledge and those that view learning as the internalization of socially established concepts belong to the same category (AM), whereas on the individual/social axis, they must be placed at opposite poles. Whereas the social dimension is salient in the PM, it is not necessarily absent from the theories dominated by the AM. It is important to understand that the two distinctions were made according to different criteria: while the acquisition/participation division is ontological in nature and draws on two radically different answers to the fundamental question, "What is this thing called learning?," the individual/social dichotomy does not imply a controversy as to the definition of learning, but rather rests on differing visions of the mechanism of learning. A schematic compari-son between the two is presented in Table 3.1.

# What can go wrong with AM, and how PM can help

It is time to ask for the reasons underlying the metaphorical shift. If we have been living with the AM for millennia, it is not all that obvious why a change should now be necessary. Well, we might have been living with AM, but have we been happy with it? The latest developments make it rather clear that the answer should probably be "no." It does not take

**Table 3.1   The metaphorical mappings**

| Acquisition metaphor | | Participation metaphor |
| --- | --- | --- |
| Individual enrichment | Goal of learning | Community building |
| Acquisition of something | Learning | Becoming a participant |
| Recipient (consumer), (re-)constructor | Student | Peripheral participant, apprentice |
| Provider, facilitator, mediator | Teacher | Expert participant, preserver of practice/discourse |
| Property, possession, commodity (individual, public) | Knowledge, concept | Aspect of practice/discourse/activity |
| Having, possessing | Knowing | Belonging, participating, communicating |

much effort to identify at least two areas in which the AM reveals a particular weakness. First, our thinking about learning has always been plagued by foundational quandaries that would not yield to the finest of philosophical minds. Second, the conception of knowledge as property, when not controlled, leads to too literal a translation of beliefs on material properties into beliefs on learning; some of the resulting norms and value judgments are likely to have adverse effects on both the theory and practice of learning and teaching. It may well be that the reason behind the conceptual unrest we are witnessing these days is the hope that the new metaphor will remedy both of these afflictions.

## Foundational dilemmas

Probably the best-known foundational dilemma obviously inherent to the AM was first signaled by Plato in his dialogue *Meno* and came to be known later as "the learning paradox" (Bereiter, 1985; Cobb, Yackel, & Wood, 1992). Although brought up in many different disguises throughout history, the quandary is always the same: how can we want to acquire a knowledge of something that is not yet known to us? Indeed, if this something does not yet belong to the repertoire of the things we know, then, being unaware of its existence, we cannot possibly inquire about it. Or, to put it differently, if we can only become cognizant of something by recognizing it on the basis of the knowledge we already possess, then nothing that does not yet belong to the assortment of the things we know can ever become one of them. Conclusion: learning new things is inherently impossible.

Philosophers and psychologists have been grappling with the learning paradox for ages, but until recently, no real attempt to transgress the boundaries of the AM was made. The metaphor just did not look like a metaphor at all. How could it be otherwise if the AM has always been engraved in language, from which there is no escape?

Thinking about the epistemological and ontological foundations of our conception of learning intensified a few decades ago, when the doctrine of radical constructivism entangled the psychologists in a new dilemma. Without questioning the thrust of the AM, the constructivists offered a new conception of the mechanism that turns knowledge into one's private possession. It is the central constructivist idea of learners as the builders of their own conceptual structures that, at a closer look, turns problematic. Whatever version of constructivism is concerned—the moderate, the radical, or the social—the same dilemma must eventually pop up: how do we account for the fact that learners are able to build for themselves concepts that seem fully congruent with those of others? Or, to put it differently, how do people bridge individual and public possessions?

One of the reasons some people may be attracted to the PM is that it seems to help us out of these foundational quandaries. It is an escape rather than a direct solution: instead of solving the problem, the new metaphor simply dissolves vexing questions by its very refusal to objectify knowledge. Here, "objectifying" means treating something as a well-defined entity that can be considered independently of human beings. It should be stressed that the doubt about the soundness of the tendency to objectify knowledge is not new and that the idea of disobjectification has been considered by many thinkers—notably Plato, Hegel, and neo-Kantians (Kozulin, 1990, pp. 22–23; Woodfield, 1993). The PM does the disobjectification job by providing an alternative to talk about learning as making an acquisition. Within its boundaries, there is simply no room for the clearcut distinction between internal and external (concepts, knowledge), which is part and parcel of objectification. By getting rid of the problematic entities and dubious dichotomies and clearing the language of an essentialist aftertaste, PMs circumvent the philosophical pitfalls of AMs in an elegant manner.

This account would not be complete without a caveat: it may well be that the PM has in store new foundational dilemmas not yet suspected by its ardent followers. The PM's present appeal stems from the fact that it brings immediate relief from the old headache. There is no guarantee, however, that it is not going to disclose its own maladies one day. The danger of finding ourselves entangled in difficulties as we go on fathoming the intricacies of the participation mechanism is only too real. After all, the physical metaphor of "turning into a part of a greater whole" has its own pitfalls and may eventually lead us to an epistemological dead end just like any other metaphor that crosses ontological boundaries.

## The question of norms and values

Whereas the impossibility of "something out of nothing" seems endemic to the property of being an object, so that dismissing the learning paradox would mean a rejection of the metaphor itself, there are MA-engendered views and opinions that are optional rather than necessary and only come to the fore if one chooses to endorse them. Metaphorical entailments that have to do with norms and values are usually of the latter kind.

If knowledge is conceived of as a commodity it is only natural that attitudes toward learning reflect the way the given society thinks about material wealth. When figuratively equated, knowledge and material possessions are likely to play similar roles in establishing people's identities and in defining their social positions. In the class-ridden capitalist society, for example, knowledge understood as property is likely to turn into an additional attribute of position and power. Like material goods, knowledge has the permanent quality that makes the privileged position of its owner equally permanent.

As a result, learning-according-to-AM may draw people apart rather than bring them together. As in a society driven by a pursuit of material goods, so in the AM-based approach to learning, learners and scientists are likely to put forward competition and solitary achievement. The American sociologist of science R. K. Morton notes that a scientist who just arrived at what may count as an important result "will be under pressure to make his *contribution to knowledge* known to other scientists and … they, in turn, will be under pressure to acknowledge *his rights to his intellectual property*" (Morton, 1973, p. 294, emphases added). In a footnote to this description, Morton seems to be apologizing for the vocabulary he uses, stating that "[b]orrowing, trespassing, poaching, credit, stealing, a concept which 'belongs' to us—these are only a few of the many terms in the lexicon of property adopted by scientists as matter of course" (p. 295). If this is the language in which this community speaks of intellectual achievement, no wonder that incidents of scientific fraud become more and more frequent in the increasingly crowded academia. While these are certainly extreme cases, there are symptoms much milder than obvious misconduct that can count as consequences of the acquisitionist approach. A not-altogether-infrequent occurrence of a self-centered, asocial attitude toward knowing, creating, and learning is certainly a case in point. If people are valued and segregated according to what they have, the metaphor of intellectual property is more likely to feed rivalry than collaboration.

It is noteworthy that within the acquisition paradigm, not only knowledge, but also the means for gaining it, counts as a highly priced possession that, if of a superior quality, can make the possessors themselves superior to others. Such terms as "gift" or "potential," often used to denote a special propensity for learning and creating, suggest that this characteristic is given, not acquired. It is a person's "quality mark." Students' achievements may depend on environmental factors, but the teachers feel they can tell students' real (permanent) potential from their actual performance. The gifts and potentials, like other private possessions, are believed to be measurable and may therefore be used for sorting people into categories. In this climate, the need to prove one's "potential" sometimes overgrows his or her desire to be useful. This is what evidently happened to the Cambridge mathematician G. H. Hardy (1940/1967) who, after confessing that his interest in mathematics was motivated by the wish to show his outstanding abilities (mathematics "gives unrivaled openings for the display of sheer professional skill," p. 80), defiantly admitted to being perfectly happy in the academy without ever doing anything "useful" (the quotes are Hardy's own).

While these distortions are definitely not a necessary outcome of the AM, the metaphor is apparently what made them possible. Attitudes like those presented in the last paragraph are most likely to appear in societies that value—or even just tolerate—the uncompromising pursuit of material wealth. As long as a metaphor enjoys full hegemony, its normative implications are usually taken for granted; the introduction of a new metaphor is often enough to bring the issue of norms to the fore and turn it into an object of explicit reflection. This is exactly what is likely to happen when the PM enters the scene as a possible alternative to the AM. The new metaphor replaces the talk about private possessions with a discourse about shared activities. This linguistic shift epitomizes the democratic nature of the turn toward the PM. The democratization of the language may lead, eventually, to a far-reaching change in awareness and in beliefs about learning.

The promise of the PM seems, indeed, quite substantial. The vocabulary of participation brings the message of togetherness, solidarity, and collaboration. The PM language does not allow for talk about permanence of either human possessions or human traits. The new metaphor promotes an interest in people in action rather than in people "as such." Being "in action" means being in a constant flux. The awareness of the change that never stops means refraining from a permanent labeling. Actions can be clever or unsuccessful, but these adjectives do not apply to the actors. For the learner, all options are always open, even if he or she carries a history of failure. Thus, quite unlike the AM, the PM seems to bring a message of an everlasting hope: today you act one way; tomorrow you may act differently.

To sum up, the *participation metaphor* has a potential to lead to a new, more democratic practice of learning and teaching. Because, however, social, normative, and ethical morals

of metaphors are not inscribed in the metaphors themselves but rather are a matter of interpretation, the intentions and skills of those who harness the metaphor to work are of central significance. In the final account, what shape the practice will take is up to interpreters
rather than to legislators. Thus, only time will tell whether the promise of a more democratic process of learning, brought by PM, is going to materialize. When it comes to social
issues, PM-based theories are not any less susceptible to abuses and undesirable interpretations than other conceptual frameworks. We can only protect ourselves from falling into
such traps by constantly monitoring our basic beliefs. It may well be that the most important merit of the PM is that it serves as an eye-opening device with respect to the *acquisition metaphor*. This relation, by the way, is symmetric: the social implications of the PM,
listed above—far from being the only possible—are brought into full relief against the
contrasting background of common beliefs induced by the AM and could be much harder
to see without it. The mutual dependence of interpretations of the metaphors is something
to be remembered when we arrive at the conclusions of the present discussion in the last
section of this article.

# Why do we need AM after all?

After pointing out the weakness of the AM and the relative advantages of the PM, I will
now argue that giving up the AM is neither desirable nor possible. When it comes to
research, some important things that can be done with the old metaphor cannot be achieved
with the new one. Besides, the PM, when left alone, may be as dangerous a thing as the
AM proved to be in a similar situation.

## Research issues: the question of transfer

The refusal to reify knowledge seems to go hand in hand with wondering about the notion
of transfer. There are two ways in which the opponents of objectifying and abstracting
argue against this notion. Some of them claim that, based on empirical evidence, transfer
is a rare event, and the most extreme among them would simply deny its existence. Others
reject the very idea of transfer, saying that it is "seriously misconceived" (Lave, 1988,
p. 39). Many opponents of the PM argue against the former type of claim (Anderson et al.,
1996), but, in fact, only the latter line of reasoning is truly consistent with the PM-based
frameworks. As Greeno (1997, p. 5) aptly notices in his contribution to the present discussion, those who overlook this point may, as a result, "talk and write past each other
because they address different questions."

   A persistent follower of the PM must realize, sooner or later, that from a purely analytical
point of view, the metaphorical message of the notion of transfer does not fit into PM-generated
conceptual frameworks. Learning transfer means carrying knowledge across contextual
boundaries; therefore, when one refuses to view knowledge as a stand-alone entity and
rejects the idea of context as a clearly delineated "area," there is simply nothing to be carried over, and there are no definite boundaries to be crossed. It is only natural that when it
comes to the centrally important controversy over transfer, many PM adherents, not yet
prepared to face the ultimate consequences of the new vision of learning, go only halfway:

they bring empirical evidence to refute the claims about the possibility of transfer rather than admit that the notion, at least as it is traditionally understood, is intractable within their framework. By doing so, they unwittingly succumb to the rules of AM-based discourse. Naturally, the discussion between the participationist and acquisitionist is bound to be futile because the former cannot convince the latter of the nonexistence of transfer, just as a physiologist would not be able to convince a psychiatrist about the nonexistence of mental illness: it takes a common language to make one's position acceptable—or even just comprehensible—to another person.

If we agree that there is no room for the traditionally conceived notion of transfer in the PM-based discourse, the long-standing controversy would disappear just as the learning paradox disappeared before. But the benefits of this new disappearance are not so obvious as those of the former one. For one thing, I doubt the very possibility of clearing the discourse on learning from any traces of the AM. Whereas growing numbers of thinkers are ready to agree that the dependence of learning on context is much too great to allow for talk about universal cross-situational invariants, nobody—not even the most zealous followers of the PM-based line of thought—would deny that something does keep repeating itself as we move from situation to situation and from context to context. Our ability to prepare ourselves today to deal with new situations we are going to encounter tomorrow is the very essence of learning. Competence means being able to repeat what can be repeated while changing what needs to be changed. How is all of this accounted for if we are not allowed to talk about carrying anything with us from one situation to another?[1]

Aware of the impossibility of circumventing these questions, some writers are trying to reconcile the idea of transfer with the PM. One such attempt has been presented by Greeno (1997) in his contribution to the present discussion. Greeno's central idea is to provide the old notion with a new interpretation. Defining learning as "improved participation in interactive systems," he proceeds to account "for transfer in terms of transformations of constraints, affordances, and attunements" (p. 12). This description, oriented toward interactions between learners and situations, may indeed be regarded as compatible with the PM framework. In spite of this, one may still wonder whether the proposal has a chance to bring the heated controversy between the two camps to a stop. Even if the new approach is welcome in acquisitionist circles, it may be unacceptable in the eyes of most devoted adherents of the PM. The latter may claim that the switch to the new framework cannot be regarded as complete until the professional discourse is thoroughly purged of expressions that bring to mind the old metaphor. Indeed, if this is what they said in response to the attempts to preserve the terms "knowledge" and "concept" (see, e.g., Bauersfeld, 1995; Smith, 1995), this is also what they are likely to say about any attempt to save the notion of transfer. Because the notion is fraught with acquisitionist connotations, some people may simply be unable to say "transfer" and "situatedness" in one breath.

Whether fully effective or not, Greeno's attempt shows that even if one agrees with the contention that any human action is a result of a dialectic between the situation and the actor rather than of any predesigned, abstract plan of that action, one may still believe that there is no satisfactory account of learning that does not take into account the actor's previous experience. Thus, if a model of learning is to be convincing, it is probably bound to build on the notion of an acquired, situationally invariant property of the learner, which goes together with him or her from one situation to another.

To sum up, it seems that even if one does not like its objectifying quality, one finds it extremely difficult to avoid the acquisitionist language altogether. Whenever we try to comprehend a change, the perceptual, bodily roots of all our thinking compel us to look for structure-imposing invariants and to talk in terms of objects and abstracted properties. We seem to know no other route to understanding. No wonder, therefore, that those who oppose objectification and try to exorcise abstraction and generalization from the discourse on learning find themselves entangled in conflicting statements. They may be making heroic efforts to free themselves from the idea of learning as acquisition, but the metaphor—engraved in the language—would invariably bounce back. Some of the proponents of the PM framework are aware of the contradictions implicit in the call for disobjectification and wonder about it explicitly: "How can we purport to be working out a *theoretical conception* of learning without, in fact, engaging in the project of abstraction rejected above?," ask Lave and Wenger (1991, p. 38, emphasis in the original). There is no simple way out of this entrapment. As I argue in the concluding section, even if one cannot solve the dilemma, one can—and probably should—learn to live with it.

Let me finish this section by saying that even if we could create an AM-free discourse, we probably shouldn't. Within the participationist framework, some powerful means for conceptualization of learning are lost, and certain promising paths toward understanding its mechanism are barred. This very article, if it resonates with the readers' thinking, may serve as evidence. This discussion on learning is founded on the theory of conceptual metaphor, according to which any new conceptualization—thus, any learning—is only possible thanks to our ability to transfer existing conceptual schemes into new contexts. The metaphor itself was defined as a "conceptual transplant." The foregoing sections abound in concrete examples of such transplants. All of this testifies to my sustained faith in the power of the AM.

## Pedagogical issues: the worry about subject matter

Whereas the above considerations deal with the inevitable implications of the *participation metaphor*, I am now going to focus on metaphorical entailments that are a matter of interpretation and choice rather than of logical necessity.

More often than not, it is not all that obvious how the request to disobjectify knowledge and "put it back into context" should be interpreted. Within the science and mathematics education communities, claims about the inherent contextuality of knowledge are often construed as contentions that scientific and mathematical concepts can be meaningfully learned only within a "real-life" context (see, e.g., Heckman & Weissglass, 1994). As it now becomes clear, however, real-life situations that would be likely to become for mathematics or science students what a craftsman's workshop is for the apprentice are extremely difficult to find. Another translation of PM-engendered theoretical ideas into the language of instructional practice is offered by those who suggest that the student should become a member of a "community of practice" (Lave & Wenger, 1991), within which he or she would have a chance to act as a (beginning) practitioner. According to Ball (1991, p. 35), "the goal [of teaching mathematics] is to help students … become active participants in mathematics as a system of human thought," whereas Schoenfeld (1996) promotes the idea of turning the mathematics class into a "community of inquiry." At a closer look, this approach also turns out quite problematic, as it is far from clear how we should construe the term "community of practice" and whom we should view as "expert practitioners" and the shapers of a given "practice."

Whichever of the two interpretations is chosen, what used to be called "subject matter" may change so dramatically that some people would begin wondering whether the things we would then be teaching could still be called science or mathematics (see, e.g., Hiebert et al., 1996; Sierpinska, 1995; Thomas, 1996). Naturally, the question of naming is not the main reason for concerns expressed by those who hold the PM responsible for current changes in mathematics education. The main problem, it seems, is that of a gradual disappearance of a well-defined subject matter. Without a clearly delineated content,[2] the whole process of learning and teaching is in danger of becoming amorphous and losing direction. No wonder, then, that current talk about "challenges for Reform" (see, e.g., Smith III, 1996)—perhaps even as a backlash to reform—indicates a growing disillusionment with what is going on in many classrooms a few years into the "participation era."

# Conclusion: one metaphor is not enough

The message of the above critical examination of the two basic metaphors for learning is rather confusing: it now seems that we can live neither with nor without either of them. In this concluding section, I wish to make it clear why it is essential that we try to live with both. Later, I make suggestions about the ways in which this seemingly impossible demand might be fulfilled after all.

## Why do we need more than one metaphor?

The relative advantages of each of the two metaphors make it difficult to give up either of them: each has something to offer that the other cannot provide. Moreover, relinquishing either the AM or the PM may have grave consequences, whereas metaphorical pluralism embraces a promise of a better research and a more satisfactory practice. The basic tension between seemingly conflicting metaphors is our protection against theoretical excesses, and is a source of power.

As was emphasized before, the metaphors we use should not be held responsible for unsatisfactory practices, but rather their interpretations. When a theory is translated into an instructional prescription, exclusivity becomes the worst enemy of success. Educational practices have an overpowering propensity for extreme, one-for-all, practical recipes. A trendy mixture of constructivist, social-interactionist, and situationist approaches— which has much to do with the *participation metaphor*—is often translated into a total banishment of "teaching by telling," an imperative to make "cooperative learning" mandatory to all, and a complete delegitimatization of instruction that is not "problem-based" or not situated in a real-life context. But this means putting too much of a good thing into one pot. Because no two students have the same needs and no two teachers arrive at their best performance in the same way, theoretical exclusivity and didactic single-mindedness can be trusted to make even the best of educational ideas fail.

What is true about educational practice also holds for theories of learning. It seems that the most powerful research is that which stands on more than one metaphorical leg (cf. Sfard,

1997). An adequate combination of the *acquisition* and *participation metaphors* would bring to the fore the advantages of each of them, while keeping their respective drawbacks at bay. Conversely, giving full exclusivity to one conceptual framework would be hazardous. Dictatorship of a single metaphor, like a dictatorship of a single ideology, may lead to theories that serve the interests of certain groups to the disadvantage of others. A metaphor that has been given hegemony serves as an exclusive basis for deciding what should count as "normal" and what is "anomalous," what should be viewed as "below average" rather than "above," and what should be regarded as "healthy" and what as "pathological." The exclusivity is often equated with certainty, whereas the very presence of a competing metaphor may be enough to disclose the arbitrary nature of some of the generally accepted classifications. This disclosure, therefore, has an immediate emancipatory effect. When two metaphors compete for attention and incessantly screen each other for possible weaknesses, there is a much better chance for producing a critical theory of learning (Geuss, 1981; Habermas, 1972). Such a theory would inquire after the true interests of all of the parties involved in the learning process and thus engage the research community in an endeavor likely to have a liberating and consolidating effect on those who learn and those who teach.

## Living with contradictions

After making the case for the plurality of metaphors, I have to show that this proposal is workable. Indeed, considering the fact that the two metaphors seem to be mutually exclusive, one may wonder how the suggested metaphorical crossbreeding could be possible at all. In fact, however, the problem is not new, and it is not restricted to the research on learning. We can turn to contemporary science for many more examples of similar dilemmas, as well as for at least two ways in which the difficulty can be overcome.

First, we can look on the PM- and AM-generated conceptual frameworks as offering differing perspectives rather than competing opinions. Having several theoretical outlooks at the same thing is a normal practice in science, where, for instance, chemistry and physics offer two different—but not incompatible—accounts of matter, while physiology and psychology bring mutually complementing outlooks at human beings. In the spirit of this approach, acquisitionists and participationists might admit that the difference between them is not a matter of differing opinions but rather of participating in different, mutually complementing discourses.

Somebody may argue, however, that the tension between the AM and the PM is too fundamental to be treated with such tolerance. After all, people may say, the AM and the PM make incompatible ontological claims about the nature of learning. To this, Kuhn, Rorty, and many other contemporary philosophers would respond that the metaphors are incommensurable rather than incompatible[3] and because "[i]ncommensurability entails irreducibility [of vocabularies], but not incompatibility" (Rorty, 1979, p. 388), this means a possibility of their peaceful coexistence. Science and mathematics are a rich source of examples showing that such an option is not purely theoretical. Thus, for instance, today's mathematicians are able to live with Euclidean and non-Euclidean geometries without privileging any of them, whereas contemporary physicists admit a mixture of ostensibly contradictory approaches to subatomic phenomena, sanctioning this decision with Bohr's famous principle of complementarity.

Remembering the metaphorical underpinnings of the claims on the nature of learning, we might find it quite easy to adopt Bohr's principle in our own research. This would mean that, ontological discrepancy notwithstanding, we could view learning as an acquisition or as participation, according to our choice. How this choice is made depends on several factors. First, there are a few necessary conditions a metaphor must fulfill to rank as a candidate. If it is to have any chance at all, the resulting theories must be found convincing and coherent. The seemingly straightforward idea of "convincing" is, in fact, rather complex, and it includes a belief in the usefulness of the theories and an expectation that they will lead to what Rorty (1991) calls an intersubjective agreement. In addition to its role as a potent sense-making tool, a theory has to be an effective producer of new insights about learning.

If the necessary conditions for the acceptance of a metaphor seem relatively easy to pinpoint, the sufficient conditions are rather elusive. Clearly, some metaphors may be more attractive than others because of their accessibility, flexibility, imaginativeness, or aesthetic value. In the final account, however, the choice made by individual researchers would probably depend mainly on what they want to achieve. If, for example, one's purpose is to build a computer program that would simulate human behavior, then the *acquisition metaphor* is likely to be chosen as one that brings forward the issue of representations—something that has to be constructed and quite literally put into a computer. If, on the other hand, one is concerned with educational issues—such as the mechanisms that enable successful learning or make its failure persistent, then the participational approach may be more helpful as one that defies the traditional distinction between cognition and affect, brings social factors to the fore, and thus deals with an incomparably wider range of possibly relevant aspects.

Finally, let me add that being aware of the essentially figurative nature of our sense-making activities, we may sometimes go so far as to merge seemingly conflicting metaphors within one theoretical framework. The merger becomes possible when acquisitionist utterances stop being read as ontological stipulations (as is usually the case within the AM framework) and are interpreted instead as bringing an "as if" message. In this case, their figurative nature is never forgotten and their use is justified pragmatically, with arguments of effectiveness and productivity.

One point cannot be overstated. With all of the flexibility of the proposed multi-metaphorical metaframework, plurality of metaphors does not imply that "anything goes;" neither does it result in a complete methodological freedom or in a reduced need for empirical evidence. To count as trustworthy, the resulting theories must still be experimentally testable and congruent with data. The only thing that changes is the relative status of data and theory. While traditionally, data were regarded as previous to, and independent of, theory, now it is assumed that they are already tinted by theory when we first set our eyes on them. As shown by the heated discussion on transfer, the very existence of "facts" may sometimes be a matter of a theoretical lens used by an observer. The relationship between theory and data is dialectic in that they have a tendency for generating each other. It is notable that the persuasive power of data may be confined to the paradigm within which they came into being. Because there is no such thing as "naked facts," the power of empirical findings may sometimes be lost in a transition from one framework to another. For that reason, empirical evidence is unlikely to serve as an effective weapon in paradigm wars.

The basic message of this chapter can now be put in a few sentences. As researchers, we seem to be doomed to living in a reality constructed from a variety of metaphors. We have to accept the fact that the metaphors we use while theorizing may be good enough to fit small areas, but none of them suffice to cover the entire field. In other words, we must learn to satisfy ourselves with only local sense-making. A realistic thinker knows he or she has to give up the hope that the little patches of coherence will eventually combine into a consistent global theory. It seems that the sooner we accept the thought that our work is bound to produce a patchwork of metaphors rather than a unified, homogeneous theory of learning, the better for us and for those lives are likely to be affected by our work.

# Notes

This article is an extended version of an invited lecture given at the Eighth International Congress of Mathematics Education in Seville, Spain, in July 1996. I wish to thank Paul Cobb, Robert Thomas, and Devorah Kalekin-Fishman for their patient reading and commenting on different drafts of the article. Special acknowledgements go to anonymous reviewers and to the editor, Dr. Robert Donmoyer, for their helpful questions and suggestions. […]

1. The range of possible situations in which we may be able to profit from the given learning sequence differs from person to person; it is interesting that we tend only to talk about transfer when the range is particularly wide. Let us not forget, however, that if so, the difference between the phenomena we recognize as simple cases of successful learning and those we regard as instances of successful transfer is qualitative rather than quantitative, and the line between the two is undefined and probably indefinable. […]
2. Please note that this notion only makes sense in an AM framework! […]
3. "By 'commensurable,'" says Rorty (1979), "I mean able to be brought under a set of rules which will tell us how rational agreement can be reached on what would settle the issue on every point where statements seem to conflict" (p. 316). In other words, incommensurability means that there is no super-theory that would provide tools for proving one framework right while refuting the other. This is certainly the case with the controversy over our two metaphors for learning: there is no possibility of solving this type of conflict with a scientific argument, as it is traditionally understood. […]

# References

Anderson, J. R., Reder, L. M., & Simon, H. A. (1996). Situated learning and education. *Educational Researcher*, 25(4), 5–11.

Ball, D. (1991). Research on teaching mathematics: Making subject-matter knowledge part of the equation. In J. Brophy (Ed.), *Advances in research on teaching: Vol. 2. Teacher's subject-matter knowledge* (pp. 1–48). Greenwich, CT: JAI Press.

Bauersfeld, H. (1995). "Language games" in the mathematics classroom: Their function and their effects. In P. Cobb & H. Bauersfeld (Eds.), *Emergence of mathematical meaning: Interaction in classroom cultures* (pp. 271–291). Hillsdale, NJ: Lawrence Erlbaum Associates.

Bereiter, C. (1985). Towards the solution of the learning paradox. *Review of Educational Research*, 55, 201–226.

Billett, S. (1996). Situated learning: Bridging sociocultural and cognitive theorising. *Learning and Instruction*, 6(3), 263–280.

Cobb, P. (1995). Continuing the conversation: A response to Smith. *Educational Researcher*, 24(7), 25–27.

Cobb, P., Yackel, E., & Wood, T. (1992). A constructivist alternative to the representational view of mind in mathematics education. *Journal for Research in Mathematics Education*, 23(1), 2–33.

Donmoyer, R. (1996). This issue: A focus on learning. *Educational Researcher*, 25(4), 4.

Geuss, R. (1981). *The idea of critical theory: Habermas and the Frankfurt school.* Cambridge, UK: Cambridge University Press.

Greeno, J. G. (1997). On claims that answer the wrong question. *Educational Researcher*, 26(1), 5–17.

Habermas, J. (1972). *Knowledge and human interests.* Boston, MA: Beacon Press.

Hardy, G. H. (1967). *A mathematician's apology.* Cambridge, MA: Cambridge University Press. (Original work published 1940)

Heckman, P., & Weissglass, J. (1994). Contextualized mathematics instruction: Moving beyond recent proposals. *For the Learning of Mathematics*, 14(1), 29–33.

Hiebert, J., Carpenter, T. P., Fennema, E., Fuson, K., Human, P., Murray, H., Oliver, A., & Wearne, D. (1996). Problem solving as a basis for reform in curriculum and instruction: The case of mathematics. *Educational Researcher*, 25(4), 12–21.

Johnson, M. (1987). *The body in the mind: The bodily basis of meaning, imagination, and reason.* Chicago: The University of Chicago Press.

Kozulin, A. (1990). *Vygotsky's psychology: A biography of ideas.* New York: Harvester Wheatsheaf.

Lakoff, G. (1987). *Women, fire and dangerous things: What categories reveal about the mind.* Chicago: The University of Chicago Press.

Lakoff, G. (1993). The contemporary theory of metaphor. In A. Ortony (Ed.), *Metaphor and thought* (2nd ed., pp. 202–250). Cambridge, UK: Cambridge University Press.

Lakoff, G., & Johnson, M. (1980), *The metaphors we live by.* Chicago: The University of Chicago Press.

Lave, J. (1988). *Cognition in practice.* Cambridge, UK: Cambridge University Press.

Lave, J., & Wenger, E. (1991). *Situated learning: Legitimate peripheral participation.* Cambridge, UK: Cambridge University Press.

Morton, R. K. (1973). *The sociology of science.* Chicago: The University of Chicago.

Reddy, M. (1978). The conduit metaphor: A case of frame conflict in our language about language. In A. Ortony (Ed.), *Metaphor and thought* (2nd ed., pp. 164–201). Cambridge, UK: Cambridge University Press.

Rogoff, B. (1990). *Apprenticeship in thinking: Cognitive development in social context.* Oxford, UK: Oxford University Press.

Rorty, R. (1979). *Philosophy and the mirror of nature.* Princeton, NJ: Princeton University Press.

Rorty, R. (1991). *Objectivity, relativism, and truth.* Cambridge, UK: Cambridge University Press.

Sacks, S. (Ed.). (1978). *On metaphor.* Chicago: The University of Chicago Press.

Schoenfeld, A. (1996). In fostering communities of inquiry, must it matter that the teacher knows the "answer"? *For the Learning of Mathematics*, 16(3), 11–16.

Sfard, A. (1997). Commentary: On metaphorical roots of conceptual growth. In L. English (Ed.), *Mathematical reasoning: Analogies, metaphors, and images* (pp. 339–372). Mahwah, NJ: Erlbaum.

Sierpinska, A. (1995). Mathematics "in context," "pure" or "with applications"? *For the Learning of Mathematics*, 15(1), 2–15.

Smith, E. (1995). Where is the mind? "Knowing" and "knowledge" in Cobb's constructivist and sociocultural perspectives. *Educational Researcher*, 24(7), 23–24.

Smith, J. P., III. (1996). Efficacy and teaching mathematics by telling: A challenge for reform. *Journal for Research in Mathematics Education*, 27(4), 387–402.

Thomas, R. (1996). Proto-mathematics and/or real mathematics. *For the Learning of Mathematics*, 16(2), 11–18.

Vosniadou, S. (1996). Towards a revised cognitive psychology for new advances in learning and instruction. *Learning and Instruction*, 6(2), 95–110.

Woodfield, A. (1993). Do your concepts develop? In C. Hookway & D. Peterson (Eds), *Philosophy and cognitive science* (pp. 41–67). Cambridge, UK: Cambridge University Press.

# 4

# Concepts of Workplace Knowledge

*John Stevenson*

This chapter presents an overview of workplace knowledge based on specific studies of […] workplace activity in a number of sites within the motel industry. Commonly recognized core workplace competencies, such as literacy, numeracy, use of technology, and problem solving, are examined. In addition, ways in which values are represented in workplaces are examined. The data pertain to front desk operations observed in a wide variety of motel types; the data consisted of transcript records of interactions among staff and between staff and customers. The results of the studies support a view of knowledge construction as a multiply mediated interaction among workplace artifacts (physical, psychological and linguistic tools and instruments), normative structures, divisions of workplace responsibility, and the social collective.

Furthermore, no matter which theoretical framework is adopted or which core competency is examined, knowledge construction was not found to be generic. Theoretical conclusions from these findings relate to the nature of workplace knowledge, knowledge use and task performance in operational settings, which contrast with alternative accounts of knowledgeable action. Findings also support the view that teaching for workplace competency must give weight to complex interactions among generic and site-specific knowledge attainments.

## Workplace knowledge

Ideas of what constitutes workplace knowledge and appropriate ways for it to be learned are dynamic and subject to powerful societal forces. The result is usually a polarization of what is considered to be vocational or related to work, from those life pursuits that are the subject of general, academic, or theoretical knowledge. That is, knowledge for work has historically been seen as a "second-best" kind of knowledge, concerned with utility: the material, the practical, the technical, and the routine. This polarization usually differentiates work and occupations into those denoted vocations (e.g., trade and clerical work) and those denoted professions (e.g., medicine, law). According to Young (1993), these polarizations can be traced to ancient forces to preserve class distinctions, i.e., to keep work and education for work separate from the pursuits of the upper classes.

Stevenson (1996, 2001) argues that, in recent history, these polarizations relate to changes in preferred societal and educational outcomes in times of societal crises such as

From: *International Journal of Educational Research*, 37 (Elsevier, 2002), pp. 1–15. Reproduced with permission.

wars and depressions. That is, more utilitarian ends are accepted for education, even general education, in times of societal crisis. It is at these times that movements such as scientific efficiency, "back to the basics," behavioral objectives, and competency-based education gain momentum; only to be counter-balanced at other times with moves under such banners as "knowledge for its own sake," "education for life," liberalism, and "development of the whole person" in times of stability and plenty. Stevenson (1998, 2001) further argues that the moves between different missions for vocational education reflect different balances in concerns for the needs of individuals, the needs of society as a whole, and the needs of industry as part of society.

This separation, however, has now become increasingly problematic for several reasons. First, the neat division of occupations into those for which learners are prepared in universities and those for which they are not has begun to collapse, with increasing university preparation for kinds of work that were previously regarded as vocational rather than professional (e.g., teaching, nursing, policing, aviation, art, music). Second, with increasing participation of young people in schooling beyond compulsory years, there has been a pressure to broaden the curriculum to include more "vocational" studies alongside more traditional academic studies and for these "vocational" studies to count towards any selection criteria for university entry. Third, the nature of work, itself, is undergoing fundamental changes. These changes give impetus to the other reasons and, consequently, are addressed in greater detail in the next section of this chapter. Fourth, and finally, theoretical assumptions about the generality (and transferability) of some knowledge and the specificity of other knowledge are increasingly difficult to sustain. This question of generic versus specific knowledge is discussed in a later section of this chapter.

## Changes in the nature of work

Changes have been occurring in the structure of economies, the nature of productivity, and access to work, with a continuum of economic conditions from core to peripheralized work (Harvey, 1989; Hirsch, 1991). There has been a rapid development and uptake of digital communications and information technologies driving the emergence of the "knowledge economy" (see, for example, Gibbons et al., 1994; Lundvall & Borrás, 1997; Stevenson, 2000). In a knowledge economy core workers are expected to be active lifelong learners who understand and embrace technological developments and respond creatively to the needs of a rapidly changing economy (Oblinger & Verville, 1998). They are expected to create new knowledge by accessing information from broad sources, developing "executive knowledge" management skills across a broad base (Oblinger & Verville, 1998), selecting the kinds of knowledge relevant to work, making choices about how this knowledge can and should be generated, and implementing strategies to contextualize general knowledge for more specific customized ends. The knowledge that is now regarded as needed for work effectiveness extends from the so-called narrow, routine, and predictable skills that have often been assumed to characterize casual, peripheral, "lower" level work in the economy, to knowledge described in new ways—intellective and connective skills, mobile knowledge workers, and symbolic analysts (Harvey, 1989; Young, 1993).

There is also claimed to be a need for "horizontal and core competencies which cut across sectors and disciplines" (e.g., interpersonal skills, the ability to take a broad view of occupational situations/production processes, the ability to learn), "transversal and personal skills" (e.g., ability to work in a team, creativity, imaginativeness, self-perception), "participatory skills" (e.g., the ability to understand the point of view of others), and "social and communication skills also referred to as 'meta-competence skills'" (Sellin, 1999, p. 70). However, such qualitative changes in the nature of work are uneven across workers, industries, and economies. Nevertheless, they do signal a problem with any attempts to separate knowledge for work from knowledge for other purposes. In responding to these changes, governments have engaged in reforms of their educational systems.

## Educational responses to changes in workplace knowledge

The path chosen in vocational education, and in education more generally, to address changing economic circumstances, in many countries, especially the United Kingdom, Australia and New Zealand, has been two-fold. First, training has been more closely aligned with industrial practice; competencies needed on the job have been identified and used as the basis for vocational educational content. Second, attempts have been made to supplement this content with knowledge that is thought to have currency across different kinds of work, even across industries and between work and other aspects of life. This latter content has been variously designated core skills (UK), essential skills (New Zealand), necessary skills (USA) and key competencies (Australia) (Mayer, 1992). These common attributes center around such ideas as communication (especially literacy and numeracy), use of technology, interpersonal activity, problem solving, and planning. The assumption that seems to underpin the development of such lists of competencies as well as their incorporation in educational and training activities is that they can be learned in such a way that they can be utilized in a variety of contexts—across changing workplace characteristics, across jobs in an industry, and even across industries.

These educational and training responses may be seen as a move to generalize aspects of workplace knowledge, i.e., to select out from work that knowledge which is commonly needed. At the same time, the move leaves intact other knowledge that is seen as workplace specific. That is, the move admits "general" knowledge to vocational education concerns while still perpetuating the polarization of general and specific knowledge. The incorporation of "general" content is founded on the idea of generic knowledge, not necessarily the "general" knowledge that forms academic disciplines, but knowledge derived from a different kind of commonness across different kinds of practice.

## Generic knowledge

The question of whether workplace knowledge can be thought of in generic terms can be examined from a number of theoretical perspectives. In the past, it has often been thought of as a question of transfer—can knowledge acquired in one context be transferred to a different one? However, more recently, in the face of situated learning and other socio-cultural research, the question of transfer of knowledge from one context to another has been displaced. The concerns are now more about equipping learners with capacities to engage in the inevitable struggles of dealing with new situations and to learn from them. Cognitive theory, socio-cultural learning theories, socio-linguistic theories and cultural–historical activity theory can each be used to examine this proposition.

In a 2002 special edition of the *International Journal of Educational Research* (Vol. 31, No. 7), the question of transfer of learning was raised and the stances taken in cognitive and socio-cultural research were discussed extensively. At one end of the debate, there are neo-Thorndikian views about how transfer of knowledge requires discernment of identical elements between learning and application situations, where the new identical elements are to be found in declarative and procedural knowledge (de Corte, 1999). The question is one of learning the correct declarative and procedural knowledge, the capacity to discern their applicability in new situations and the activity of engaging in this application. At the other end of the debate are those socio-cultural researchers whose situated cognition perspective is that "knowledge and skills cannot transfer because they are so strongly embedded in and tied to the context in which they are acquired" (de Corte, 1999, p. 556). The question is one of functional, purposive learning in an authentic context so that knowledge is meaningful; plural diverse experiences of different contexts, and active reflection on these experiences for the extraction of principles which might assist in new (but not so unfamiliar) contexts.

The contemporary view seems to lie between these two extremes, with transfer seen as an interpretive or constructive activity. In fact, the concept of transfer itself may be too restrictive. The questions of interest are how learning can enable individuals to be productive in new situations (Hatano & Greeno, 1999) and how instruction can facilitate this type of learning. Moreover, according to Hatano and Greeno, the quest for transfer is too ambitious. The history of transfer studies shows "not that school learning has seldom been successful, but that human competencies are so much dependent on socio-cultural enablements" (p. 653). Thoughts on the kinds of paradoxes that learners face when engaging in near or far transfer and the kinds of instructional strategies that can be adopted in confronting these paradoxes have also been advanced (Simons, 1999).

The paradoxes identified by Simons are interpretive or constructive in nature and can be summarized in terms of finding relevant and productive prior knowledge, using only applicable tacit knowledge, reading the similarities of new situations in terms of prior knowledge, aiming for near or far transfer, and selecting the appropriate knowledge as the target of transfer. That is, they relate to learner capacity to construct interpretations of new situations that are culturally appropriate (Pea, 1987) and that enable productive use of existing tacit and explicit knowledge. Similarly Bransford and Schwartz (1999) argue that we should be more concerned with transfer as preparation for future learning through developing the idea of "knowledge with" (that is, ways in which we use our cumulative knowledge and experiences in perceiving, interpreting and judging new situations).

Thus, there is growing recognition that it is too simplistic to view transfer as the direct, unproblematic application of declarative and propositional knowledge, acquired in situation A to tasks and problems in situation B discerned as similar to those in situation A. There is much more involved than the acquisition and application of inert knowledge. There is a growing recognition of the "cultural situatedness" of activity—the ways in which knowing is derived from socio-cultural activity and its historical construction, and the ways in which the socio-cultural features of new situations are read afresh when individuals seek to address them on the basis of previous learning and other experiences in order to engage in successful activity.

Beach (1999) argues, that for such reasons, the concern for transfer should be replaced by one for "continuity and transformation in knowledge, skill, and identity across changing forms of social organization" (p. 130). For Beach, transfer becomes a "consequential transition" when there is a developmental change in the relation between an individual and one or more social activities; and when the eventual outcome of the struggle and reflection is a change in one's sense of self and social positioning. This position takes the emphasis away from considering the application of knowledge learned in situation A to situation B, to a consideration of the construction and transformation of self, practice and knowledge. To illustrate, Beach sees moves between school and work as lateral transitions—moves between two historically related activities in a single direction. In this transition, knowledge is not applied directly, but transformed in and for the new social organization. On the other hand, work experience, as part of a school curriculum would involve collateral transitions— simultaneous participation in two or more historically related activities. But again, the differences in social organization and the transformations of knowledge and self, rather than direct applications of declarative and procedural knowledge, become the central concern. Beach also defines encompassing transitions where there is a sense of progress in the transition, e.g., towards the center of a community of practice; and mediational transitions that involve simulations or projections of to-be-experienced situations.

Thus, the search for generic knowledge, whether it be codified in the form of academic or theoretical disciplines, as school curricula or in the form of key, core, essential, or necessary skills and/or competencies, is one of whether or how such knowledge would promote participation in familiar and unfamiliar cultural practices and the transformation of oneself, one's practice and one's knowledge based on the struggles in which one engages in new experiences. Cultural–historical activity theory (Engeström, 1987, 1999; Leont'ev, 1981) is a powerful perspective from which to examine participation in cultural practices, including those of work. Two aspects of this theory salient for the present discussion are mediation and transformation. Engeström's depiction of activity theory is one of mediation of collective activity directed at an object (motive) by instruments (cultural, psychological and physical), rules, the division of labor, and the community. Activity theory is based on the assumption that activity systems (defined as bounded sets of collective activity aimed at the same motive) are inherently in tension. This tension is within and between elements as well as with other activity systems. Transformation occurs in the processes of resolving such tensions.

Thus, a learner engages in a struggle when engaging in a new activity. For instance, when undertaking an activity for the first time (e.g., using a motel database), the learner struggles to understand the tasks, the demands (e.g., rules and responsibilities) of the setting represented in the culture which has been transformed over time, and the place of the database work in the overall scheme of things). The learner may come to terms with using the database in a culturally appropriate and effective way, over time, but will in the process have undergone some personal transformations with respect to his or her place in the work routines, with respect to the artifacts in the setting (especially the computer, its software, and its functions). Similarly, the activity itself will have undergone some changes, especially as a result of the person's individual interactions with the computer and others in the setting. Moreover, the consequent transformations in the learner's knowledge and practice, upon confronting new situations, relate to interactions which are not passive. Rather, they involve tensions within elements of an activity system (e.g., tensions in the various tools, in the object, in the community), as well as among such elements. This is a far cry from the image of "transferring knowledge" from setting A to setting B. Thus, activity theory situates, both culturally and historically, the learner's "consequential transitions" or attempts at "transfer" or aims to apply "generic" or "specific" knowledge.

# The studies

These studies […] illuminate the nature of knowledge in a single area of practice, and explore the senses in which such knowledge could be considered to be generic or transferable across similar practices in different sites in the same industry. The aspects of practice that were examined were those commonly found in statements of key or core skills or competencies outlined above: literacy (Searle, 2002), numeracy (Kanes, 2002), the use of technology (Beven, 2002), and problem solving (Middleton, 2002). Because practice is normative and the relevant values are usually not made explicit in the respective generic statements, values in practice were also examined (Middleton, 2002).

## Sites

The sites chosen for investigation were the front office and reception operations of small accommodation-based enterprises (e.g., motels) within the field of tourism. However, a pilot study established that collecting suitable data for the complex problem-solving study would be difficult. Interviews with managers during the pilot study indicated that complex, ill-defined problems are most likely to occur during the start-up phase of a new business. Gibbs (1987) found that failure rates in small business were high in the first two years of operation. Managers interviewed for this project indicated that problems that caused failure were related to two factors. The first was the degree of experience of the manager/operator and the second was contextual features of the business such as location, seasonal factors, and target markets. It was thus established that the sites selected would need to include new tourism industry sectors, such as eco-tourism, as well as sites that contained rich contextual features, such as isolated locations, urban and rural locations, and a mix of owner operated and employed managers. Thus, two sets of sites were identified—one for examining literacy, numeracy, technology and values, and the other for examining complex problem solving. A list of sites and descriptions of their characteristics is summarized in Table 4.1. […]

As Table 4.1 indicates, a wide range of characteristics was reflected in the chosen sites. Thus, these features were taken to be adequate to provide work situations where the activity in the same kind of job could be examined across sites with different characteristics. Prospective sites were contacted, information about the research studies was provided, and site details were exchanged. Arrangements for site visits were negotiated once the suitability and availability of sites were determined.

## Data collection

The main source of data was observations of practice. These data were supplemented by concurrent participant verbalization of their practice (when there were no customers involved) and interviews. Observations of a full day's activities were undertaken at each of the sites (between 7 a.m. and 6 p.m.). The purpose of conducting observations was to record the activities performed by front office staff, as they performed them, and in so doing, to document the contexts in which these activities were performed. An inventory of the resources used in performing the tasks was collected. The specific day selected for the observation was negotiated with each site according to the spectrum of tasks typically performed on that day and the ability of the site to accommodate the presence of the research team.

**Table 4.1  Site characteristics**

| Site | No. of rooms | FO staff/ total incl. pt & casual | Owner/operator configuration | Period of current management (months) | Location | Client groups | Booking office | Front office system |
|---|---|---|---|---|---|---|---|---|
| *Data set 1 = interviews + full observation* | | | | | | | | |
| A | 130 | 6/50 | P,C | 18 | L | 1 = C | On-site | Computer |
| B | 23 | 1/4 | F,H | 42 | R, L | 1 = T | On-site | Manual |
| C | 57 | 6/15 | P,H | 19 | L | 1 = T 2 = C | On-site | Computer |
| D | 48 | 9/86 | P,M | 8 | I | 1 = E | On-site | Computer |
| E | 14 | 2/46 | P,H | 24 | I | 1 = E | Remote | Computer |
| F (i) | 6 | 4/16 | P,H | 6 | I | 1 = S | Remote | Manual |
| F (ii) | 6 | 1/2 | P,H | 6 | L | 1 = S | Remote | Computer |
| *Data set 2 = interviews + limited observation* | | | | | | | | |
| G | 4 | 3/3 | P | 24 | I | 1 = T | On-site | Manual |
| H | 17 | 2/7 | P,H | 17 | I | 1 = E | Remote | Manual |
| I | 2 | 2/2 | P | 60 | I | 1 = T | On-site | Manual |
| J | Interview conducted with business facilitator of regional small business development board | | | | | | | |

*Note*: P = privately owned, C = chain managed, F = foreign owned, H = hired management, L = large city, R = regional, I = isolated, 1 = main, 2 = other, T = tourist, C = corporate, E = eco tourist, S = special tourist.

The observation sessions concentrated on the activities of an experienced front office staff member and, where possible, interactions with less-experienced staff were also recorded. Observational sessions were recorded in audio, video and written forms. During the front office observation sessions, practitioners described and explained procedures as they performed them. The participants also described and explained the resources they used and discussed the full range of tasks and interactions required of them in the discharge of their duties. Semi-structured interviews were also conducted with front office staff after the observation sessions. Where possible, these interviews included stimulated recall regarding activities performed during the observation sessions. Interviews with back office and accounting staff focused on the practitioner's use of computer software. Discussions with managers and owner-operators ranged over problem-solving skills, staff training, and contextual and operational features of the business. All interviews and discussions were audio-recorded. [...]

## Summary of major findings

Each site was found to be dynamic, with tensions in the object (motive) of the collective work [...]. That is, while activity seemed to be directed at profit (through the goals of increasing funds and efficiency), return trade (through customer satisfaction and professional appearances), and accountability, there were tensions in these various facets of the object (e.g., between achieving a profit and keeping customers satisfied; between accountability and efficiency). Thus, activity was value-laden and aimed at normative ends (which were in tension). Sets of value labels could be constructed to describe the kinds of values found in these workplace sites. However, the values in operation in the activity that was taking place did not consist in the direct application of cognitions about values labeled in this way. That is, the labeled norms were not abstracted ideas, explicitly being called upon to guide activity. For example, it was not the case that a person applied the value of "be persistent" [...] to directing activity towards a named goal of "acquiring funds" for "profit" to "ensure the business was successful." Rather, these normative aspects of activity were derived from observing the practice as a post hoc way of understanding what norms were implicit in activity. That is, there were motives and goals that were shared within sites. The imputed object and its various aspects provided the momentum for activity.

Moreover, the norms in activity seemed to take their form from the setting. That is, the normative actions directed at the goal of efficiency or the normative actions of being courteous in one setting were different from those in another. Indeed the norms were so embedded in each activity system that normative activity and the value labels that could be abstracted to describe them appeared to be largely unrelated to personal values or wider societal concerns.

Irrespective of the theoretical lens used by the authors of the studies or their specific subjects of investigations, there are some common findings about the ways in which knowledge can be considered generic or site-specific, and the instructional implications that follow. Using a context-text model of language in use approach to the examination of literacy, Searle (2002) found that the multi-literacies were highly contextualized, situated within the specific discourses of the individual workplaces. This was the case for spoken and written languages, as well as for reading. She concluded that a focus on sets of decontextualized skills in labeling and assessing literacy competencies loses sight of the social components of work through which work practices are generated and sustained and how effectiveness in those workplaces is acquired. Kanes (2002), drawing upon Activity Theory, shows how numerical concepts were mediated by workplace tasks and were themselves mediated by artifacts generated within the workplace.

Using a situated cognition lens, Beven (2002) found that data work was essentially functional, being dependent not only on the particular software but the particular worksite. For instance, operators at different sites used entirely different keystrokes to reach the check-in screen. An observer could construct conceptual labels to describe similarities in some of the ways in which databases were used, but these similarities were not apparent at the functional level when operators were interacting with customers or directly with the databases. That is, the knowledge utilized in practice was not known in terms of the various abstract labels that could be constructed on it by observers, software designers, or curriculum developers. Rather, if it were known in such terms, it would be inadequate for functional effectiveness. Middleton (2002), using cognitive theory to conceptualize complex problems and their solution, found that the complex problems encountered in the various workplaces could be conceptualized as similar at only a superficial (non-functional) level. Rather, they were fundamentally different from each other in that the problem that could be "found" (conceptualized for solution), and the solutions that could be generated were site-specific. Moreover, strategies used for generating solutions to the complex problems were also site-dependent.

Thus, irrespective of the theoretical lens or of the topic of the investigation, each researcher found that labeling workplace activities in common ways across sites created a considerable distance between the labels, on the one hand, and the actual activity and the capacities needed for that activity, on the other. Clearly, labels could be generated, but what was known was not known by or used in those terms. Any capacities known in some abstract or generic way could conceivably be utilized as a mediating tool, but would have to be discerned as relevant to the tasks at hand, interpreted in terms of the cultural context, and transformed for utility. Moreover, what constituted activity usually drew upon more than one topic area and was dependent on the cultural and physical nature of the setting.

In addition, each setting had its own history embedded within the history of the hospitability industry itself. In and through the struggles of everyday practices of work, over time, practitioners had transformed themselves (including their identities) and the ways in which they knew and acted. These transformations developed out of their knowing "with" their experiences. Knowledge construction involved a multiply mediated mediation among workplace artifacts (physical, psychological and linguistic tools and instruments), normative structures, divisions of workplace responsibility and the social collective.

# Discussion

The findings reported in these various studies challenge traditional views of the relationships between knowledge and practice, dualistic constructions of knowledge, the abstraction of workplace competence into clusters of specific and generic skills, and simplistic views of transfer.

## Knowledge and practice

From the studies, knowing was difficult to separate from the activity. It could not easily be separated even in terms of the topic areas identified for the study (that is, as literacy, numeracy, problem solving, use of technology, and values). Rather, practice was a set of activities (e.g., greeting a customer, finding out what is required, entering information in the database, giving the customer directions). For each activity, there was content across the various areas of literacy, numeracy, technology, values, and so on. It was not a case of calling upon some literacy knowledge and using it to execute an action. Rather, activity was mediated not only by various kinds of knowing and their interpretation for the situation, but by the physical, psychological, and linguistic tools and instruments in the setting itself, as well as the implicit and explicit rules and working arrangements. Thus, how a guest was directed to a room would be courteous, informative, involve numeracy, and be in accord with the database information. The knowing was, in practice, the consequence of many transitions where self, experience, and knowing had been transformed and become intrinsically related—a kind of knowing "with" in Bransford and Schwartz's (1999) terms.

## Dualistic constructions of knowledge

It is reasonable to propose that the activities that constitute work in all walks of life involve the kind of mediation found in these studies. That is, it is apparent that it is not just one class of workers (e.g., vocational), as opposed to other classes (e.g., professionals), whose practice is aimed at a collective motive and mediated by artifacts, rules, responsibilities, and a community of practice. It is clear, for example, that professionals also work in settings, that these settings function as activity systems, and that activity within these settings is multiply mediated. It follows then that the ways in which people "know" in other walks of life are as related to the activities of their practice as are found here. Hence, the idea that there is one type of knowledge (e.g., theoretical knowledge) for academic or professional work that is qualitatively different from the kind of knowledge needed for vocational activities such as those examined here would need to be argued.

There is already evidence that knowledge for professional activity is actually practice-based, rather than learned theory-based. For instance, Boshuizen, Schmidt, Custers, and Van De Wiel (1995) found that the knowledge of expert medical practitioners is experiential. They transform their theoretical, discipline-based knowledge into knowledge for practice that is much like the knowledge found here—knowledge that is related to the kinds of experiences that the practitioner had encountered in manifold activities and that is the result of mediation by artifacts and other aspects of the socio-historical settings of medical practice. Viewed in this way, the knowledge that is the subject of academic work would also be used simply as one of a number of tools or instruments to mediate a particular practice. When applied in professional practice, academic or theoretical knowing simply becomes an instrument to utilize (along with other tools and elements of an activity system) until it is transformed in relation to the various cultural–historical demands of the practice. Moreover, other forms of knowledge (e.g., tacit knowledge, for instance a routinized skill) would be instrumental in the same way.

## Specific and generic skills

The ability to engage in effective practice in these studies was site-specific. While one could assign labels to abstractions of what an observer could construct as general across sites, these abstractions were not the ability as it was concretely utilized in practice. Where generic knowledge was called upon, it was in interaction with site-specific knowledge. Abstractions in functional terms, such as those to be found in lists of key or core skills or competencies, were at a distance from practice, as were concepts drawn from such theoretical disciplines as mathematics, linguistics, engineering, and so on. Furthermore, practical knowledge was not only specific to sites. The normative motives and goals at which it was directed also took their form from the individual sites.

## Transfer

The findings of the studies [...] suggest that ideas of transfer as the direct application of generic procedural and declarative knowledge from a prior learning experience to a new situation are too simplistic. Rather, operators grapple with the complex demands of their work settings, and their activity is mediated by a complex of artifacts and other workplace elements. Among the artifacts may well be some concepts and procedures from other places, but they would have no privileged or stable position in the setting. Rather, there would simply be some placed among the many tools that could be drawn upon if discerned as culturally appropriate and relevant. Moreover, they would be transformed as a consequence of challenging activity—consequential transitions. In the process of individuals coming to terms with their place in, and contributions to activity systems, their identities, selves, knowledge and the practice itself underwent transformation. That is, as Beach (1999) suggests, there was a developmental change in the relation between the individual and the social activities.

In summary, the various studies explore the nature of practical activity in a number of settings, and find that concepts of workplace knowledge need revision if they are to accommodate the findings. Revisions are needed in dualistic ideas about qualitative differences in "vocational" and "professional" knowledge, ideas of knowledge as specific and general, and ideas of the transfer of knowledge. In order to overcome some of the conceptual problems in understanding the nature, use, and development of workplace knowledge, suggestions are made concerning needed reconceptualizations (e.g., workplace knowledge construction as a multiply mediated interaction among workplace artifacts; divisions of responsibility and the social collective; transfer as a consequential transition).

# References

Beach, K. (1999). Consequential transitions: A socio-cultural expedition beyond transfer in education. In A. Iran-Nejad, & P. D. Pearson (Eds.), *Review of Research in Education*, 24, 101–140.

Beven, F. (2002). The knowledge required for database software use. *International Journal of Educational Research*, 37(1), 43–66.

Boshuizen, H. P. A., Schmidt, H. G., Custers, E. J., & Van De Wiel, M. W. (1995). Knowledge development and restructuring in the domain of medicine, the role of theory and practice. *Learning and Instruction*, 5, 269–285.

Bransford, J. D., & Schwartz, D. L. (1999). Rethinking transfer: A simple proposal with multiple implications. In A. Iran-Nejad, & P. D. Pearson (Eds.), *Review of Research in Education*, 24, 61–100.

de Corte, E. (1999). On the road to transfer: New perspectives on an enduring issue in research and practice. *International Journal of Educational Research*, 31, 555–559.

Engeström, Y. (1987). *Learning by expanding: An activity theoretical approach to developmental research*. Helsinki: Orienta-Konsultit Oy.

Engeström, Y. (1999). Expansive visibilization of work: An activity-theoretical perspective. *Computer Supported Cooperative Work*, 8, 63–93.

Gibbons, M., Limoges, C., Nowotny, H., Schwartzman, S., Scott, P., & Trow, M. (1994). *The new production of knowledge; The dynamics of science and research in contemporary societies*. London: Sage.

Gibbs, A. (1987). Designing effective programmes for encouraging the business start-up process: Lessons from UK experience. *Journal of European Industrial Training*, 11(4), 24–31.

Harvey, D. (1989). *The condition of postmodernity: An enquiry into the origins of cultural change*. Oxford: Blackwell.

Hatano, G., & Greeno, J. G. (1999). Commentary: Alternative perspectives on transfer and transfer studies. *International Journal of Educational Research*, 31, 645–654.

Hirsch, J. (1991). Fordism and post-Fordism: The present social crisis and its consequences. In W. Bonefield, & J. Holloway (Eds.), *Post-Fordism and social form: A Marxist debate on the post-Fordist state* (pp. 8–34). London: Macmillan.

Kanes, C. (2002). Delimiting numerical knowledge. *International Journal of Educational Research*, 37(1), 29–42.

Leont'ev, A. N. (1981). *Problems of the development of the mind*. Moscow: Progress.

Lundvall, B. -Å., & Borrás, S. (1997). *The globalising learning economy: Implications for innovation policy*, TSER programme. DG XII, Commission of the European Union.

Mayer, E. (Chair) (1992). *Key competencies*. Report of the committee to advise the Australian Education Council and Ministers of Vocational Education, Employment and Training on employment-related key competencies for postcompulsory education and training. Australian Education Council and Ministers of Vocational Education, Employment and Training.

Middleton, H. (2002). Complex problem solving in a workplace setting. *International Journal of Educational Research*, 37(1), 67–84.

Oblinger, D., & Verville, A. (1998). *What business wants from higher education*. Phoenix, AZ: The Oryx Press.

Pea, R. (1987). Socializing the knowledge transfer problem. *International Journal of Educational Research*, 11, 639–663.

Searle, J. (2002). Situated literacies at work. *International Journal of Educational Research*, 37(1), 17–28.

Sellin, B. (1999). *European trends in the development of occupations and qualifications*. Vol. 1. Thessalonika: European Centre for the Development of Vocational Training (CEDEFOP).

Simons, P. R. J. (1999). Transfer of learning: Paradoxes for learners. *International Journal of Educational Research*, 31, 577–589.

Stevenson, J. C. (1996). The metamorphis of the construction of competence. *Studies in Continuing Education*, 18(1), 24–42.

Stevenson, J. C. (1998). Finding a basis for reconciling perspectives on vocational education and training. *Australian and New Zealand Journal of Vocational Education Research*, 6(2), 134–165.

Stevenson, J. C. (2000). Codification of tacit knowledge for the new learning economy. In F. Beven, C. Kanes, & D. Roebuck (Eds.), *Learning together, working together: Building communities for the 21st Century*. Brisbane: Australian Academic Press.

Stevenson, J. C. (2001). Constituting and connection vocational knowledge. In F. Beven, C. Kanes, R. Roebuck (Eds.), *Knowledge demands for the new economy*, Vol. 2. Proceedings of the ninth international conference on post-compulsory education and training (pp. 261–268). Brisbane: Australian Academic Press.

Young, M. F. D. (1993). A curriculum for the 21st Century? *British Journal of Educational Studies*, 31(3), 203–222.

# Section 2

## Thinking about Curriculum

# 5

# Constituting the Workplace Curriculum

*Stephen Billett*

There is an urgent need for workplace curriculum practices and principles to be identified, elaborated, and evaluated. This need arises partially from the acknowledgement of the crucial role that workplaces play in individuals' initial learning and further development of vocational knowledge throughout their working lives. Without the identification, conceptualization, and acknowledgement of a workplace curriculum, workplaces will remain misunderstood, open to easy criticism, and delegitimized as learning spaces. However, much, if not most, learning in the course of working lives will be acquired, refined, and developed in workplace settings as individuals deploy and extend their knowledge through their everyday work activities. Consequently, workplaces need to be conceptualized more clearly as learning environments—through identifying their characteristics and qualities (i.e. their capacities to assist developing vocational practice) and considering how their contributions can be best organized to assist the learning required for work. […]

This chapter attempts to address part of this need through identifying and discussing factors that shape the organization and enactment of a workplace curriculum. Three conceptions of curriculum often used to understand practices in educational institutions are exercised for this purpose. These are: the *intended curriculum*—what is intended to occur; the *enacted curriculum*—what actually happens when the curriculum is enacted; and the *experienced curriculum*—what learners experience, construe, and learn as a result of its enactment. […]

Although this chapter utilizes and is informed by curriculum concepts and theorizing premised on activities in educational institutions, it is not intended that the workplace curriculum be hostage to constructs and practices arising from those institutions. What is advanced here as bases for a workplace curriculum have a genesis that both predates and extends beyond efforts to organize learning in educational institutions. Moreover, it is proposed that these bases are not reserved for what happens in workplaces or educational institutions. Rather, they can be applied and have meaning in social practices wherever participation in and the remaking of these practices occurs. […]

Because of this, it is quite erroneous to refer to workplaces as informal learning environments (Billett, 2002a). Workplace learning experiences are shaped by structural factors associated with work practices. These regulate and are reproduced by the division of labour and by the distribution of opportunities for participation in work, and learning about

From: *Journal of Curriculum Studies*, 38 (1), 2006, pp. 31–48. Reprinted by permission of the publisher (Taylor & Francis Ltd, http://www.informaworld.com).

it. This structuring, and its contestation, are no more evident than in accessing or learning about work-tasks that are highly valued or remunerated. This structuring underpins the need to identify ways of intervening in workplaces to assist in the equitable distribution of learning experiences.

For the purposes of identifying bases of a workplace curriculum, I use these conceptions of curriculum and of sentiments about their enactment to discuss three questions:

- How should a workplace curriculum be best organized?
- What factors are likely to influence its enactment?
- How will workers experience and learn from engagement in workplaces?

These questions are framed by larger questions about how individuals participate in and learn through engagement in social practices.

In preview, the 'intended' workplace curriculum takes as its starting point an anthropological conception of curriculum as participation in social practice, Lave's (1990) 'learning curriculum'. This comprises the sequencing of a pathway of activities that leads the worker-learner from novice status to being able to participate effectively in, and potentially transform, the particular social practice (e.g. workplace). Movement along this pathway needs to account for the kinds of knowledge to be learned in order to engage fully— particularly that which cannot be learned alone or requires practice to secure proficiency. Considerations of the knowledge to be learned to become an effective and productive practitioner, and how this learning can be best supported, constitute key elements of the ideal 'intended' workplace curriculum. In adapting this concept to contemporary workplace settings, current work organization, and employment practices, as well as the problem of learning knowledge that is hidden or otherwise 'hard-to-learn', need to be elaborated and accommodated.

A central proposition underlying the conceptualization of a workplace curriculum is that workplaces will invite workers to engage and learn, insofar as that participation serves its goals and/or the interests of those within it, that is the continuity and/or development of the workplace or affiliates or individuals within it. Therefore, the bases for the enactment of workplace curriculum are likely to be shaped by: (1) particular interests (e.g. affiliations, cliques) in the workplace and their capacity to influence the enactment of the workplace curriculum; and/or (2) individuals' goals for participation and advancement. For fear of being displaced, existing and more experienced workers may resist the participation and learning of new or other workers. Individuals' gender, race, aspirations, or personal affiliations may also shape how their participation and learning are supported through work activities. Management may elect to either support or resist workers' learning because of either the need for those skills or concerns about financial cost or loss of control. However, individuals themselves will ultimately determine how they participate in and learn through what is afforded them, premised on their values, goals, and experiences. Hence, both the enactment and experiencing of a workplace curriculum are likely to be contested and negotiated. Such negotiation between the social structuring of knowledge and individual agency is commonly acknowledged in many accounts of human cognition and action within psychology (e.g. Valsiner and van der Veer, 2000), sociology (e.g. Giddens, 1984) and philosophy (e.g. Taylor, 1985). Perhaps the ideal workplace curriculum is one in which the goals and interests of the workplace (intents) and those of individuals who participate in it are shared. [...]

# Workplace curriculum as intentions

In conceptualizing a workplace curriculum, some existing curriculum concepts can also be applied directly or analogously to identify the bases for proposing what might be the 'ideal' intended curriculum—that which is supposed to be enacted. Thus, the issue of the ideal raises the question: From what perspective is it ideal? It is unusual for educators or students to initiate educational institutions or programmes (Skilbeck, 1984). It is often powerful interests that organize education as a means of regulating their continuity (Bernstein, 1996). Just as the intended curriculum (e.g. syllabus documents, curriculum standards, and frameworks) in educational systems is typically regulated by powerful and external forces (e.g. government, religious orders, industry, pressure groups), so too is the intended workplace curriculum. Many definitions of curriculum refer explicitly to being primarily about achieving the school's goals—that is its continuity. In this way, the educational institutions' programmes and goals will reflect their particular niche in the educational sector (e.g. securing academic achievement, providing vocational preparation, enhancing sports proficiency, accessing higher education, supporting particular religious or educational values, etc.). An educational institution that makes a claim for high academic achievement is unlikely to champion its remedial or vocational programmes. The emphasis of learning experiences and acknowledgement of student achievement will be directed towards those goals and, ultimately, its continuity.

An approach to an intended workplace curriculum is also focused on how learners would acquire the knowledge (e.g. concepts, procedures, dispositions) to perform functionally and effectively in their workplace role and develop further their potential through workplace experiences. The latter concern is important. As Dewey (1916) notes, there is no greater waste than individuals not being able to exercise their full potential within their vocational practice. *A goal for vocational curriculum is to assist individuals to identify and realize their full vocational potential.*

Thus, the curriculum for the workplaces Lave (1990, 1993) observed comprised pathways of activities in which the novice workers participated as learners. This participation ultimately led to effective performance with tasks that had a high error-cost. Their employers, master tailors to whom they were apprenticed and in whose workshop they lived throughout the duration of their indenture, regulated the sequencing and pace of the individual apprentices' movement through these activities. [...]

It is noteworthy that the pathway constituting the curriculum that Lave (1990) identified is analogous to the original meaning of the term curriculum: *Currere*—'the track to be run', the course of learning (Marsh and Willis, 1995). From an anthropological account of learning, through participation in practice, the course of learning is not presented as a set of subjects to be undertaken and passed, as in educational institutions. Instead, there is a sequence of tasks to be successfully learned and practiced on the way to learning to perform more complex and demanding tasks that are central to the continuity and survival of the community (Pelissier, 1991). So, the sequencing of workplace activities is premised on securing the continuity of the work practice (i.e. the enterprises' goals, or those of cliques and affiliates in workplaces) through learning. These considerations likely take two forms: first, addressing a need to develop the kinds of skills that the enterprise requires to function effectively to survive and prosper; and secondly, developing these skills in ways that do not jeopardize the enterprise's survival.

Although not stated in the form of a syllabus, these pathways, seen as a curriculum, have purposes (i.e. intents). They function in similar ways to a syllabus: setting out the activities, the goals to be achieved, and the means by which progress and attainment can be secured. […]

In hairdressing salons, the tasks apprentices engage in and their progress through these hairdressing tasks are regulated by the salon's approach to hairdressing (Billett, 2001). In one salon, where clients are attended to by a number of hairdressers, the apprentices first engage in 'tea-and-tidy', providing hot beverages for clients and keeping the salon clean and tidy. These tasks are necessary components in understanding and performing as a hairdresser. Through these activities, apprentices learn about, and practice, procedures for determining client needs and hygiene, and maintaining cleanliness. For instance, identifying clients' needs and providing them with tea or coffee assist in building the apprentices' capacities and confidence in negotiating with clients. Next, apprentices engage in washing clients' hair and later rinsing the chemicals used to shape and/or colour clients' hair. Engagement in these tasks develops further the apprentices' capacities to communicate and negotiate with clients. Throughout, the apprentices learn inter-psychologically through direct interpersonal interactions with experienced hairdressers and through more indirect kinds of participation (i.e. observation and listening) in order to understand both the salient aspects of each task (e.g. the importance of removing all the chemicals), and each task's place in and significance to the hairdressing process. Later, apprentices work with experienced hairdressers in placing rods and curlers in clients' hair. Then, before being permitted to cut women's hair, they commence cutting men's hair. This is held to be less difficult and of lower accountability (i.e. lower error-cost) than cutting women's hair. The apprentices continue on this path of activities and engagement in practice until they can style hair independently. In other words, there is a track providing incrementally more demanding tasks (i.e. new learning), and then practice (i.e. refinement) in those tasks that assist in the development of the apprentices' workplace practice. This track of activities constitutes a central principle of a workplace curriculum, and one founded on maintaining the workplace's viability. This principle may prove to be broadly applicable across different kinds of work.

However, because the work requirements are not uniform, curriculum pathways may be quite particular to each workplace, even across the same occupational practice. For instance, in another salon, there is a different division of labour, with each hairdresser undertaking the entire hairdressing task. There, the apprentice is required to learn to cut and colour independently far earlier than in the first salon. The structuring of activities in the second salon includes gaining competence with procedures that permit early independent practice (Billett, 2001). Therefore, in the same vocational practice the particular workplace's goals and practices will shape the structuring and sequencing of the activities that constitute the kinds of tasks to be undertaken and to what standard: the intended workplace curriculum. The two salons have distinct hairdressing goals and practices, and different bases for their continuity. These differences reinforce the localized factors that constitute a particular workplace curriculum. […]

These examples also highlight the pedagogic qualities that can constitute the intended workplace curriculum. These include assisting learners to understand the requirements for effective work: the curriculum goals. Like those stated in syllabuses, these goals may need to be made explicit and be the subject of intentional guided activities in the workplace, because what constitutes effective work-practice is often hidden or hard-to-learn. Novice police officers may not understand the kinds of detail required at a crime scene or an arrest until they are questioned in court many months later; coalminers may be quite unaware of the consequences of the amount of foreign matter in what they extract from a mine site unless they are made aware of the processes at the coal-washing and -grading facilities (Billett, 2001). In one warehouse, workers who pack and load pallets onto delivery trucks were sent with the trucks to understand the requirements for the pallets to remain intact during their transportation and unloading at the stores. Without this experience, these workers would be less likely to understand the requirements for packing the pallets.

It may also be necessary to intentionally support hard-to-learn knowledge in the workplace. That learning may be demanding because the task is complicated, multi-faceted, difficult to manage, or hard to access and learn about. In these circumstances, close guidance by a more experienced co-worker may be required to support this learning. However, this provision of guidance needs to be preceded by identifying what tasks are hard-to-learn and why they are hard-to-learn. The evidence suggests that it is worth securing more than one perspective on what comprises hard-to-learn tasks. When both experienced and relative novices were asked to rate the difficulty of a range of work tasks, there were differences in the views between the two groups (Billett and Boud, 2001), suggesting that more experienced workers may not always be the best judges of what comprises difficult workplace tasks for learners.

In summary, an ideal intended workplace curriculum comprises the identification and sequencing of work activities that represent the 'course to be run'—that lead to full participation in the particular work-practice. This process is likely to be shaped by the requirements of the workplace, including how work is organized and labour divided, as well as the goals that are to be realized through permitting individuals to learn more about that practice. [...]

In other words, the focus of the intended curriculum in addressing the intents and requirements of a social practice is not restricted to educational institutions or workplaces. It is a more general curriculum concern. Yet, it is how the intended curriculum is enacted—what is—that ultimately shapes what learners experience.

# The enacted workplace curriculum

As with educational institutions, conceptions of a workplace curriculum need to go beyond what is intended. There is also a need to understand how factors associated with the enactment of those learning experiences shape what workers experience and engage with. Within educational practice, it has long been understood that no amount of external control, or mandates, can ensure that what is intended will be enacted with 'fidelity' (Hall and Loucks, 1977). The decisions that teachers make in enacting the curriculum are based on their experience, values, preferences, and competence. Their interpretation of a syllabus, how best its goals might be achieved, and the selection of possible learning experiences cannot be prespecified. Moreover, the contributions of teachers in augmenting what is presented in curriculum documents can provide rich experiences, making up the *effective curriculum* (Skilbeck, 1984). For instance, in a study of how vocational educators had assisted developing vocational knowledge that transferred from the college setting to the workplace, students frequently reported the importance of stories and examples provided by teachers (Billett and Beven, 1999). Moreover, beyond the teachers' contributions are the kinds of opportunities, interactions, resources, and infrastructure that are available to provide appropriate learning experiences. Even with the best and most faithful intent, learners' experiences may be constrained by these factors, by the *available curriculum*. So, for instance, nurses being prepared in university health faculties may not be able to access the depth and array of nursing experiences that hospital-based nurse education provides.

In a similar way, the learning experiences enacted in workplaces may vary from what was intended, or is ideal. Thus, the factors determining the enacted workplace curriculum include the concerns and continuities of those who organize activities in the workplace. The intended learning curriculum may well reflect a desired track of experiences; but it is others in the workplace who regulate learners' access to activities and interactions and provide the support that regulates learners' progression. Decisions about and support for learners' access to these experiences will most likely come from three sources: employers/managers; co-workers; and service and production factors.

First, employers may either deliberately support or restrict workers' participation in and learning about work activities. If there is a need for a particular task to be performed, workers might be actively supported and encouraged to learn that task because it is in the enterprise's interest. With changes in production or in legislated requirements, even enterprises that are normally reluctant to expend funds on training will support that learning (Billett, 2000). Employers might also want to extend the workers' skills to make them more broadly deployable within the workplace, or aim to secure a greater sense of attachment to the workplace through a process of developing their skills and understanding about its particular requirements. Some evidence suggests that this kind of involvement sustains enterprises over time: the securing of their survival and continuity (Rowden, 1995).

However, conversely, if employers or managers perceive threats to their continuity and control of the enterprise arising from the development of workers' skills, they may act to restrict that development. Because of such fears, Danford (1998) reports that management dismantled the self-managed teams that were securing productivity improvement. As Braverman (1974) contends, management may subordinate efficiency and productivity to maintaining the control of the means of production. In each workplace there will be a limit on the number of highly remunerated workers it can sustain. Therefore, to remain viable or secure a desired level of profitability, employers may work to limit the amount of skill development that occurs, particularly when that development is structurally rewarded through higher pay levels. Thus, in a study of coal-workers' mine-site learning, Billett (2001) found that management was concerned about workplace arrangements that linked levels of remuneration to the acquisition of training modules when this learning did not lead to productivity enhancements commensurate with the increased wage costs. Progress towards full participation may be constrained to avoid the workplace becoming unviable, or operating with reduced profit.

It may not be feasible to provide the range of learning opportunities that workers desire. The required level of practice on equipment or engagement in tasks may simply be unavailable through a lack of opportunity. For instance, in open-cut coalmines, becoming a dragline operator is a prized role. However, there is little worker turnover and few opportunities to practice on a multi-million-dollar piece of equipment that needs to operate productively 24 hours a day and 7 days a week. So there may be unresolvable conflicts between individuals' desire for skill development and the needs for those skills in the workplace, an internal supply and demand problem.

Employers or owners are also selective about how they direct their support for learning among their employees (Groot *et al.,* 1994). Employers appear unwilling to provide opportunities for learning for part-time or contractual workers (Brunello and Medio, 2001). Lacking workplace support to advance their skills, these contingent workers are doubly disadvantaged. In other words, just as the institutional practices of schools may influence who participates in what activities, the actions of owners and managers shape the range of learning opportunities in workplaces.

The second set of influences upon how the workplace affords learning experiences is the beliefs and actions of co-workers. Workplaces are not benign environments. Co-workers may not support other workers' development and progression. The degree of support is likely to be dependent on how learning and advancement are seen to affect co-workers' interests. For instance, expert workers may be unwilling to assist other workers if they believe that they may be displaced by those whom they have supported (Lave and Wenger, 1991). In uncertain times, those with skills may be reluctant to share their expertise with other workers, particularly those paid at a lower rate.

The interests of workplace affiliations and cliques also regulate who is afforded learning support and in what ways. Full-time workers may restrict the activities of part-time workers (Hughes and Bernhardt, 1999), 'old-timers' restrict those of 'newcomers' (Lave and Wenger, 1991), and professional or trade affiliations may work to support their affiliates while marginalizing others (Billett, 2001). There are the inevitable workplace factions that serve to regulate the distribution of activities, interactions, and judgements about others' performances. Workers' gender, race, and language also shape how they are supported in the workplace by management and co-workers (Hull, 1997; Bierema, 2001). In short, workplaces are contested learning environments in which relations among workers and support for learning are unlikely to be benign, because the learning and development of some workers may threaten others.

The effort and support of co-workers are salient for learning through work. In a year-long study of guided learning in three work areas in a workplace that prided itself on learning support for its employees, the support available to learners was largely shaped by the efforts and skills of more experienced co-workers (Billett, 2003). Ultimately, it was the personal qualities and characteristics of co-workers that regulated the support for learning provided in the workplace. In a manufacturing plant that offered little in the way of support, a co-worker, through his own efforts, was able to provide rich learning experiences to workers who had not previously experienced any support.

Where evidence exists of strong support for co-workers' learning, it is often in circumstances where the person providing the support is in some way an affiliate. Senior female public servants or executives form relationships with younger women to advise them on work choices and difficult career decisions in order to assist their career development (Arnold and Davidson, 1990; Vincent and Seymour, 1994). Support is also likely to be provided where there is no risk to individuals' employment or standing (Dore and Sako, 1989; Hughes and Bernhardt, 1999), or when those assisted will become supporters of their mentor (Allen *et al.,* 1997). However, even with the most well-intentioned and best efforts of co-workers, there remains the risk that co-workers working alone and without support may themselves be unaware of all the kinds of knowledge that need to be learned. Worse still, they may guide the development of practices that are short-term and habits that may even be dangerous. So, whether the workers' learning experiences and progression are constrained or promoted by management practices or co-workers, they are usually shaped by particular sets of interests.

The third source of influences is factors beyond employers' and co-workers' influence which may also regulate the kind of learning experiences that are afforded individual workers or cohorts of workers. There are demarcations that arise from societal expectations. Dental assistants are expected only to assist; nurses to nurse, not to diagnose, etc. Also, the level of production or service can influence the kinds of opportunities that are made available. For instance, the reduced demand for a product saw one team of workers lose the opportunity for further skill development and another team lose access to the training funds that were used to support time-release for training in their work area (Billett and Boud, 2001). However, the opposite can occur when there is a labour shortage. For instance, in many parts of rural Australia, nurses are required to perform medical tasks that would be only undertaken by physicians in provincial and metropolitan centres. The shortage of physicians has led to a demand for nurses to provide a wider range of services and be trained to conduct those services safely. And, as noted above, there is the simple availability of plant and equipment. If such infrastructure is not available, it may be difficult to provide the kind of practice that is often so important in developing skillful performance: the available curriculum would be weak.

In other words, as with educational institutions, there can be no guarantee that the 'intended' workplace curriculum will be realized. The actions of individuals and co-workers in enacting a workplace curriculum are directed by particular interests and focused on particular continuities (e.g. the workplace, their personal, or affiliate's continuities). These may serve to either support or inhibit access to the kinds of activities and interactions required to assist individuals' development. The concern for the organization of the enacted workplace curriculum is to attempt to find ways to improve and enrich workplace learning experiences through guidance and the ordering of experiences in order to secure fair and positive outcomes for all workplace learners (Billett, 2001). This can include guided participation in activities and the provision of direct guidance by more expert co-workers.

However, while influential, whatever is enacted is not the sum of a workplace curriculum. It is learners who determine whether what was enacted constitutes worthwhile learning experiences worth engaging with, and in what ways.

# The workplace curriculum as experienced by workers

Beyond the experiences that are intended and enacted, learners will interpret and construct meaning in ways that may or may not be consistent with the intentions of those who enacted those experiences. In educational settings, for instance, tasks set for students as problem-solving activities may become a basis for guessing or trial-and-error (Posner, 1982), a competition to finish first, to please the teacher, or to 'look smart' (Dweck and Elliott, 1983). The experiences may be premised on whether learners have the confidence to proceed with the task as intended (Belenky *et al.*, 1986). Similarly, there can be no guarantee that individuals participating in workplace activities will learn what was intended or enacted. Individuals decide how they engage with what the particular social practice affords them (Goodnow, 1990). Valsiner (1998: 393) contends that 'most of human development takes place through active ignoring and neutralization of most of social suggestions to which the person is subjected in everyday life'. This is essential to buffer individuals' personality against the constant demands of the social suggestions. This suggests that the regulatory practices (Bernstein, 1996) enacted in educational institutions and workplaces alike are subject to individual agency and intentionality.

The significance and implications of this exercise of individual agency go beyond how individuals behave or perform in educational institutions or workplaces. Activity structures cognition (Rogoff and Lave, 1984), and the degree to which individuals elect to engage in a particular task or interaction has cognitive consequences for the kind of change or learning that occurs (Newell and Simon, 1972). Learning is highly effortful, particularly in learning new knowledge that requires some restructuring of existing understandings and practices (van Lehn, 1989). Therefore, the degree of self-directed interest and engagement that individuals enact will probably have specific implications for the learning (Perkins *et al.,* 1993; Tobias, 1994).

Moreover, individuals participate and learn in ways directed towards the continuity of *their* interests and goals (Somerville, 2002). Their agentic action is influenced by their goals, subjectivities, and identities. How their agentic action is directed will have consequences for their learning. In one worksite, a production worker went to extraordinary lengths to understand the work of fitters (Billett, 2001). The source of his agentic action was that he was a fitter by trade and wanted to be employed as a fitter in this workplace. His goal was to participate more fully than existing staffing levels permitted. Similarly, a grief counsellor was, by force of personality and persistence, able to reshape the counselling practice in his workplace in ways aligned to his particular beliefs about counselling. This action reshaped the operation of the workplace in ways that had impact upon other workers (Billett *et al.*, 2004). The important point is that individuals exercise agency in how they participate in the workplace, including potentially transforming the work practice and what they learn through their participation. [...]

Thus, individuals also decide what constitutes workplace affordances. This may occur in ways that are counter to the best intentions or most invitational qualities of the workplace. For instance, one worker refused to participate as a workplace mentor because he could identify no personal advantage from expending effort in this way. Another rejected the support and interactions provided by his new workplace because he believed his expertise to be superior to that of his assigned mentor and that his standards of skill were higher than that practiced in the workplace—so he had nothing to learn from them (Billett, 2001). In essence, both these workers rejected the opportunities and support afforded by their workplaces; they had concluded, rightly or wrongly, that the kind of engagement was not in their interests or career trajectory.

In highly contested work environments, workers' construal of affordance may be premised on suspicion and distrust. At one coal mine, the management's offer of additional safety training was firmly rejected by the miners (Billett, 2001). Such was the distrust in the workplace that these miners viewed the safety training as a ploy to further transfer the responsibility for mine-site safety to the workers. That is, they viewed this offer of training as being most uninviting, and complicit in eroding the traditional responsibility of mine-site management for workplace safety. Darrah's (1996) study of a computer manufacturing plant in California demonstrated how workers of Vietnamese heritage resisted teamwork because it countered their cultural beliefs about being judged as an individual, not as a team member. These workers believe the social system they despised and had fled from (i.e. communism) had followed them to Silicon Valley. Even if forced to work under team-based arrangements, these workers would likely only master the concepts about teamwork that their employer intended.

Even when action by workers is precipitated by the threat of redundancy, the kind of learning that occurs may be premised more on survival, placating managers or supervisors, than learning richly about work performance (Billett, 2002b). The important point here is that learning experiences are something construed and judged by individuals through *their* interactions with the workplace. Ultimately, they will make judgements about what constitutes workplace affordances and how they might engage with what is afforded. So, just as with education institutions, conceptions of a workplace curriculum have to include the idea that individuals are not passive recipients of knowledge. They decide what they make their own (Leont'ev, 1981).

In considering the workplace curriculum as something to be experienced, concerns about continuity arise in the form of individuals' goals, identities, and subjectivities. This directs how they decide to participate in and learn from the experiences they encounter in the workplace, and how they elect to exercise their agentic action. Moreover, it emphasizes that finding ways of securing individual's interests and identities is likely to be central to the task of engaging them in appropriating the kinds of learning that are important both to themselves and the workplace. This is not always an easy goal. A marriage between the two sets of continuities—the workplace's and the individual's—is perhaps the ideal for the workplace curriculum. [...]

# A curriculum for the workplace and beyond

In this chapter, some bases and prospects for a workplace curriculum have been advanced. I hope that they can contribute to broaden the debate about curriculum more generally, *and within educational institutions.*

Thus, I proposed that an ideal 'intended' curriculum comprises pathways towards full participation within a social practice as a learning outcome and the support for learning required to progress along these pathways. In its ideal form, the needs of both the individual and the social practice (workplace) are addressed. However, the degree by which any intentions can be realized is likely premised on the support for their enactment by interests within the social practice of the workplace. The exercise of these interests is directed towards the continuity of the social practice and those individuals, affiliation, and interests that operate within it. Together, the concepts of the affordances of the social practice and individual engagement emphasize the significant role that the social practice's norms and regulations play in individuals' engagement in learning, and their learning itself. Practices that invite, structure, support, and guide participation are likely to engage workers in the kinds of thinking, acting, and learning that are important for effective vocational practice. Moreover, the degree of consonance between individuals' interests and what the workplace affords will be salient in shaping individuals' engagement in the kind of learning which they desire—in ways consistent with increasing the quality of their learning experience.

These tentative bases for understanding the workplace curriculum are founded in empirical work and are consistent with many curriculum concepts and practices used in appraisals of learning experiences in educational institutions. They may provide a useful way of under-standing how the purposes of social practices, such workplaces *and* educational institutions, as well as community organizations and even perhaps families, aim to reproduce them-selves, and how such processes are complicated by circumstances in which different inter-ests, power relationships, and influences are embedded and enacted. Moreover, even powerful forms of social pressure are not immune from the exercise of human agency. Individuals' agentic actions will likely interpret and construe meaning in ways that are con-sistent with their own personal goals and trajectories (Valsiner, 1998). [...]

# References

Allen, T. M., Poteet, M. L. and Burroughs, S. M. (1997) The mentor's perspective: a qualitative inquiry and future research agenda. *Journal of Vocational Behaviour*, 51(1), 70–89.

Arnold, V. and Davidson, M. (1990) Adopt a mentor: the new way ahead for women managers? *Women in Management Review*, 5(1), 22–27.

Belenky, M. F., Clinchy, B. M., Goldberger, N. R. and Tarule, J. M. (1986) *Women's Ways of Know-ing: The Development of Self, Voice, and Mind* (New York: Basic Books).

Bernstein, B. B. (1996) *Pedagogy, Symbolic Control and Identity: Theory, Research, Critique* (London: Taylor & Francis).

Bierema, L. L. (2001) Women, work, and learning. In T. Fenwick (ed.), *Sociocultural Perspectives on Learning Through Work* (San Francisco, CA: Jossey-Bass), 53–62.

Billett, S. (2000) Defining the demand side of VET: industry, enterprises, individuals and regions. *Journal of Vocational Education and Training*, 50(1), 5–30.

Billett, S. (2001) *Learning in the Workplace: Strategies for Effective Practice* (Sydney, Australia: Allen & Unwin).

Billett, S. (2002a) Critiquing workplace learning discourses: participation and continuity at work. *Studies in the Education of Adults*, 34(1), 56–67.

Billett, S. (2002b) Workplace pedagogic practices: co-participation and learning. *British Journal of Educational Studies*, 50(4), 457–481.

Billett, S. (2003) Workplace mentors: demands and benefits. *Journal of Workplace Learning*, 15(3), 105–113.

Billett, S. and Beven, F. (1999) Introduction. In S. Billett, C. McKavanagh, F. Beven, L. Angus, T. Seddon, J. Gough, S. Hayes and I. Robertson (1999) *The CBT Decade: Teaching for Flexibility and Adaptability* (Leabrook, Australia: National Centre for Vocational Education Research), 1–14. Available online at: http://www.ncver.edu.au/publications/368.html (visited 21 March 2005).

Billett S. and Boud, D. (2001) Participation in and guided engagement at work: workplace pedagogic practices. Paper presented at the 2nd International Conference on Learning and Work (Calgary, Canada: University of Calgary). Available online at: http://www.ucalgary.ca/cted/confer2001/con_paper.html (visited 21 March 2005).

Billett, S., Barker, M. and Hernon-Tinning, B. (2004) Participatory practices at work. *Pedagogy, Culture and Society*, 12(2), 233–258.

Braverman, H. (1974) *Labour and Monopoly Capital: The Degradation of Work in the Twentieth Century* (New York: Monthly Review Press).

Brunello, G. and Medio, A. (2001) An explanation of international differences in education and workplace training. *European Economic Review*, 45(2), 307–322.

Danford, A. (1998) Teamworking and labour regulation in the autocomponents industry. *Work, Employment and Society*, 12(3), 409–431.

Darrah, C. N. (1996) *Learning and Work: An Exploration in Industrial Ethnography* (New York: Garland).

Dewey, J. (1916) *Democracy and Education: An Introduction to the Philosophy of Education* (New York: Free Press).

Dore, R. P. and Sako, M. (1989) *How the Japanese Learn to Work* (London: Routledge).

Dweck, C. S. and Elliott, E. S. (1983) Achievement motivation. In E. M. Hetherington (ed.), *Handbook of Child Psychology*, Vol. 4 (New York: Wiley), 643–691.

Giddens, A. (1984) *The Constitution of Society: Outline of a Theory of Structuration* (Cambridge: Polity Press).

Goodnow, J. J. (1990) The socialization of cognition: what's involved? In J. W. Stigler, R. A. Shweder and G. H. Herdt (eds), *Cultural Psychology: The Chicago Symposia on Human Development* (Cambridge: Cambridge University Press), 259–286.

Groot, W., Hartog, J. and Oosterbeek, H. (1994) Costs and revenues of investment in enterprise-related schooling. *Oxford Economic Papers*, 46(4), 658–676.

Hall, G. E. and Loucks, S. F. (1977) A developmental model for determining whether the treatment is actually implemented. *American Education Research Journal*, 14(3), 263–276.

Hughes, K. and Bernhardt, A. (1999) Market segmentation and the restructuring of banking jobs. IEE Brief number 24 (New York: Columbia University, Institute on Education and the Economy). Available online at: http://www.tc.columbia.edu/iee/briefs/Brief24.htm (visited 21 March 2005).

Hull, G. (1997) Preface and introduction. In G. Hull (ed.), *Changing Work, Changing Workers: Critical Perspectives on Language, Literacy, and Skills* (Albany, NY: State University of New York Press), 3–39.

Lave, J. (1990) The culture of acquisition and the practice of understanding. In J. W. Stigler, R. A. Shweder and G. Herdt (eds), *Cultural Psychology: The Chicago Symposia on Human Development* (Cambridge: Cambridge University Press), 259–286.

Lave, J. (1993) The practice of learning. In S. Chaiklin and J. Lave (eds.), *Understanding Practice: Perspectives on Activity and Context* (Cambridge: Cambridge University Press), 3–32.

Lave, J. and Wenger, E. (1991) *Situated Learning: Legitimate Peripheral Participation* (Cambridge: Cambridge University Press).

Leont'ev, A. N. (1981) *Problems of the Development of the Mind* (Moscow: Progress Publishers).

Marsh, C. and Willis, G. (1995) *Curriculum: Alternative Approaches, Ongoing Issues* (Englewood Cliffs, NJ: Merill).

Newell, A. and Simon, H. A. (1972) *Human Problem Solving* (Englewood Cliffs, NJ: Prentice-Hall).

Pelissier, C. (1991) The anthropology of teaching and learning. *Annual Review of Anthropology*, 20, 75–95.

Perkins, D. N., Jay, E. and Tishman, S. (1993) Beyond abilities: a dispositional theory of thinking. *Merrill-Palmer Quarterly*, 39(1), 1–21.

Posner, G. (1982) A cognitive science conception of curriculum and instruction. *Journal of Curriculum Studies*, 14(4), 343–351.

Rogoff, B. and Lave, J. (eds) (1984) *Everyday Cognition: Its Development in Social Context* (Cambridge, MA: Harvard University Press).

Rowden, R. (1995) The role of human resources development in successful small to mid-sized manufacturing businesses: a comparative case study. *Human Resource Development Quarterly*, 6(4), 335–373.

Skilbeck, M. (1984) *School-based Curriculum Development* (London: Harper & Row).

Somerville, M. (2002) Changing masculine work cultures. In J. Searle and D. Roebuck (eds), *Envisioning Practice: Implementing Change: Proceedings of the 10th Annual International Conference on Post-compulsory Education and Training*, Vol. 3 (Brisbane, Australia: Australian Academic Press), 149–155.

Taylor, C. (1985) *Human Agency and Language: Philosophical Papers 1* (Cambridge: Cambridge University Press).

Tobias, S. (1994) Interest, prior knowledge, and learning. *Review of Educational Research,* 64(1), 37–54.

Valsiner, J. (1998) *The Guided Mind: A Sociogenetic Approach to Personality* (Cambridge, MA: Harvard University Press).

Valsiner, J. and van de Veer, R. (2000) *The Social Mind: The Construction of an Idea* (Cambridge: Cambridge University Press).

van Lehn, V. (1989) Towards a theory of impasse-driven learning. In H. Mandl and A. Lesgold (eds), *Learning Issues for Intelligent Tutoring Systems* (New York: Springer-Verlag), 19–41.

Vincent, A. and Seymour, J. (1994) Mentoring among female executives. *Women in Management Review*, 9(7), 15–20.

# 6

# Emotion, Functionality and the Everyday Experience of Music: Where Does Music Education Fit?

*John Sloboda*

## Introduction

This chapter is intended to raise broad issues about the nature and purpose of general music education. Although it is grounded in an empirically observable phenomenon (the decline of engagement of young people in traditional forms of music activity), it goes far beyond scientifically validated data in an attempt to locate the phenomenon we observe within a broad historical and cultural context. I am, however, not a social historian, and I am painfully aware that I may be doing badly what others unknown to me have done much better. I hope readers will take this as an opening contribution to a debate in which not enough people in music education research appear to be participating, rather than a polished and finalised set of positions.

## Why do children drop out of instrumental music?

A phenomenon which has been reported with concern by observers of UK music education is the decline of engagement by young people with those forms of musical activity which have been traditionally encouraged and supported within the school system (particularly the playing of traditional acoustic musical instruments). This decline may be mirrored in other countries, but the focus of this chapter is on data from the UK, and its implications for music education in the UK.

The transition from primary to secondary education appears to be a point of particular vulnerability. Many children appear to 'leave instrumental music behind' as they make this transition. This has recently been confirmed by data from a large-scale study of young

From: *Music Education Research*, 3 (2), 2001, pp. 243–253. Reprinted by permission of the publisher (Taylor & Francis Ltd, http://www.informaworld.com).

people's participation in music (cf. Ryan, Boulton, O'Neill & Sloboda, 2000). In this longitudinal study, we have been able to collect data from 684 school-aged children (aged 11–12 years) at three points in time: (a) in the last half of the final year at primary school; (b) in the first half of the first year at secondary school; and (c) in the second half of the first year at secondary school.

Children were asked the same question at each point: 'do you play a musical instrument?'. Among these 684 children, 420 answered 'yes' at point (a). By point (c) only 229 of these were still playing; 191 children (45% of the players) had given up playing.

Although detailed quantitative analysis of the correlates of this massive 'drop-out' is still under way, I would like to present here two illustrative vignettes, drawn from intensive interviews with two of the children concerned. A sample of 76 children was interviewed at point (a) and again at point (c). The vignettes presented here are from two children who showed a very high degree of instrumental engagement at point (a) but who had given up playing by point (c), 1 year later.

'Mary' was receiving weekly group violin lessons at school when we first interviewed her. She had learned the violin for 2 years, but had not taken any Grade exams. She reported playing the violin for upwards of 21 hours per week (3 hours per day).

'Lucy' was receiving weekly individual piano lessons at her teacher's home when we first interviewed her. She had been learning the piano for 3 years, and had passed Grade 3. She reported playing the piano for between 11 and 15 hours per week (2 hours per day).

Mary and Lucy's weekly investment in their playing puts them both in the top 5% in terms of instrumental time investment within the playing cohort. These levels of investment equal or exceed the age-average (2 hours per day) for the highest achieving players in the study of practising time carried out by Sloboda, Davidson, Howe and Moore (1996). Mary and Lucy could, therefore, have been expected to be on a trajectory similar to that reported for those children in Sloboda et al.'s study who succeeded in competitive entry to a nationally recruiting specialist music school.

Three significant features characterise the accounts given by Mary and Lucy at point (a) while identifying as players.

1. *'Fun' is a key motivating concept, both for individual playing and participation in lessons.*

When asked 'What does being involved in music mean to you?', Mary responded: 'It gives me a chance to practise because I like playing my violin, and most children in my class play instruments, so I just thought it would be fun.' In response to the question: 'What do you like about playing the violin?' she said, 'I just like practising it, and I like playing it.' To a similar question, Lucy answered, 'Well it's just fun really. I just enjoy doing it. It's a hobby, something to do.'

2. *While playing, achievement is valued (e.g. grade success, being able to play a difficult piece, playing in front of people).*

Mary expanded her liking of playing the violin by saying 'sometimes the music we have to play is quite hard but it seems easy after a while.' When asked, 'What do you like about playing in front of people?' , Lucy replied 'Um, it's just that you can show off your talent because you only do that to like your family and music teacher really'. Later she explained: 'I enjoy playing the piano. You can get different grades for it and things, so like all your hard work to pay off when you get to pass an exam or something.'

3. *Parents and instrumental teachers are key players in the discourse concerning support.*

In response to the question: 'What did your parents think when you first started playing the violin?', Mary said: 'Me dad was quite interested and happy for me, me mum, she doesn't like the violin because its screechy, she says I'm happy for you, and she's glad that I've got an instrument because I've been on about it all like for a long time, she says I'm happy that you've got the instrument, the violin, because you've always wanted it … .'. In response to the same question, Lucy said 'they were really pleased and they said that I was making good progress as well.'

Of her violin teacher, Mary said; 'She's really kind. I did have one teacher and I didn't like her much because if we forgot our violins she used to go tell secretary and then we were in real trouble. But that wasn't all the reason. She didn't give us the chance to pick what music we wanted to play.' Lucy described her piano teacher thus: 'He's always like cheery, and he doesn't shout at you or anything if you get it wrong, he buys books for you to play out of and he just helps you work out notes and things.'

When asked if they thought they would still be playing their instruments in secondary school, they both said yes.

Five new features characterise the discourse of these two interviewees at point (c).

1. *Playing an instrument is seen as 'boring'.*

When asked 'Can you tell me why you decided to give up the violin?', Mary said 'Cos I didn't like it.' 'What didn't you like about it?' 'I don't know. When I first started playing it, I used to really like instruments but then I just went off it. I just found it boring. …' In response to the question, 'Why did you give up the piano?', Lucy said 'Well I'd been playing since year 2, and I'd got up to grade 3, and I just got bored with doing exams and that.'

2. *Previously valued achievements are discounted.*

Mary, who at point (a) had enjoyed practising, now 'hated' it. When asked how her teacher reacted to her giving up, she said 'I think she was a bit upset really 'cos I had been doing quite well just before I quit, and she was like a bit upset that I was, she said I was making good progress, and if I'd carried on a bit longer I would have got some more grades.' 'And how do you feel about having given up now?' 'I feel quite glad actually.' When Lucy was asked 'Do you ever regret having given up?', she replied: 'No … It was … the exams and practising all the different ones I didn't like doing.'

3. *Other activities are valued more highly than music (e.g. academic lessons, homework, seeing friends).*

Mary said 'I hated practising, and I had other things to do, like homework and going outside and playing with my friends, and it's just like that took over.' In response to a question about whether she might take up an instrument the following year, Lucy said no, because 'the first year at high school, when you do instruments you miss your lessons, and then you have to catch up, so you worry about having to catch up on your lessons.'

4. *Dropping out of music is associated with discourses of autonomy and self-determination.*

When asked whether she missed playing, Mary said no 'because I always used to play at 5 o'clock till 6 o'clock, an hour every night. My mum used to push me about doing my practice. I just missed it for a bit, but then I got used to it, doing things I really wanted to do.' Lucy got explicit support from her mother for the autonomous choice to stop – 'I told my mum first, and she said she wouldn't make me do anything I didn't want to do. So she told my (private) teacher for me.'

5. *Future engagement in music is not ruled out but is conceptualised in terms of instruments and social networks that were marginal to (and possibly conflicting with) previous involvement.*

When asked 'if you were to take up an instrument again, is there anyone who you think would be particularly helpful or supportive to you?' Mary nominated her grandmother. In the earlier interview, Mary had told us that she used to play the piano, which she actually preferred to the violin (although she found it more difficult). Her grandmother played the piano, and Mary sometimes went to her grandmother's house to play the piano there, which used to be in Mary's house. When Lucy was asked whether there was any instrument she might consider taking up in the future, she nominated the saxophone because 'my friend plays cornet, and I go to their jazz concerts, and I like the sound of the saxophone.'

# The sociocultural environment for young people

In gaining a clearer understanding of how a well-embedded daily activity can collapse like a house of cards within a 12-month period, I'd like to propose four conjectures which link these vignettes to wider social and cultural trends.

## Conjecture 1
Instrumental playing is a 'hobby'. It is in the nature of hobbies to 'grow out of them'. Therefore, an understanding of the 'take' that a lot of children have on musical activities requires a broader understanding of the psychology and sociology of hobbies.

## Conjecture 2
Instrumental playing 'comes from' the culture of the primary school, where musical activity is just 'part of the furniture'. Its underpinnings are undermined through the transition to secondary school because:

- instruments are 'less important' than 'academic' subjects;
- the peer groups through which instrumental activities are reinforced have been disrupted;
- secondary music teachers are (for structural and cultural reasons) in a less good position than their primary colleagues to maintain a shared set of values and expectations within which positive engagement can proceed.

## Conjecture 3

Instrumental playing is associated with parental control and a focus of everyday life on the home. The desired focus of the pre-adolescent shifts in the direction of increasing assertions of autonomy, identification with peer groups and life outside the home.

## Conjecture 4

For many young people, instrumental playing has no inherent 'purpose' which relates to their activities and goals, even those which might involve music in other ways.

For these conjectures to be validated, evidence from a number of sources will be relevant. Some of this evidence exists already. One of the most important sources of evidence comes from detailed studies on the musical lives of individuals in different sub-cultures within UK society. This shows how people appropriate music for their specific personal and social uses in ways which are often unique, and which have little to do with the forms and activities of music which are found within educational establishments. Two major examples of this approach are provided by Green (2001) in relation to the lives of popular musicians, and De Nora (2000) in relation to the personal lives of adult non-musician women. Another example is given by Sloboda, O'Neill and Ivaldi (2001) who obtained a 1-week 'diary' of musical engagement from adult non-musicians using an 'experience sampling methodology' (originated by Czikszentmihalyi & Lefevre, 1989). Participants carried pagers with them at all times for a week, and made a structured entry into a 'diary' every time the pager sounded. They were required to report on concurrent activity and the nature, purpose and effect of any music happening in the context of that activity. The study showed that the vast majority of music takes place in the context of (and subsidiary to) non-musical activity. The most common types of activity are what we call 'maintenance' activities, those essential routines of everyday life that everyone has to perform many times each day (e.g. washing, cleaning, cooking, travelling, etc.). Usually these activities are enacted alone, and music seems to be a resource through which the individual addresses issues of personal autonomy and identity. Because of this, the accounts of participants from a range of studies suggest that music is often a source of conflict where different individuals occupying the same space have different relationships to, and needs from, the music. The same music that affirms and reinforces one person's psychological agendas can simultaneously threaten another's.

Sloboda, O'Neill and Ivaldi (2001) also investigated change in emotional state as a result of the music experienced. In general, participants experienced greater and more positive change when the music was chosen by them.

Unfortunately, all the studies of this sort known to us have been undertaken with adult participants. The details of the intimate hour-by-hour musical lives of children in contemporary society are almost unknown to us. We really need to know much more about what children autonomously use music for in their everyday lives. In particular, we need to know what are the 'natural' varieties of performance that are given meaning within their solitary, family and social settings. Then we can begin to understand better how formal instrumental playing maps (or fails to map) onto these natural categories.

# The goals and attitudes of classroom music teachers

A second source of evidence relevant to an understanding of why children drop out of formal music relates to the nature of what it is they are running from. An important new source of information on this matter comes from a recent survey of 750 heads of music in UK high schools catering for ages 12–16 (York, 2001).

Seventy-eight per cent of respondents had degrees based in classical music with 50% being classical pianists, organists or singers. The most commonly used public sources of support and resources for their teaching were Radio 3, Classic FM and *BBC Music Magazine*. The most commonly used specialist sources of information were: the Qualifications and Curriculum Authority (55%) and the Local Music Service (50%).

Use of agencies such as the British Phonographic Institute, the Musicians Union, or the Performing Rights Society was almost nonexistent.

Respondents were asked if they knew 20 pieces of music from various genres and periods, and if they could name the most associated composer or performer. Although over 95% could correctly answer for classical titles such as 'The Four Seasons' (Vivaldi) or 'The Ode to Joy' (Beethoven), only half answered correctly for 'Wannabe' (Spice Girls), and only tiny numbers were correct for 'Kind of Blue' (Miles Davies – 15%) and 'Rockafeller Skank' (Fatboy Slim – 9%).

York concludes from these and other data that

> school music culture tends to be introverted and avoids looking for models of current practice from the art of music rather than relying on the received knowledge of music education. … Many teachers seem to be engaged in using pop and rock to extend pupils' musical interests into other styles … but the vast majority of teachers are doing this with little or no training or professional experience in pop or rock.

Although York's analysis focuses on the genres used by music teachers, there is implicit in his data the assumption that this is about more than genres. It is about different approaches to music, including ways of thinking about it and responding to it. One cannot just insert a popular genre into the set of classroom practices that have been developed to deal with classical music.

Musical sub-cultures are defined by much more than the style of music they use (it is also how they are used, in what contexts, for what purposes, assuming what type of interpersonal relationships, and accruing what meanings). Labels like 'pop' and 'rock' are coarse grained and uninformative. Take, for instance, the case of 'techno'.

Techno is not 'performed', 'composed' or 'appraised' within parameters that fit neatly with the UK's National Curriculum formulations. The music is constructed in real time out of computer-manipulated elements at the disposal of a DJ. Its primary function is to support communal (but individualistic) dancing designed to induce certain altered states of awareness. Dancers may only experience the intended effects after several continuous hours of engagement. A short extract experienced in a classroom setting provides an incomplete, even misleading, basis for appraisal. The basis for valid appraisal exists only for someone attending a techno club and dancing to the music. No classroom teacher could hope to adequately address issues relating to techno with their students without specific understanding of, and exposure to, that sub-genre and its role for its habitual users. The same point can be made for almost any other sub-genre.

# Determining the place of music in education

Music education in schools cannot function effectively without an implicit agreement between stakeholders (e.g. teachers, student, parents, government, etc.) about what it is for. The 'meaning of music' is a constantly shifting function of the discourses of these diverse groups, which may coalesce around a 'dominant ideology' which gains enough inter-group consensus to generate a stable educational agenda. I would argue that such a stable agenda existed in mid 20th-century music education, but its underpinning consensus collapsed as a result of major cultural shifts, most evident from the 1960s onwards.

At risk of caricature, but emboldened by the analyses of writers such as Cook (1998) and Small (1998), the dominant paradigm of the early to mid-20th century might be described as follows.

Classical artworks (as epitomised by Bach or Beethoven) represent the pinnacle of musical value. Deeper appreciation and understanding of such artworks is the most important (and universally applicable) aim of music education. Such appreciation and understanding is most accessible to those who have the technical and theoretical skills to perform these works. All performance-based education is oriented towards enabling a significant minority (or even a majority) to acquire the necessary skills to be able to perform at least some works from the 'canon'. The most profound end result of a musical education trajectory is the development of the ability to add to the canon of masterworks through compositional activity. This is necessarily confined to the few. Music is necessarily best taught by people trained in the understanding and performance of the classical canon.

A revised version of this characterisation emerged in the 1960s–1980s, primarily articulated through the liberal educational establishment, justifying some broadening of the syllabus but still very much framed by the pre-existing dominant paradigm. It ran something like as follows.

Lesser forms of musical activity (e.g. world music, pop, jazz, etc.) have their legitimate place within the syllabus, and may be necessary 'stopping points' for many people. A wide range of musical activities and genres permits the development of valuable skills, including technical skills relating to the perception and production of organised sound, the ability to subordinate the personal to the goals of a group, self-discipline, etc. Music can be a useful vehicle for interdisciplinary education, relating it to its cultural, historical and scientific context. *But*, whatever broadening of the syllabus is contemplated, music education must remain controlled by those who have been through a full classical training themselves, since this remains the pinnacle of the musical pyramid, to which all, in the end, aspire.

Our present dilemmas may be an indication of the unsustainability of even this liberalised view of music education. It may be no longer possible to muster stakeholder consensus around any version of the educational enterprise that prioritises the classical canon. Strong cultural forces have been at work which account for the collapse of this consensus. I identify seven such forces. There may, of course, be more.

# Seven key cultural trends

## 1. Multiculturalism

An important consequence of the multiculturalism that increasingly has characterised the UK since the Second World War is the fact that European history and culture no longer define British history and culture. The classical canon is the product of European history and culture, and its defence therefore increasingly becomes identified with a xenophobic 'fortress' mentality which places it on the margins of the cultural spectrum.

## 2. Youth culture

First-world prosperity gives young people unprecedented freedoms and spending power. This allows them to set cultural agendas rather than accept agendas laid down by others. The effects of this are being felt throughout secondary education, not just in music, but it is arguable that stakeholder consensus is still holding together (just) in disciplines where the educational agendas relate more directly to occupationally relevant skills. Parents and children will ally themselves with school management where the earning potential of their child is at stake. They are less likely to do this when neither school management nor government is able to articulate a shared vision of the value of music which is stronger than the child's own lived experience.

## 3. Electronic communication

Unprecedented choice, and the miniaturisation of delivery technology, give much greater individual autonomy in musical experience than has been possible hitherto. Young people can easily and cheaply create their own musical 'worlds'. Institutions such as schools no longer comprise a privileged route to access.

## 4. Feminism

This movement has had many profound effects on culture. One important effect is the progressive replacement of the hierarchic by the democratic as the paradigm of cultural organisation. In the context of music, this has rendered the paradigm forms of the classical canon increasingly problematic. The symphony concert represents the pinnacle of such forms. Everything from the nature of the building to the social organisation of symphony orchestras points to the subjugation of the entire cultural project to the will of the (overwhelmingly and predominantly male) 'maestro' who is himself subjugated to the will of the (male) composer. Feminism foregrounds alternative modes of organisation where leadership is more shared and fluid, and where the musicians are as likely to have generated their own music as they are to be reproducing the music of others. Although the pop group is not without major contradictions as an expression of feminism (not least because the membership of such groups is still overwhelmingly male, and because the music industry attempts to be far more controlling of pop musicians than classical patrons ever had the power to be), it is hard to imagine major industrial nations according symphony orchestras the explicit or implicit role as 'cultural ambassador' that is now accorded to a country's major popular artists. When the London Symphony Orchestra visits the USA, no-one notices or cares. When the Spice Girls visit, it is front-page news.

## 5. Secularism

Christianity (along with all forms of organised religion) has suffered a massive decline as a social force in the last 40 years (Brown, 2001). People look within themselves and their personal networks rather than outside for sources of personal meaning and fulfilment. Personal emotional work, rather than confirmation of the social/divine order, becomes a key focus of musical activity. Key musical organisations to which almost all children used to be exposed (the church choir) are no longer experienced by most children. I have argued elsewhere that churches have probably been responsible for keeping alive a 'ladder of opportunity' for classical music performers in every town and village for the last century. This ladder now has many missing rungs (Sloboda, 1999), and schools have neither the resources nor the social influence to bridge the gaps.

## 6. Niche cultures

In the age of easy electronic communications, affiliations between individuals are increasingly based on 'special interests' rather than shared social or civic obligations (and the geographical proximity which these presuppose). Young people can be swapping information (and music clips) with people on the other side of the world. Schools, which could easily relate to the civic (e.g. village brass bands, the church, the Town Hall) are 'cut out of the loop' of shifting 'grass-roots' affiliations. The decline of the 'civic' has been most prominently documented by Puttnam (2001).

## 7. Postmodernism

All the above are sometimes considered as key manifestations of a post-modern society, characterised by a free, even anarchic cultural 'market' in which the conditions for one segment to acquire cultural dominance do not exist. There are significant national differences in all these factors. For instance, the cultural homogeneity of small-town America, with the far stronger grip of religion, and relatively weak incursions of feminism, can probably still sustain a music education system that meets more dominant cultural needs.

The consequence of cultural fragmentation is that we music educators no longer occupy a privileged position. We represent a small (and increasingly marginal) subset of these sub-cultures that co-exist in the population. Furthermore, it is an assumption of postmodernism that the conditions for the re-establishment of a new 'dominant cultural ideology' do not exist. We cannot hope for any easy return to the stability we once enjoyed. A national curriculum for music was probably introduced at the very moment in history when its sustainability had never been less certain. The classical conservatoire culture is vibrant and valuable. It just won't do for the majority of our children. In this context it is important to defend teachers, who are not to blame for the 'failure' of music education. The present rapid rate of cultural change is leaving many public institutions 'high and dry' in one way or another.

# What should viable and engaging UK music education look like?

On the basis of the above, it is at least conceivable to hypothesise that classroom music, as currently conceptualised and organised, is an inappropriate vehicle for mass music education in 21st-century Britain. Hints of the parameters of a more effective music education environment may well be found within the somewhat anarchic mixed economy of out-of-school music provision in this country. Such anarchy may be a crucial breeding-ground for the celebration of personal autonomy and cultural differentiation that is a prerequisite for focused and goal-directed musical engagement in a post-modern society. This is not simply an anarchy of musical styles and genres, or even of technologies, but an anarchy of social relationships, where boundaries between the teacher and student role are creatively redrawn.

Variety may well be the key concept. I indicate eight areas where it may be possible to significantly increase the variety available to our young people:

## 1. Varied providers
There should be no monopolies of provision but a healthy alliance of national, regional and local interest groups.

## 2. Varied funding
There should be a mixture of state, voluntary and commercial funding, reflecting the different interests that have a legitimate stake in music education.

## 3. Varied locations
Music education should be delivered throughout the community, in schools, music centres, community centres, shops, homes and cultural centres (e.g. libraries and museums).

## 4.Varied roles for educators
To support a wider range of musical cultures and activities, those supporting young people need to adopt a wider range of roles than has traditionally been conceived. These should include teacher, animateur, coach, mentor, impresario, fund-raiser, programmer, composer, arranger and studio manager.

## 5. Varied trajectories

Young people need a wide range of 'entry and exit' points for musical engagement. These should vary from long-term syllabi for some, but should include a far wider variety of short-term projects for others, who may dip in and out according to the needs and parameters of the project, rather than be subject to the tyranny of the school term or year.

## 6. Varied activities

The range of activities available to young people should mirror more closely the types of musical activities available in the sub-cultures they value. This will involve a wider menu of visits, workshops, concerts, talks, programme planning and assistance in activities such as DJ-ing. It is probable that the DJ is the most common 'deliverer' of music within the community. How many young people get meaningful help in developing the role of DJ?

## 7. Varied accreditation of achievement

A range of certificates of participation/competence is needed to accredit and document participation. Existing agencies need to broaden the range of qualifications on offer, and new agencies should develop them. There is nothing wrong with graded music exams or GCSEs. We just need more choices for young people who value accreditation.

## 8. Varied routes to training competence (beyond, for instance, GRSM, BMus or PGCE)

If people are to be suitably trained to support young people's music making, then a far wider range of training and continuing professional development opportunities must be on offer than the traditional 'teacher education' model. Indeed, until this happens, it is hard to see how major change will occur.

It is quite difficult to predict what the final role of schools might be in a wider, more inclusive view of music education. However, school music is the one aspect of the provision that we can guarantee all children receive. Perhaps its most useful role is to provide a core 'anchor-point' where diverse experiences may be reflected upon, integrated and co-ordinated.

# Acknowledgement

Part of the research presented in this chapter was supported by a grant (R 000237231) from the Economic and Social Research Council awarded to Susan O'Neill, John Sloboda and Michael Boulton at the University of Keele.

# References

Brown, C. (2001) *The Death of Christian Britain* (London, Routledge).
Cook, N. (1998) *Music: A Very Short Introduction* (Oxford, Oxford University Press).
Czikszentmihalyi, M. & Lefevre, J. (1989) Optimal experience in work and leisure, *Journal of Personality and Social Psychology*, 56, pp. 815–822.

De Nora, T. (2000) *Music in Everyday Life* (Cambridge, Cambridge University Press).

Green, L. (2001) *How Popular Musicians Learn: A Way Ahead for Music Education* (London, Ashgate).

Puttnam, R. (2001) *Bowling Alone: The Collapse and Revival of American Community* (New York, Simon & Schuster).

Ryan, K., Boulton, M., O'Neill, S. A. & Sloboda, J. A. (2000) Perceived social support and children's participation in music, in: C. Woods, G. Luck, R. Brochard, F. Seddon & J. Sloboda (Eds) *Science, Music, & Society: Proceedings of the 6th International Conference on Music Perception and Cognition* (Newcastle, Staffordshire, Keele University).

Sloboda, J. A., Davidson, J. W., Howe, M. J. A. & Moore, D. G. (1996) The role of practice in the development of performing musicians, *British Journal of Psychology*, 87, pp. 287–309.

Sloboda, J. A. (1999) Music: where cognition and emotion meet, *The Psychologist*, 12(4), pp. 450–455.

Sloboda, J. A., O'Neill, S.A. & Ivaldi, A. (2001) Functions of music in everyday life: an explanatory study using the experience sampling methodology, *Musical Scientiae*, 5(1), pp. 9–32.

Small, C. (1998) *Musicking: The Meanings of Performance and Listening* (Hanover, NH, Wesleyan University Press).

York, N. (2001) *Valuing School Music: A Report on School Music* (London, University of Westminster and Rockschool Ltd.).

# 7

# Information and Communications Technology, Knowledge and Pedagogy

*Robert McCormick and Peter Scrimshaw*

## Introduction

The focus of the use of information and communications technology (ICT) in schools has changed over the past decade, as more has become known about what is required for successful implementation and in response to the introduction of quite new technologies, such as the Internet and computer conferencing. These new technologies extend the range of possibilities in exciting but often unpredictable ways. To cope with these developments in technology and effectively implement curriculum change, more attention must be given to the impact of ICT on the classroom. Traditional approaches to the use of computers in education have given insufficient attention to this impact, partly because of the lack of a clear enough model of pedagogy. We present a model that helps in the analysis of impact. Any implementation of ICT in schools requires a level of change in practice. We examine three such levels, namely, where existing practice is made more efficient or effective, where it is extended in some new way, and where it is transformed. Each level has different implications for pedagogy and we use our model to examine these. The understanding that this analysis reveals will help those who are implementing change, for example, by revealing possible conflicts between goals. A more sophisticated idea of change, we argue, will be needed to ensure that ICT has a significant impact on the classroom, whatever the goals.

## 'Traditional' approaches to ICT in the school

A variety of approaches have been used to analyse and support the integration of new technologies in schools, but none of these pays sufficiently detailed attention to issues of pedagogy. We begin by examining a set of 'traditional' approaches, most of which focus on interactions at and around a computer. The first set is adopted by those who think about innovation models. Here the increasing take-up and enthusiasm for the use of ICT,

From: *Educational Communication and Information*, 1 (1), 2000, pp. 39–57. Reprinted by permission of the publisher (Taylor & Francis Ltd, http://www.informaworld.com).

characterised in the stages 'entry, adoption, and invention' (Sandholtz *et al.*, 1997) or 'localised, co-ordinated, transformative, embedded, and innovative' (National Council for Educational Technology [NCET], 1996) are seen as central. A second set focuses on the complexity of the technologies themselves, moving from simple word processors to web pages, with the implication that the impact on pedagogy is directly related to the complexity of the technology. A third set of approaches focuses on the computer interface and interaction with the learner. This set builds on ideas about learning, focusing on the move from simple question and response approaches (of drill and practice software) to complex tutorial systems that try to model the learner's understanding and the knowledge area being taught.

The approaches that focus on the computer–learner interactions, which represent the bulk of the research, do deal with teaching and learning issues. They often assume, however, that the software and the interaction with the learner are isolated from the surrounding pedagogy of the classroom or school. Research has shown that, even with highly 'self-contained' types of software such as Integrated Learning Systems, the success of the use of ICT is dependent upon the way in which the other elements of the classroom pedagogy relate to it (Wood, 1998). Such elements include other supporting classroom work, classroom discussion and how, if at all, students interact around the computer as they use the software (Wegerif & Scrimshaw, 1997). Recent publications in the area of collaborative learning involving computers have explored some of these issues (e.g. Littleton & Light, 1999).

Traditional concerns of computer-aided learning become somewhat out of date as ICT use in the classroom becomes integral to a range of learning activities. The use of networks and communications software also makes this 'machine–learner(s)' analysis inadequate. Similarly, the use of general-purpose software, such as word processors, points up the need to consider a more complex analysis, because the learner and teacher have more control over the learning, rather than that control resting with the program itself. Scrimshaw (1997) has taken this analysis one stage further by exploring a variety of software used in schools in terms of how knowledge, the learner, the relationships with other learners, and the role of the teacher is viewed. Whilst this work offers a more sophisticated approach, in later sections of this chapter we will extend the analysis to reflect contemporary views of learning, knowledge and pedagogy (Edwards & Mercer, 1987; Leach & Moon, 1999; McCormick & Paechter, 1999; Murphy, 1999; McCormick & Murphy, 2000).

Such contemporary views, commonly referred to as social constructivist and situated perspectives, emphasise the social aspects of learning, through ideas such as participation in communities and the social construction of knowledge. Rather than simply acquiring concepts (the process of 'internalisation' to cognitive constructivists), from a situated perspective learners are seen as creating identities by learning to participate in communities. Knowledge, as seen from this perspective, is not constructed as an object acquired by individual learners (in the way cognitive constructivists would argue [Bredo, 1997]) but is a social process of knowledge construction. Meaning is created through participating in social activity. From this perspective, there is, therefore, not an individual notion of a concept, but a distributed one. The learning process is viewed not as the transmission of knowledge from the knowledgeable to the less knowledgeable, but as engagement in culturally authentic activity, participation in a community of practice. Such participation can be considered at different levels, as we will show later. This perspective posits a close relationship between particular views of learning, of knowledge and pedagogy. Just as social constructivist or situated perspectives have an interrelated set of views of knowledge, learning and pedagogy, so cognitive constructivists have a different set of views on these matters that start from a view of learning as the individual acquisition of concepts.

Although we are inclined to the social constructivist and situated perspectives, there remains much debate about the relevant merits of the various theoretical stances. (See Anderson *et al.*, 2000, for some points of agreement in a 4-year debate.)

Not only do traditional approaches to ICT integration need to respond to these increasingly sophisticated views of learning, they also have to respond to the way in which national curricula are being implemented. The adoption of national curricula in many countries has led to a focus on subjects, both as content and as ways of organising the curriculum. Internationally, at elementary school level, there is an increasingly strong concern about the key areas of literacy, mathematics and science. It is also the case that contemporary views of learning and knowledge indicate the importance of domains, whether these domains are subjects or areas of human activity (Glaser, 1984, 1992). In the realm of teachers' knowledge and professional development, it is evident (as we discuss later) that subject identity and knowledge are central features (Banks *et al.*, 1999). In addition to a concern for general issues of learning, knowledge and pedagogy, we must, therefore, also consider the way in which subjects affect pedagogy and hence the use of ICT.

Recent initiatives in the use of ICT in schools exhibit a growing range of ways in which curriculum developers approach the implementation of ICT.[1] These go beyond the narrow focus on computer–student interaction. Such approaches attempt to cope, in different ways, with some of the issues noted earlier. They pay attention, although with different emphasis, to a number of issues:

- how to provide school-level support;
- the role of district, regional or national bodies in coordinating development;
- the integration of ICT with the wider classroom context;
- the importance of pedagogy.

However, in our view, these initiatives still do not provide a full enough analysis of the nature of pedagogy. This is likely to limit their impact and effectiveness. Attempts in the UK to relate pedagogy and the use of ICT have gone some way towards illustrating such an analysis (e.g. Moseley *et al.*, 1999) but do not explore pedagogy in terms of contemporary views of learning and knowledge. Nor have they related to teachers' knowledge in a way that reflects more complex models. An exploration of teacher knowledge is necessary in order to indicate the way in which teachers need to change, which has implications for implementation strategies. In the two sections that follow we therefore present our views of pedagogy and of teachers' knowledge.

# The dimensions of pedagogy

To locate the place of ICT in teaching and learning, we need to see the use of ICT as part of a teacher's pedagogy. Further, a sophisticated understanding of that pedagogy is required to ascertain the impact of ICT on practice. In particular, pedagogy has to be seen in terms of several interrelated dimensions:

- educational goals and purposes;
- a view of learning;
- a view of knowledge;

- the learning and assessment activities required;
- the roles and relationship among learners and between the teacher and the learner;
- the classroom discourse.

(adapted from Leach & Moon, 1999, p. 268)

Each of these dimensions is complex, and a full exploration is beyond the scope of this chapter. Here we say a few words on the more obvious ones, dealing with the more complex dimensions of learning and knowledge and discourse in more detail later.

*Goals and purposes* state the intentions and rationale of the educational encounter, both in general terms (e.g. for a subject) and for particular activities. Curriculum designers, teachers and learners might all vary in what they see as goals and interpret those specified by the curriculum in different ways. *Learning and assessment activities* define and structure the classroom activity (and that outside it). They will also be a manifestation of the other dimensions, particularly the first three. For example, if activities are 'open', learners may be encouraged to define the goals of learning or what is learned (which will also demonstrate a particular view of knowledge and a particular relationship between the learner and teacher). *Roles of learners and teacher* include such aspects as who controls the learning and the extent of collaboration among learners. The remaining three dimensions are particularly important and difficult to characterise. We examine them in more detail below, before going on to explore how the implementation of ICT may affect each of the six dimensions.

## Views of learning

How teachers act in the classroom will depend upon how they think learning takes place. If they take the view that learning is the individual construction of knowledge (cognitive constructivism), then their focus will be on individual learners. However, there is a range of views of learning that is eligible for consideration. While notions of information processing or constructivism are well known, the ICT community has not kept up to date with those views that emphasise the social dimension of learning. For example, Pachler (1999) considers behaviourism and cognitive constructivism in some detail, but, more briefly, what he calls 'social interactionism', when referring to Vygotsky. Pachler acknowledges the sociocultural aspects of learning, and the importance of peer and teacher–student interaction, but fails to carry this forward to more contemporary ideas of 'learning as participation', as represented by those who take a situated view of cognition (e.g. see Murphy, 1999).

At the peer or teacher–student level of interaction, the idea of joint construction of knowledge is important, but this also needs to be considered at the community level (Rogoff, 1995). At this level, learning is 'learning to participate in a community', and this community may be represented by a subject (e.g. a community of scientists) or an occupational group (e.g. health visitors). From this perspective, learning to be part of a community is not just the acquisition of concepts, but ways of behaving, values and hence identity. Schools, and classrooms within them, form special types of communities and learning in them is, in part, learning to be a student. Thus, classroom and school cultures are part of the 'content' of learning, in addition to the norms, values and practices of communities represented by school subjects (which are not in themselves the same as the subjects as represented in life outside school). Students have to learn about carrying out a science experiment as scientists do, whilst also learning that the way validity of outcomes is arrived at may not be the same as in religious studies. They also have to learn that the science laboratory has rules that are peculiar to schools, and that these may not be the same as those operating, for example, in the English or mathematics class.

# Knowledge

Complexities also arise in relation to the dimension of knowledge, not least because views of knowledge are related to those of learning. For example, those who take a 'radical constructivist' view of learning (von Glasersfeld, 1995) see students as constructing an individual knowledge structure that is tested (for its validity) against its viability in making sense of the individual's world. Such an approach sees the objectivity of knowledge as an untenable concept ('viability' individually tested is their focus). Those who take a mainstream cognitive constructivist view, on the other hand, see knowledge as in the head, and matching reality outside the head; i.e. there is a form of objectivity. Those who emphasise the social dimension of learning, and hence knowledge, focus on the shared creation of knowledge (at the interpersonal or the community level) and consider subjective (or intersubjective) views of knowledge. From a situated perspective, therefore, objectivity of knowledge is rejected. (Sfard [1998] reviews how views of learning that vary from individual to participatory in their focus relate to different views of knowledge.) At the very least, we need to consider issues such as whether we take knowledge to be:

- objective;
- reflecting reality;
- reflected in a reality, that is, an individual's reality or one which is socially shared.

Different views of learning take different stances towards each of these properties of knowledge (objectivity, match to reality, individual or social). (Sfard [1998] notes that this is not always done consistently, for good reason.)

# Discourse

The dimension of discourse is also related to these views of learning and knowledge, including a number of strands that we have already alluded to in the discussion on classroom and school cultures. Discourse is usually seen in terms of the *language* of the classroom. However, we want to extend the notion of discourse to include the way subjects and classrooms are represented by both speech and action in the norms and behaviours of particular classrooms. Cobb *et al.* (1997) represent a classroom as a micro-culture that contains a variety of levels of norms. Some of these norms derive from the school level and some from particular classrooms. This dimension includes the way language is used, but also extends to the way students are expected to behave and the ways in which they carry out activities. We have already noted that different school subjects may exhibit differences in the micro-culture of particular classrooms; the way students act in the science laboratory is not the same as in the English or mathematics classroom, for example. Similarly, different subjects in the world outside school may have different cultures in the way they deal with activity and hence may have different ways of working. Scientists have empirical methodologies, including tests of truth, as well as a code of ethics in the way they work, for example. This may contrast with what engineers do; for example, engineers may have to work within different legal and economic tests from scientists. Such differences are reflected (usually imperfectly) in the differences found in the practice of school subjects. In addition, different kinds of schools and classrooms (e.g. elementary compared to a high school) have their own varieties of discourse. For example, by the end of elementary school, students may have a degree of independence of movement around the classroom, which disappears when they attend the first year of middle or high school. Thus, we need to see discourse as a kind of micro-culture shaped by such factors as the school, teacher and subject (Cobb *et al.*, 1997).

## Teacher knowledge and pedagogy

When we consider different approaches to the use of ICT in the classroom, we must therefore be able to see how, if at all, these affect each of the interrelated dimensions of pedagogy. Teachers' knowledge is, in part, made up of these dimensions; Figure 7.1 indicates a way of representing the different facets of teacher knowledge. The model draws on Shulman (1986), who was concerned to explain the transformation that teachers have to carry out to render their subject knowledge into a form that can be learned by students. The model in Figure 7.1, a development of Banks *et al.* (1999),[2] goes beyond Shulman's ideas, particularly in not seeing knowledge as objective and in trying to take account of the situated nature of knowledge and learning. This representation of teacher knowledge acknowledges teachers' multiple identities as: subject expert (subject knowledge), subject teacher (school knowledge), teacher (pedagogical knowledge) and individual (personal construct). The model also depicts pedagogy in the way we outlined earlier, indicating that a teacher's knowledge of pedagogy is made up of a series of dimensions that govern their views, decisions and practice in the classroom. The justification and exploration of this model are beyond the scope of this chapter, but they indicate the complexity of teacher knowledge and these three aspects of subject, school and pedagogic knowledge.

   Such representation enables us to see what the implications are for a teacher when ICT is introduced into schools. Teachers may have to change their views of the subject, what they count as school knowledge, and how they view (and implement) pedagogy. The element of personal identity in the model is a critical aspect of how teachers react to change that has the potential to be as threatening or as stimulating as that posed by ICT.

## Three levels of change in relation to the use of ICT

Earlier, we indicated that traditional approaches to the use of ICT were inadequate to deal with the complexities that the technologies bring, as well as with the requirements of a sophisticated view of pedagogy. The use of ICT may entail three levels of change to

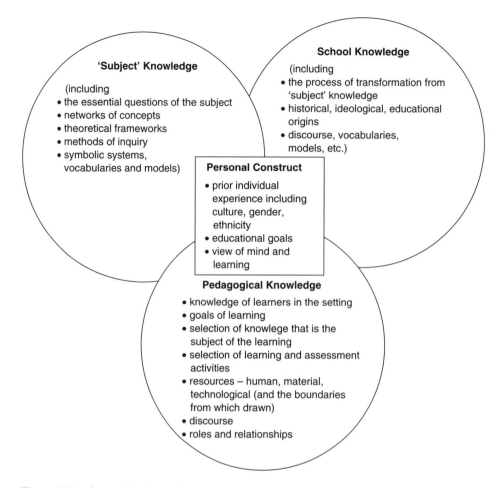

**Figure 7.1   A model of teacher knowledge (Banks *et al.*, 1999)**

current practice, namely, to improve efficiency of conventional teaching, to extend the reach of teaching and learning, and to transform teachers' and learners' conceptions of the subject itself.[3] In the following, we explore the implications of each of these levels and analyse how teacher knowledge and pedagogy need to change.

## Improving efficiency with ICT

The first level aspires to provide a more effective means of doing what is already being done. The assumption is that *ICT replaces some conventional resource, but that the other elements in the situation remain largely unchanged*. As one writer puts it:

When the children used databases and spreadsheets they didn't just draw graphs, they could go on to interpret them. And when they worked together with a word processor, they started talking with zeal, not the usual gossip, but about science. Children who were challenged by doing things 'the old way' were able to move on. The tools

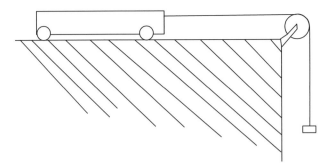

**Figure 7.2 Trolley pulled by a mass suspended over a bench**

that started life as information processing tools became really special tools to enhance our teaching. These were tools for the mind.

And for all the speed of computers, I doubt if anyone saved any time. What was saved—by not having to draw tables, or colour-in graphs, or 'write it out neatly', or take thermometer readings—was spent straight away examining the science that had started to open up. (Frost, 1998, p. 9)

Yet, even in what is primarily an efficiency-raising approach, there can be unexpected effects. Consider, for instance, the use of computer-based data recording in science. A classic experiment to explore Newton's laws of motion involves measuring the acceleration of a trolley pulled along a table by a mass suspended over the end of a bench (Figure 7.2), in order to show that the acceleration of a mass is proportional to the force acting on it.

The use of ICT allows the experiment to be carried out more efficiently and accurately than previous methods, and produces a graph that has points on a smooth curve (Figure 7.3), indicating a non-linear relationship, something apparently at odds with Newton's law.[4] This outcome requires explanations that are not usually dealt with in such a science lesson and which may, in addition, be unfamiliar to teachers.[5] Thus, the teachers' subject knowledge may be challenged by knowledge that is not part of the school knowledge they normally deal with. Even if teachers are familiar with the explanation, they may still have the pedagogic problem of trying to explain it to students. A reassessment of the way the knowledge is introduced (i.e. new pedagogic knowledge) is therefore required.

## Extending the reach of teaching and learning with ICT

The second level of change is to use ICT to provide a major extension to what can be achieved, one that goes well beyond the efficiency level. In this case, *the ICT extends the reach of the teacher, the learners or both*. The Internet provides one medium for doing this:

Common classroom activities can be enhanced by access to the internet. It could provide a global audience or test bed for work normally carried out in the classroom or give up-to-date information in an easily accessible form.

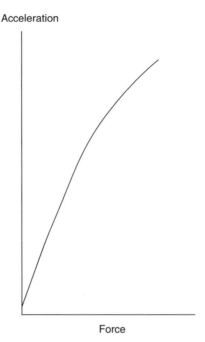

Figure 7.3   **A plot of acceleration against mass obtained using light gates**

One example is a simple survey of television viewing habits. Perhaps a class could keep a diary of their television viewing for a week. Typical classroom activities based around this would include working out averages, comparing boys' habits with girls' and drawing graphs to illustrate the results. By contacting other schools around the country, or even in different countries, other possibilities arise. For example, comparing the results of rural areas with urban or the results from different countries. The ease of collecting and disseminating such work on the internet allows the teacher to add this extra dimension with little extra effort. (Cunningham *et al.*, 1997, pp. 21–22)

This amounts to more than doing more effectively what was done before. If, for instance, students are put in touch with a professional social scientist by e-mail, to discuss their current work, this is not simply a more motivating form of textbook work. Such an experience is likely to move their understanding of what being a social scientist involves into a quite different framework. Similarly, when students use computer conferencing to compare life in their local community with the experiences of peers in New Mexico, Tokyo or Finland, they are doing more than simply learning more efficiently about a different society. In such cases, who counts as teacher and learner is altered, as is the relationship between knowledge creation and knowledge acquisition.

If, for example, an investigation based on a web site is carried out in history, then we see an extension of the history that is offered to students, who can go to sites that may be used by historians, or which are created for historians. Such sites may not follow the careful structuring of knowledge that is characteristic of school learning. For example, see the following example of how a major (and very good) site on Anglo-Saxon history and archaeology introduces materials on Sutton Hoo. (This is the richest Anglo-Saxon burial site so far excavated in Britain, and is frequently mentioned in English school history textbooks and resources covering the period.)

> Sutton Hoo is a multi-period site in Suffolk, near Woodbridge (TM 288487). The main periods represented are the neolithic–early Bronze age (Beaker) and early Medieval (7th–8th centuries AD). The prehistoric site extends to fourteen hectares and is a settlement with round houses, pits and field-boundaries, producing very large assemblages of flint and pottery. The early medieval site is a barrow cemetery with flat graves. The barrows are rich although often disturbed, one famous find from 1939 being the undisturbed Sutton Hoo Ship burial. 14 barrows are visible, the more numerous other features being cut into sand under turf. (Sutton Hoo Research Project, 2000)

These six introductory sentences to the site include several obviously technical terms that many students would be unlikely to understand, and several more ('round houses', 'pits', 'barrow cemetery', 'flat graves') that, although couched in ordinary language, are likely to be misinterpreted or downright baffling.

Students are likely to come across historical terms and interpretations in material of this sort that they do not understand, and which a teacher may have to explain. One possible response to this is for the teacher to download selected web pages onto an intranet on a school network (or onto a disk for use on stand-alone machines). This approach leaves the teacher in exclusive control of the knowledge that students have access to. Alternatively, the teacher may educate students to use the Internet for themselves to research agreed questions. Through the use of the web sites they locate, students will enter a world of history where there is controversy, and perhaps a lack of certainty. This may be in contrast with the world of history knowledge in that particular school. As students get older, they will inevitably experience this controversy, but with web access they may be exposed to it at any time. Indeed, they may even, in political and socially controversial areas, have to distinguish bona fide sites from those where opinion masquerades as evidence-based interpretation. Thus, issues of teacher control and views on knowledge are challenged by the technology, and teachers may have to decide how to deal with these from a pedagogical perspective.

## Transforming conceptions of the subject with ICT

Beyond the level of extending learning lies another possibility. Some subjects (for instance, music, literacy, and art) are largely defined by the media they use. Here new technologies may transform the nature of a subject at its most fundamental level. As one author points out in relation to literacy teaching:

> Our current definitions of literacy are quite narrow: text read and text written, with some critical awareness of others' work, covers much of it. Multimedia, however, offers us many corridors to support communication, many corridors for success: music, speech, aural ambience, text, video, animation, graphics and symbols, a second language or more, synchronous or asynchronous time and more. It allows us this portfolio of communication possibilities individually, collaboratively, in private, in public,

in the same place or in different locations. The problem this brings is of a need for a much broader definition of literacy, clearly now encompassing oracy and graphicacy for example. …

The problem for our curriculum is to decide which subsets of these multiple media we will encourage or how small a set we are prepared to tolerate and at which ages. Again it is because the rapid advances in technology have made so much possible that we are now faced with the unenviable task of deciding what is essential. Different regions of Europe place different values on the various components of multimedia (some stressing oracy far more than others for example). Rather than striving for an increasingly elusive common agreement, perhaps we should simply recognize that multimedia has guaranteed diversity and concentrate instead on identifying subsets of media capability which are demonstrably dysfunctional and need remedial interventionist support. A text-based curriculum built around individual endeavour would arguably produce dysfunctional learners in a technological world, which is a highly controversial conclusion to emerge from the promise of multimedia technology. (Heppell, 1998, pp. 8–9)

As part of our exploration of the introduction of technologies into art (as an example of the above), it should be noted that ICT is sometimes used to mimic an existing technique, as was the case initially with photography in relation to painting. This is a kind of efficiency use, where considerations such as the ease with which a work can be changed and stored may or may not outweigh the costs of having to learn the new ICT techniques. In some cases, the tools are not as flexible or as easy to control as the original physical objects (e.g. a 'mouse' compared to a 'pencil' to sketch). New tools have been introduced to allow this mimicry to work more naturally (e.g. the use of electronic sketchpads with pens to enable freehand sketching). Thus, the technique base may be extended, although it may not be obvious what the gains in efficiency or effectiveness are. However, the electronic medium can also be seen as a new artistic medium (as video has become in contemporary art), thus transforming the nature of art itself by extending the range of media available to artists (Loveless, 1997). The techniques of filtering and image manipulation, for instance, may have no parallel in conventional techniques. Further, when interactivity is built into the medium (for example, a web site), then the 'image' has only an electronic life. The first, almost prosaic, effect of this in a school situation is to make assessment problematic. The student must submit an electronic version. This is particularly difficult for public examinations where sheets of paper and three-dimensional works are more commonly submitted to examiners and moderators. (Parallel problems exist in subjects that include graphic design, where a web site can be an example of such design.) Such examples are compounded by the fact that the work of other artists, including famous painters, can be electronically manipulated, so in effect a 'dialogue' is set up with that original artist. One art teacher we observed saw this as an important artistic experience for her:

The course I attended focused on communication. I began to realise that using ICT was not an 'instead of' way of working, but facilitated approaches that I feel are good practice—connecting to artists, use of sketch books, independent working and research. After I scanned in my own images, I explored a variety of other artists' images. It was like poring over images in a book, only these images were on screen, alongside my own, and it was at this moment that I began to feel excited. I sensed that the technology was offering something new and dynamic and, though my confidence with that technology was still virtually non-existent, I glimpsed a connection with images and ideas that felt exhilarating. (Learning Schools Programme, 1999, Exemplar A, Section 2)

The underlying issues for our general argument are that the knowledge that is taken to be 'art' (e.g. techniques and effects) is changed in ways in which teachers trained in conventional media may not have experienced. We have encountered examples of teachers experiencing a significant change in their own artistic identity when they come to learn to work in these new media. To see this process as merely learning to use a computer, as you would a word processor, is to underrate the personal change that a teacher has to undergo (the symbol system of the subject may be changing for the teacher). Such a change may affect their personal identity (related to the 'personal construct' in Figure 7.1). With such change, however, may come experiences that fire teachers and which they also want their students to experience. They may in the process have to reassess all that constitutes their knowledge of school art, and some elements of pedagogy may also be profoundly affected. For example, the discourse of an art studio may be around the individual creating ideas and learning to use (or not depending on the school of art) the techniques of the medium. The teacher will explore these ideas through discussion, along with instruction in the use of techniques. Teachers and students can look jointly at the object. When the medium is an interactive electronic medium, not only are the techniques different (those associated with using software), but in addition, the experience of the product may be individual, particularly if the electronic art object is complex. What, then, becomes of the role of the teacher in supporting the development of critical and aesthetic awareness? Such a situation is further complicated by the potential of web publishing, where reactions to and use of the work can be carried beyond the confines of the classroom and the teacher.

## The levels compared

How, then, do these levels of changes to practice in the use of ICT relate systematically to the dimensions of pedagogy identified at the outset? Table 7.1 summarises the differences as we see them, although it inevitably simplifies the picture.

The transformative level illustrates the most significant impact on pedagogy, so it is worth exploring this column of Table 7.1 in a little more detail. In the following, we highlight the pedagogy dimensions in italics to indicate the effects on each dimension. Take again the example of the creation of an electronic medium in art, parallel to a written artefact where electronic 'dialects' may be created, as in the case of e-mail (Tweddle et al., 1997). The transformation, which is what this new medium represents, goes further when communication is involved. The Virtual Identities project, for example, involves children being allocated an unknown remote partner to work with electronically.[6] The first student creates an image that is personal and sends it to a partner (one student scanned her hand and sent the image). The second student must use 20% of the original image received. This image can be combined with the second student's chosen image and

**Table 7.1   How different levels of change in the practice of ICT affect dimensions of pedagogy**

| Dimensions of pedagogy | ICT as efficiency aid | ICT as extension device | ICT as transformative device |
|---|---|---|---|
| Educational goals and purposes. | Stay the same, they are just easier to achieve. | Largely stay the same, although either information skills or supporting learner independence become important. | These are transformed, e.g., the creation of knowledge becomes a goal. |
| A view of learning. | 1. Constructivists would see more time for making sense of data, etc. (making meaning).<br>2. Those who take an information processing view see that increased time on using ideas will allow better learning.<br>3. Those who take a situated cognition view may find the implied instructional approach inappropriate. | 1. Constructivists would see more time and perspectives for making sense of data, etc.<br>2. Those who take an information processing view see that increased time on using ideas will allow better learning.<br>3. Those who take a situated cognition view would see the involvement of communities of practice, with a focus on participation, as helpful. | Those with constructivist and information processing views would not see any change, but those who support a participatory approach (as in situated cognition) would see, entering into communities of practice as central. |
| A view of knowledge. | No new view of knowledge is required for this. | Extension to new areas may bring with it the need to be clear about who gives validity to knowledge. | Knowledge may become contested, and validation procedures unclear; hence a need for learners to have explicit criteria for what counts as valid knowledge, or processes to arrive at this knowledge. |

*(Continued)*

manipulated by various electronic layering and filtering effects. Thus, not only is the medium changed, but also the creative process. In school art this process is often seen as purely individual, but now it can be collaborative, something which is happening increasingly in the world of art outside school. Such collaborations might include students working with professional artists.

| Dimensions of pedagogy | ICT as efficiency aid | ICT as extension device | ICT as transformative device |
|---|---|---|---|
| The learning and assessment activities required. | Activities remain largely the same, but may be delivered using electronic means. Dynamic assessment can be used (where the assessment interacts with student responses). | Additional activities required for working with others at a distance. Issues of collaborative learning and group assessment may be important, as well as new outcomes being involved. | New outcomes will require new learning activities are assessment methods. Additional activities are required for working with others at a distance. Issues of collaborative learning and group assessment will be important; learners may have to develop self-assessment strategies and the ability to cope with non-teacher/non-school assessment. |
| The roles and relationship between learners and between the teacher and the learner. | Roles and relationships remain largely the same. | Roles and relationships changed by the addition of new teachers and/or learners elsewhere. Teacher's role as source of knowledge displaced somewhat and learner independence may be important. | Distinction between teacher and learner may change, with community of learners and of practice being important. Teacher may be replaced on occasions by outside sources and agents. |
| Discourse. | No change. | As the classroom may be extended, there may be different non-school discourses involved. | The creation of a discourse may be part of the learning (e.g. for a community of learners). |

The pedagogy involved in such a case will depend on how a teacher currently views the dimensions of pedagogy. Established *goals* in art will include such things as learners developing an aesthetic sense, learning to express themselves and perhaps learning specific techniques. Using ICT, students are able to create new artwork and publish it (e.g. on the web), participating in the art world rather than replicating it in the classroom (this makes it culturally authentic). This may constitute a new goal. *Learning activities* will need to allow for participation and the assessment will need to reflect criteria of judgement and self-confidence, as well as collaborative skills (which may in turn be new goals for art education). The technical skills involved will be different from those of traditional media and hence the *assessment system* will need to change radically (e.g. the submission of electronic assessment items, as noted earlier).

The degree and nature of transformation envisaged by teachers will depend upon their *views of learning and knowledge*. If a teacher takes an information processing or even a cognitive constructivist view of learning, then knowledge will be seen as objective, and matching reality, with little by way of social construction being considered. Thus, the creation of art knowledge may be rendered problematic. Those who share a social constructivist or situated perspective will recognise the social construction of knowledge element, although the way they carry out the analysis will be different. They will therefore welcome the transformation as a chance to involve students in communities of practice outside the school environment. In contrast, teachers may find the transformation into new media takes students away from an interest in artistic heritage and traditional forms of art, which may be a goal for most teachers, irrespective of their views of learning and knowledge.

The effect of ICT on *discourse* may be complex and exhibit strong subject differences. We have already noted that school subjects have different sets of rules from those of the 'parent' subject, embedded, in particular, in the assessment system. Science laboratories have a process of testing knowledge through empirical investigation. In a school context, such investigations are a ritual because the knowledge is already established (i.e. shared by the science community). However, when students find themselves trying to establish the truth of, say, the safety of nuclear waste (i.e. what constitutes a safe dosage or exposure) through an Internet search, then the right and wrong of scientific knowledge may be open to challenge. Disputes or uncertainties become more important still, given the international nature of the Internet. Students may encounter and have to cope with knowledge that is local in significance or which is presented by a variety of interest groups, for example, in religious education, web sites of religious cults or splinter groups from a mainstream religion. Even in the controlled discourse of school knowledge (where what is important, who says it is right, and how it is represented is not normally problematic or discussed), there will be exposure to local discourses whose rules are different from the classroom where students are physically located. Thus, a web site where students can discuss environmental issues together many raise one set of expectations for a child in England, who thinks such issues are a subset of science. A quite different set of expectations may be raised for a child in Scotland who is familiar with a school subject called 'Environmental Studies' (that includes science, history, geography and other social studies). Discussion taking place on such a site will be carried out by students who will bring differing expectations of the discourse. This is a relatively prosaic example; where there are deep-seated cultural and religious differences, however, the discourse may be mutually unintelligible.

At this transformative level, learners have a degree of independence, and the teachers' role will be to develop students' judgements and their ability to appraise critically what is of particular importance. Such an approach does not remove the need for students to understand accepted science concepts. For example, if students find a spoof web site, such as the one for the substance dihydrogen oxide, http://www.dhmo.org (5/10/00), they will need an understanding of chemical concepts to be able to realise that a seemingly legitimate web site can be completely misinterpreted. (This applies to ICT as both an extension and transformatory device.) This particular spoof web site presents the 'dangers' of the substance dihydrogen oxide (which is actually water), implying that it is a hazardous chemical. The dangers are obvious enough (flooding), but when presented as a 'chemical', the discourse becomes different.

This example illustrates just how complex the impact on pedagogy can be in relation to the use of ICT. The different levels of changes in practice in using ICT affect each dimension of pedagogy in different ways, but, in addition, the interactions among the dimensions are also related in complex ways to these different levels. Thus, a teacher's view of learning (e.g. as information processing) might not accommodate the participatory approaches engendered by ICT as a transformative device. A teacher must decide how to accommodate these approaches and for what reasons. One response might be to reject such a use of ICT; another might be to include participation, but to focus on individual acquisition (e.g. through the assessment system). More radically, a teacher might re-examine their view of learning to recognise that participation might require students to discuss and examine their own understanding (a cognitive constructivist rather than an information processing view of learning). Addressing these problems requires teachers to make pedagogic choices. Teachers need to be able to justify their choices. For example, a teacher may decide to control the use of a web site that takes students into a controversial subject area, either by downloading only certain aspects of it onto a school intranet or by limiting student access to web sites. There are controversies surrounding these issues within schools (e.g. that this does not prepare students for use of the Internet outside school) and teachers legitimately differ in how they respond to these issues.

## Concluding reflections

The analysis we have presented has a number of implications for the implementation of ICT in schools. First, those responsible for any initiative must be clear about what they are trying to do with ICT and, crucially, why they want to use it in any future approach to curriculum development. Our analysis may help them. For example, in the UK, the approach adopted by government agencies in implementing a national training initiative to support the use of ICT in teaching reveals a strong preference for an 'efficiency' level of change. Yet, as we have seen, ICT will bring other levels of change too, for which such training may not necessarily prepare teachers. If governments want to implement ICT in particular ways, they need to be clear about the implications and prepare teachers appropriately. They will need to make these implications clear to teachers, as well as to those supporting them in this implementation. Second, attention needs to be given to the effects on pedagogy. For policy-makers, there will be issues relating, for example, to home use of computers that may well be one consequence of the extending and transforming levels of change. Teachers and schools need to develop pedagogy in productive ways, and how this will come about is one element of curriculum change. This leads to our third implication, that it is necessary to see any such initiative as curriculum change, a change that must engage with fundamental views of learning, knowledge and pedagogy.

## Notes

1. For example, the Technology in Learning and Teaching (TILT) programme in Australia (http://www.tdc. nsw.edu.au/tilt/about/policy.htm, 5/10/00), the Co-nect network in the USA (http://www.co-nect.org/, 5/10/00) and The Learning Schools Programme in the UK (http://www.learningschools.net/, 5/10/00).

2.  We would like to acknowledge the contributions of Jenny Leach and Bob Moon, who developed this model.
3.  We acknowledge the Learning Schools Programme team for the development of these three levels, in particular, Peter Twining. This is one of several similar analyses that are evolving (e.g. Streibel, 1993; Twining, 2000).
4.  The traditional method, involving ticker tape, produces a scatter of points through which students draw a straight line to follow Newton's law.
5.  These explanations relate to the changing mass of the system caused by adding mass to accelerate the trolley.
6.  http://www.digital-collaborations.co.uk/thebridge/(5/10/00).

# References

Anderson, J. R., Greeno, J. G., Reder, L. M. & Simon, H. A. (2000) Perspectives on learning, thinking and activity, *Educational Researcher*, 29(4), pp. 11–13.

Banks, F., Leach, J. & Moon, B. (1999) New understandings of teachers' pedagogic knowledge, in: J. Leach & B. Moon (Eds) *Learners and Pedagogy*, pp. 89–110 (London, Paul Chapman).

Bredo, E. (1997) The social construction of learning, in: G. D. Phye (Ed.) *Handbook of Academic Learning: construction of knowledge* (San Diego, CA, Academic Press).

Cobb, P., Gravemeijer, K., Yackel, E., McClain, K. & Whitenack, J. (1997) Mathematizing and symbolizing: the emergence of chains of signification in one First-grade classroom, in: D. Kirshner & J. A. Whitson (Eds) *Situated Cognition: social, semiotic, and psychological perspectives* (London, Lawrence Erlbaum).

Cunningham, F., Kent, F. H. & Muir, D. (1997) *Schools in Cyberspace: a practical guide to using the internet in schools* (London, Hodder & Stoughton).

Edwards, D. & Mercer, N. (1987) *Common Knowledge: the development of joint understanding in the classroom* (London, Methuen). (Also published 1988 as *El conocimiento compartido*, Barcelona, Ediciones Paidos/MEC.)

Frost, F. (1998) *IT in Primary Science* (London, IT in Science, distributed by the Association for Science Education, Hatfield, UK).

Glaser, R. (1984) Education and thinking: the role of knowledge, *American Psychologist*, 39, pp. 93–104.

Glaser, R. (1992) Expert knowledge and processes of thinking, in: D. F. Halpern (Ed.) *Enhancing Thinking Skills in the Sciences and Mathematics*, pp. 63–75 (Hillsdale, NJ, Erlbaum).

Heppell, S. (1998) Making IT work for schools, *European Schoolnet Launching Conference Report 1998* (Brussels, IBM).

Leach, J. & Moon, R. (Eds) (1999) *Learners and Pedagogy* (London, Paul Chapman).

Learning Schools Programme (1999) *Art Teacher Folder (CD-ROM)* (Milton Keynes, Open University).

Littleton, K. & Light, P. (Eds) (1999) *Learning with Computers: analysing productive interaction* (London, Routledge).

Loveless, A. (1997) Working with images, developing ideas, in: A. McFarlane (Ed.) *Information Technology and Authentic Learning: releasing the potential of computers in the primary classroom* (London, Routledge).

McCormick, R. & Murphy, P. (2000) Curriculum: a focus on learning, in: B. Moon, S. Brown & M. Ben-Peretz (Eds) *International Companion of Education*, pp. 204–234 (London, Routledge).

McCormick, R. & Paechter, C. (Eds) (1999) *Learning and Knowledge* (London, Paul Chapman).

Moseley, D., Higgins, S. & Newton, L. *et al.* (1999) *Ways Forward with ICT: effective pedagogy using information and communications technology for literacy and numeracy in primary schools* (Newcastle, University of Newcastle).

Murphy, P. (Ed.) (1999) *Learners, Learning and Assessment* (London, Paul Chapman).

National Council for Educational Technology (NCET) (1996) *Managing IT in Primary Schools* (Coventry, NCET [now BECTa]).

Pachler, N. (1999) Theories of learning and ICT, in: M. Leask, & N. Pachler (Eds) *Learning to Teach Using ICT in the Secondary School*, pp. 3–18 (London, Routledge).

Rogoff, B. (1995) Observing sociocultural activity on three planes: participatory appropriation, guided participation and apprenticeship, in: J. V. Wertsch, P. Del Rio & A. Alverez (Eds) *Sociocultural Studies of Mind*, pp. 139–164 (Cambridge, Cambridge University Press).

Sandholtz, J. H., Ringstaff, C. & Dwyer, D. C. (1997) *Teaching with Technology: creating student-centred classrooms* (New York, Teachers' College Press).

Scrimshaw, P. (1997) Computers and the teacher's role, in: B. Somekh & N. Davis (Eds) *Using Information Technology Effectively in Teaching and Learning*, pp. 100–113 (London, Routledge).

Sfard, A. (1998) On two metaphors for learning and the dangers of choosing just one, *Educational Researcher*, 27(2), pp. 4–13.

Shulman, L. S. (1986) Those who understand: knowledge growth in teaching, *Educational Research Review*, 57, pp. 4–14.

Streibel, M. J. (1993) Instructional design and human practice: what can we learn from Grundy's interpretation of Habermas' Theory of Technical and Practical Human Interests? In: R. Muffoletto & N. N. Knupfer (Eds) *Computers in Education: social, political and historical perspectives*, pp. 141–162 (Cresskill, NJ, Hampton Press).

Sutton Hoo Research Project (2000) Online at www.york.ac.uk/depts/arch/staff/sites/sutton_ hoo.htm (accessed 28 February 2008).

Training and Development Directorate, New South Wales Department of Education and Training, *Information about TILT;* http://www.tdc.nsw.edu.au/tilt/about/policy.htm 5/10/00.

Tweddle, S., Adams, A., Clarke, S., Scrimshaw, P. & Walton, S. (1997) *English for Tomorrow* (Buckingham, Open University Press).

Twining, P. (2000) Pedagogic re-engineering: issues surrounding the use of new media to support a move from 'didactic' to 'constructivist' models of transaction on an Open University course, in: M. Selinger & J. Wynn (Eds) *Educational Technology and the Impact on Teaching and Learning* (Oxford, Research Machines).

Von Glasersfeld, E. (1995) *Radical Constructivism: a way of knowing and learning* (London, Falmer Press).

Wegerif, R. & Scrimshaw, P. (1997) *Computers and Talk in the Primary Classroom* (Clevedon, Multilingual Matters).

Wood, D. (1998) *The UK ILS Evaluations: Final Report* (Coventry, BECTa).

# 8

# Students' Experiences of Ability Grouping: Disaffection, Polarisation and the Construction of Failure

*Jo Boaler, Dylan Wiliam and Margaret Brown*

## Introduction and background

In the UK there is a long tradition of grouping by 'ability'—a practice founded upon the idea that students have relatively fixed levels of ability and need to be taught accordingly. In the 1950s, almost all the schools in the UK were 'streamed'— a process by which students are segregated by 'ability' and taught in the same class for all subjects. A survey of junior schools in the mid-1960s (Jackson, 1964) found that 96% of teachers taught to streamed ability groups. The same study also revealed the overrepresentation of working-class students in low streams and the tendency of schools to allocate teachers with less experience and fewer qualifications to such groups. This report contributed towards a growing awareness of the inadequacies of streamed systems, supported by a range of other research studies (most notably the longitudinal study carried out by Barker *et al.*, 1970) which highlighted the inequitable nature of such systems. Studies by Hargreaves (1967), Lacey (1970) and then Ball (1981) all linked practices of streaming and setting (whereby students are divided into different classes by 'ability' for individual subjects) to working-class underachievement.

The late 1970s and early 1980s witnessed a growing support for mixed-ability teaching, consistent with the more general public concern for educational equality that was pervasive at the time. But in the 1990s, concerns with educational equity have been eclipsed by discourses of 'academic success', particularly for the most 'able', which has meant that large numbers of schools have returned to the practices of ability-grouping (Office for Standards in Education [OFSTED], 1993). Indeed ability-grouping is now widespread in the UK, not only in secondary schools, but also in primary schools, with some children as young as 6 or 7 being taught mathematics and science (and occasionally other subjects) in different classrooms, by different teachers, following different curricula with different schemes of work. This phenomenon may also be linked directly to a number of pressures from government. The 1988 Education Reform Act (ERA) required schools to adopt a

From: *British Educational Research Journal*, 26 (5), 2000, pp. 631–648. Reprinted by permission of the publisher (Taylor & Francis Ltd, http://www.informaworld.com).

national curriculum and national assessment which were structured, differentiated and perceived by many schools to be constraining. Research into the effects of the ERA on schools has shown that a number of teachers regard this curriculum as incompatible with mixed-ability teaching (Gewirtz *et al.*, 1993). The creation of an educational 'market place' (Whitty *et al.*, 1998) has also meant that schools are concerned to create images that are popular with local parents and 'setting' is known to be popular amongst parents, particularly the middle-class parents that schools want to attract (Ball *et al.*, 1994). The White Paper *Excellence in Schools* (Department for Education and Employment ([DfEE], 1997) revealed the new Labour government's commitment to setting:

> Unless a school can demonstrate that it is getting better than expected results through a different approach, we do make the presumption that setting should be the norm in secondary schools. (p. 38)

In mathematics however, relatively few subject departments have needed to change *back* to ability-grouping as the majority have remained faithful to practices of selection, even when they have been the only subject department in their particular school to do so. An OFSTED survey in 1996 reported that 96% of schools taught mathematics to 'setted' groups in the upper secondary years (*Guardian*, 1996). This has non-trivial implications for students' learning of mathematics. Despite this, our understanding of the impact of ability-grouping practices upon mathematics teachers' pedagogy and, concomitantly, students' understanding of mathematics, is limited.

Previous research in the UK has concentrated, almost exclusively, upon the inequities of the setting or streaming system for those students who are allocated to 'low' sets or streams. These are predominantly students who are also disadvantaged by the social system because of their 'race', class or gender (Hargreaves, 1967; Lacey, 1970; Ball, 1981; Tomlinson, 1987; Abraham, 1989). The majority of these research studies used qualitative, case study accounts of the experiences of students in high and low streams to illustrate the ways in which curricular differentiation results in the polarisation of students into 'pro'- and 'anti'- school factions. Such studies, by virtue of their value-based concerns about inequality (Abraham, 1994), have paid relatively little attention to the effects of setting or streaming upon the students' development of *subject* understandings. Furthermore, many of the studies have concentrated on 'streaming', in which students are allocated to the same teaching group for a number of subjects—what Sorensen (1970) termed a wide *scope* system— rather than on 'setting', which is carried out on a subject by subject basis (narrow scope).

Research in the USA has provided a wealth of empirical evidence concerning the relative achievement of students in academic, general and vocational tracks. Such studies have consistently found the *net* effects of tracking on achievement to be small (Slavin, 1990), with evidence that tracking gives slight benefits to students in high tracks at the expense of significant losses to students in low tracks (Kerchkoff, 1986). Comprehensive reviews of studies of the general effects of ability-grouping have been published in the UK recently (Hallam & Toutounji, 1996; Harlen & Malcolm, 1997; Sukhnandan & Lee, 1998), but the existing research has tended to report the effects of ability-grouping practices, rather than providing detailed insights into the way that tracking and setting impact upon students' learning of mathematics, the processes by which it takes effect, or the differential impact it has upon students. This is partly because quantitative methods have been used almost exclusively, with no classroom observation and no analysis of the mechanisms by which tracking influences learning. Many of the studies into tracking have also focused upon differences in group means, masking individual differences within groups (Oakes, 1985; Gamoran & Berends, 1987).

This chapter reports upon interim data from a 4-year longitudinal study that is monitoring the mathematical learning of students in six UK schools. It develops and expands themes arising from a study of two schools that offered 'traditional' and 'progressive' approaches to the teaching of mathematics (Boaler, 1997a, 1997b, 1997c). Although ability-grouping was not an initial focus of that study, it emerged as a significant factor for the students; one that influenced their ideas, their responses to mathematics, and their eventual achievement. One of the schools in that study taught to mixed-ability groups, the other to setted groups, and a combination of lesson observations, questionnaires, interviews and specially-devised assessments revealed that students in the setted school were significantly disadvantaged by their placement in setted groups. A complete cohort of students was monitored in each school over a 3-year period from the beginning of year 9 until the end of year 11 (ages 13–16). The disadvantages affected students from across the spectrum of setted groups and were not restricted to students in low groups. The results of that study relevant to the current study may be summarised as follows:

- Approximately one-third of the students taught in the highest ability groups were disadvantaged by their placement in these groups because of high expectations, fast-paced lessons and pressure to succeed. This particularly affected the most able girls.
- Students from a range of groups were severely disaffected by the limits placed upon their attainment. Students reported that they gave up on mathematics when they discovered their teachers had been preparing them for examinations that gave access to only the lowest grades.
- Social class had influenced setting decisions, resulting in disproportionate numbers of working-class students being allocated to low sets (even after 'ability' was taken into account).
- Significant numbers of students experienced difficulties working at the pace of the particular set in which they were placed. For some students the pace was too slow, resulting in disaffection, while for others it was too fast, resulting in anxiety. Both responses led to lower levels of achievement than would have been expected, given the students' attainment on entry to the school.

A range of evidence in that study linked setting to underachievement, both for students in low *and high* sets, despite the widely-held public, media and government perception that setting increases achievement. Indeed, the evidence was sufficiently broad ranging and pronounced to prompt further research in a wider range of schools.

# Research design

The six schools in the present study have been chosen to provide a range of learning environments and contexts. All are regarded as providing a satisfactory or good standard of education in mathematics, as evidenced by the inspection reports of OFSTED, and all are partner schools with higher education institutions for initial teacher training. The schools are located in five different local education authorities, all in the Greater London area. Some of the school populations are mainly white, others mainly Asian, while others include students from a wide range of ethnic and cultural backgrounds. The General Certificate of Secondary Education (GCSE) performance of the schools ranges from the upper quartile to the lower quartile, nationally, and the social class of the school populations ranges from mainly working class, through schools with nationally representative distributions of social class, to strongly middle class. One of the schools is an all-girls school and the other five are mixed.

All six schools teach mathematics to mixed-ability groups when students are in year 7 (age 11). One of the schools allocates students to 'setted' ability groups for mathematics at the beginning of year 8 (age 12), three others 'set' the students at the beginning of year 9 (age 13), and the other two schools continue teaching to mixed-ability groups. At the time of writing, the cohort of students in our study has completed the end of year 9, so that students in four of the six schools have been taught mathematics in setted groups for at least a year.

The data collection methods included 120 hours of observation of mathematics lessons within the schools, the administration of questionnaires relating to attitudes to and beliefs about mathematics at the end of both year 8 and year 9, and a total of 72 interviews with pairs of students towards the end of year 9.

The lesson observations were conducted throughout years 8 and 9, and evenly distributed across the schools, resulting in approximately 10 hours of observations per school per year; the detailed notes for each lesson observed were transcribed in full.

In May and June of both years 8 and 9, a questionnaire relating to attitudes and beliefs in mathematics was administered by members of the project team, in order to ensure confidentiality. The questionnaire included eight closed items, and two open items ('Describe your maths lessons' and 'How could your maths lessons be improved?') From approximately 1000 students in the cohort, a total of 943 questionnaires were completed in year 8, and 977 in year 9, with matched questionnaires for both years from 843 students.

During June and July of year 9, we also conducted six interviews in each school with pairs of students—a pair of boys and a pair of girls from each of the top, middle and one of the lower sets, and with students from a comparable range of attainment in the mixed-ability schools. Each interview lasted approximately 30 minutes, and followed an agreed protocol which identified 18 prompts. Students were chosen for interview by asking teachers of the selected classes (who were aware of the focus of the research) to nominate pairs of students who would be relaxed and happy to talk. Each interview was transcribed in full. We have also collected data on attainment, social class, gender and ethnicity although these are still being analysed.

The qualitative data form the open items in the questionnaire, the interview transcripts and the lesson observation notes were coded using open coding (Glaser & Strauss, 1967), from which the three themes to be discussed emerged.

# Research results

When students moved from year 8 to year 9 in our study, it became clear from questionnaire, lesson observation and interview data that many students in the setted schools began to face negative repercussions as a result of the change from mixed-ability to setted teaching. Forty of the 48 students interviewed from setted groups wanted either to return to mixed-ability teaching or to change sets. The students reported that teaching practices emanating from setting arrangements had negatively affected both their learning of mathematics and their attitudes towards mathematics. Three major issues that were raised by students are discussed.

## High sets, high expectations, high pressure

In Boaler's (1997b) study, at least one-third of the students taught in the highest set were disadvantaged by their placement in this group, because they could not cope with the fast pace of lessons and the pressure to work at a high level. The students that were most disaffected were able girls, apparently because able girls, more than any others, wanted to understand what they were doing—in depth—but the environment of set 1 classes did not allow them to do this.

We chose to observe set 1 lessons and interview set 1 students in this study to determine whether the environment of set 1 lessons in other schools was similar to those in Boaler's study and whether students were disadvantaged in similar ways. Early evidence suggests that this is the case. Every one of the eight girls interviewed from set 1 groups in our study wanted to move down into set 2 or lower. Six out of eight of the set 1 boys were also extremely unhappy, but they did not want to move into lower groups, presumably because they were more confident (although no more able) than the girls, and because of the status that they believed being in the top set conferred. Observations of set 1 lessons make such reactions easy to understand. In a range of top-set classes the teachers raced through examples on the board, speaking quickly, often interjecting their speech with phrases such as 'Come on, we haven't got much time' and 'Just do this quickly'. Set 1 lessons were also more procedural than others—with teachers giving quick demonstrations of method without explanation, and without giving the students the opportunity to find out about the meaning of different methods or the situations in which they might be used. Some of the teachers also reprimanded students who said that they did not understand, adding comments such as 'You should be able to, you're in the top set'. Before one lesson, the teacher told one of us that about a third of his class were not good enough for the top set and then during the lesson proceeded to identify the ones that 'were not academic enough', with the students concerned watching and listening. The following are descriptions of 'top-set' lessons, from students in the four setted schools:

*School E: mainly white, working-class school with low attainment*

If we can't answer the question or something, he'll say 'Oh yeah, you're not going to be in set 1 next year—you are the set 1 class, you shouldn't be doing this, you should be doing this'. (Graham, school E, set 1)

*P*: He likes being successful.

*G:* He wants to turn up a number 1 set—but he's going too fast, you know, a bit over the top.

*P*: He explains it as if we're maths teachers. He explains it like really complex kind of thing, and I don't get most of the stuff. (Paul and Graham, school E, set 1)

I want to get a good mark, but I don't want to be put in the top set again, it's too hard and I won't learn anything. (Molly, school E, set 1)

*School F: ethnically diverse, middle- and working-class school with average attainment*

The teacher says 'You'd better do this, by like 5 minutes time' then you start to rush and just write anything. (Lena, school F, set 1)

You don't even get time to think in the maths lessons. (school F, girls, set 1)

I want to go down because they can do the same work but just at a slower pace, so they understand it better, but we just have to get it into our head the first time and that's it. (Aisha, school F, set 1)

*School A: mainly white, middle- and working-class school with average attainment*

A: Sometimes they work too fast for me and I can't keep up with the rest of the class.

J: And all your other friends are in different groups so you can't really ask them for help, because you're the top set and you're supposed to know it all. (Ayla and Josie, school A, girls, set 1)

S: Most of the difference is with the teachers, the way they treat you. They expect us to be like, just doing it straight away.

M: Like we're robots. (Simon and Mitch, school A, set 1)

*School C: mainly white, middle-class school with very high attainment*

L: This year I find it really hard and I haven't been doing as well as I wanted to be.
I [Interviewer]: Did you enjoy it more last year? [in mixed-ability groups]

L: Yeah definitely, because it's a whole different process, you're doing different books, you're able to be taught more, you just feel that you're not being rushed all the time. (Lena, school C, set 1)

I used to enjoy maths, but I don't enjoy it anymore because I don't understand it. I don't understand what I'm doing. So if I was to move down I probably would enjoy it. I think I am working at a pace that is just too fast for me. (Andrea, school C, set 1)

This is just a small selection of the complaints raised by students in top sets, who characterised their mathematical experiences as fast, pressured and procedural. The four schools that are represented by the foregoing comments were not chosen because of the way that they taught mathematics and the schools are quite different in many respects. Yet, the students' perceptions of set 1 lessons were similar in each of the schools. Boaler (1997b) found that teachers change their normal practices when they are given top-set classes to teach, appearing to believe that being a 'top-set' student entails a qualitative and meaningful difference from other students, rather than simply being in the highest-attaining range of students in the school. Top-set children, it seems, do not need detailed help, time to think, or the space to make mistakes. Rather, they can be taught quickly and procedurally because they are clever enough to draw their own meaning from the procedures they are given. In questionnaires, students in the six schools were asked, 'Do you enjoy maths lessons?' Students in top sets were the most negative in the entire sample, with 43% of set 1 students choosing 'never' or 'not very often', compared with an average of 36% of students in other sets and 32% of students in mixed-ability classes. Students were also asked whether it was more important 'to remember work done before or think hard' when answering mathematics questions. The set 1 groups had the highest proportion of students who thought remembering was more important than thinking. In the set 1 classes, 68% of students prioritised memory over thought, compared to 56% of students in the other setted groups and 51% of students in mixed-ability groups.

In the same article, Boaler also argued that the fast, procedural and competitive nature of set 1 classes particularly disadvantages girls and that the nature of high-set classes contributes to the disparity in attainment of girls and boys at the highest levels. Despite media claims that girls are now overtaking boys in all subjects (Epstein *et al.*, 1998), boys still outnumber the number of girls attaining A or A* grades in mathematics GCSE by 5 to 4. As the majority of able girls are taught within set 1 classes for mathematics in the UK (*Guardian*, 1996) and the four schools in this study are unlikely to be particularly unusual in the way that they teach set 1 lessons, it seems likely that the underachievement and non-representation of girls at the highest levels are linked to the environments generated within top-set classrooms.

## Low sets, low expectations and limited opportunities

Students in low sets at the four schools appear to be experiencing the reverse of the students in high sets, with repercussions that are, if anything, even more severe and damaging. Indeed, the most worrying reports of the implications of the setting process for students in our sample came from students in lower groups. These students reported a wide range of negative experiences, substantiated by observations of lessons. These included a frequent change of teachers (in one school, the 'bottom' set had been taught by three different teachers in the first nine months), the allocation of non-mathematics teachers to low sets and a continuous diet of low-level work that the students found too easy. Examples (in which a new paragraphs denotes a change of speaker) include:

It's just our group who keeps changing teachers.

*I*: Why?

Cause they don't think they have to bother with us. I know that sounds really mean and unrealistic, but they just think they don't have to bother with us, cause we're group 5. They get say a teacher who knows nothing about maths, and they'll give them us, a PE teacher or something. They think they can send anyone down to us. They always do that. They think they can give us anybody. (Lynne, school E, set 5)

*R*: We come in and sir tells us to be quiet and gives us some work and then he does them on the board and then that's basically it.

*J*: Even though we're second from bottom group, I think it would be much better if we didn't have the help with it.

*R*: Because he thinks we're really low.

*J*: Really stupid or something. (Ramesh and Jack, school A, set 6)

Students were particularly concerned about the low level of their work and talked at length about teachers ignoring their pleas for more difficult work, making students who had finished the work in the first five minutes of the lesson sit and wait with nothing to do for the remaining 55 minutes. In some cases, students were told things like, 'You can't have finished, you're set 5' (school E, set 5 girl). In some lower-set lessons, the students were not given any mathematics questions to answer—only worked solutions to copy off the board.

> *L*: We come in, sit down, and there's like work on the board and he just says copy it. I think it's all too easy.
>
> *R*: It's far too easy.
>
> *I*: What happens if it's too easy? Do they make it any harder?
>
> *M*: No, we just have to carry on. We just have to do it. If you refuse to do it he'll just give you a detention. It's just so easy.
>
> *R*: Last year it was harder. Much harder. (Lee and Ray, school E, set 5)
>
> *C*: He just writes down the answers for us from the board, and we say to him, we say we can do it, but he just writes them down anyway.
>
> *I*: So what are you meant to do?
>
> *C*: Just have to copy them down. That's what we say to him, 'cause a lot of people get frustrated from just copying off the board all the time. (Carol, school A, set 6)
>
> *L*: We do baby work off the board.
>
> *N:* Yeah, it's just like what we already know, you know, 1 add 1.
>
> *L:* Say it's three times something equals nine.
>
> *N:* It's easy and it's boring. (Lynne and Nelly, school E, set 5)

In questionnaires, 27% of students taught in the lower sets in the setted schools reported that work was too easy, compared with 7% of students in the upper sets and 14% of students in the schools using mixed-ability teaching in year 9. Students in lower groups were upset and annoyed about the low level of the work they were given; in addition to finding lessons boring, they knew that their opportunities for learning were being minimised.

> Sir treats us like we're babies, puts us down, makes us copy stuff off the board, puts up all the answers like we don't know anything.
> And we're not going to learn from that, 'cause we've got to think for ourselves.
> Once or twice someone has said something and he's shouted at us, he's said, 'Well you're the bottom group, you've got to learn it', but you're not going to learn from copying off the board. (school A, set 6, girls)

The students' reports were consistent with our observations of low-set lessons, in which students were given answers to exercises a few minutes after starting them or required to copy work off the board for the majority or all of lessons. In response to the questionnaire item 'how long would you be prepared to spend on a maths question before giving up?' 32% of students in the lower sets chose the lowest option–'less than 2 minutes'—compared with 7% of students in sets in the top half and 22% of students in mixed-ability groups. The polarisation in the students' perceptions about mathematics questions in the setted schools probably reflects the polarisation in their experiences of mathematics. We have not yet interviewed teachers to talk to them about the choices they make about the level of work but the students were convinced that teachers simply regarded students in low sets as limited:

> *Im*: Sir used to normally say, 'You're the bottom group, you're not going to learn anything'.
>
> *I*: He says that to you?
>
> *Im*: Yeah.
>
> *I*: Why?
>
> *Im*: I don't know, I don't think he's got—maybe you'd call it faith in us, or whatever, he doesn't believe we can do it. (Imran, school A, set 6)

All four schools that use ability-grouping have told us that the system is flexible and that students will change groups if they are inappropriately placed, but the students in low groups believed there to be little hope of moving to higher groups. They believed that they were trapped within a vicious circle—to move up they needed good end of year test results, comparable with students in higher groups, but they could not attain good results because they were not taught the work that was assessed in the tests:

> *R*: In our class it was very easy and as soon as we got into the SATs, it was just like we hadn't done it.
>
> *L*: I want to be brainy, I want to go up, but I won't go up if this work is too easy. (Lee and Ray, school E, set 5)

In the same way as the 'top-set' teachers had fixed ideas about the high level and pace of work students should have been able to do, the teachers of the lower sets had fixed ideas about the low level of work appropriate for 'bottom-set' students. The students reported that teachers continued with these ideas, even when students asked them for more difficult work:

> *N*: I say 'Oh, I've done this before already'.
>
> *L*: And he says 'Well you can do it again'. He's nothing like 'Oh, I'll set you with some harder work or nothing'. (Nelly and Lynn, school E, set 5)

The students were clearly disadvantaged by the diet of low-level numeracy work that they were given. This problem seemed to derive partly from the teachers' perceptions about the level of work appropriate for low-set students but also from an idea that is intrinsic to setting policies and will be discussed in the final section—that students in setted groups have the same mathematical capabilities and learning styles and may be taught accordingly.

## Restricted pedagogy and pace

In mixed-ability classes, teachers have to cater for a range of students whose previous attainment varies considerably. Most teachers respond to this challenge by providing work that is differentiated either by providing different tasks for different students within the same class ('differentiation by task'), or by giving all students a task that can be attempted in a variety of ways and at a variety of different levels ('differentiation by outcome'). Teachers often let students work 'at their own pace' through differentiated books or work-sheets. In setted classes, students are brought together because they are believed to be of similar 'ability'. Yet, setted lessons are often conducted as though students are not only similar, but *identical*—in terms of ability, preferred learning style and pace of working. In the setted lessons we have observed, students have been given identical work, whether or not they have found it easy or difficult, and they have all been required to complete it at the same speed. This aspect of setted lessons has distinguished them from the mixed-ability lessons we have observed, even when the 'setted' lessons were taught by the same teachers. The restrictions on pace and level of work that are imposed in setted lessons have also been a considerable source of disaffection, both for students who find the pace of lessons too fast and for those who find it too slow.

In interviews, students talked at length about the restrictions imposed upon their pace of working since changing to setted groups, describing the ways in which they were required to work at the same speed as each other. Students reported that if they worked slower than others they would often miss out on work, as teachers moved the class on before they were finished:

> *D*: People who are slow they don't never get the chance to finish because she starts correcting them on the board already.
>
> *S*: You don't finish the module. (David and Scott, school A, set 4)

Students also described the ways in which teachers used a small proportion of the students as reference points for the speed of the class (cf. Dahllöf, 1971), and the detrimental effect this could have on their learning:

> *A:* Sometimes you can do it fast, and at the end, you don't really know it.
>
> *L:* But if she knows some people have finished, then she tells the class, 'OK you've got even less time to do the work'. She's like, 'Look at these five people, they have finished, hurry up!' (Aisha and Lena, school F, set 1)

Students also reported that if they worked quickly they were disadvantaged, as teachers made them wait for the rest of the class:

> *D*: Now we are sort of, people can be really far behind and people can be in front. Because it is sort of set, and we have these questions, say 'C', we have to all start.
>
> *I*: So you all start at the same, you all start at C?
>
> *S*: Yeah, but then the people who work fast have to wait for the people at the end to catch up.
>
> *D*: Because I finished, nearly before half the class and I had a lesson to do nothing. (David and Scott, school A, set 4)

Again, the students linked these restrictions to the norms generated within setted groups:

> *C*: Last year it was OK but when we finished our work or anything miss would give us harder work to do. But in this year when you finish it you just got to sit there and do nothing.
>
> *L*: Yeah, because in sets you all have to stay at one stage. (Craig and Liam, school F, set 3)

Such problems were not caused by teachers simply imposing an inappropriate pace upon their groups—some students found lessons too fast whilst other students in the same groups found the same lessons too slow. The two boys in school F, quoted above, described the problem well—in mixed-ability classes, students would be given work that was chosen for them; if they finished the work, teachers would give them harder work; in setted lessons, 'you all have to stay at the same stage'. Being able to teach the whole class as a single unit is the main reason that teachers put students into 'ability' groups, and it was also one of the main sources of the students' disaffection. The students also described an interesting phenomenon—that some teachers seemed to hold ideas about the pace at which a class should work that were independent of the capabilities of the students who were in that set. For example:

> If you're slow she's a bit harsh really, I don't think she really can understand the fact that some people aren't as fast as others. Because if you say that I don't understand the work—she'll just say something like 'You're in the middle set, you had to get here somehow, so you've got to do middle set work'. (David, school A, set 4)

The teachers of the top sets also exemplified this phenomenon with the frequent remarks they made to students in the vein of:

> You are the set 1 class, you shouldn't be finding this difficult. (Peter, school E, set 1)

It seems that the placing of students into 'ability' groups creates a set of expectations for teachers that overrides their awareness of individual capabilities. This is a particularly interesting finding given that the main argument that the ex-Prime Minister, Tony Blair, and other government ministers have given for supporting setting is that children need work that is at an appropriate pace and level for their particular 'ability'.

But the process of ability-grouping did not only appear to initiate restrictions on the pace and level of work available to students. It also impacted upon the teacher's choice of pedagogy. Teachers in the four schools in our study that used ability-grouping responded to the move to setted teaching by adopting a more prescriptive pedagogy and the same teachers who offered worksheets, investigations and practical activities to students in mixed-ability groups concentrated upon chalk-board teaching and textbook work when teaching groups with a narrower range of attainment. This is not surprising given that one of the main reasons mathematics teachers support setting is that it allows them to 'class teach' to their classes, but it has important implications for the learning of students. When students were asked in their questionnaires to *describe their maths lessons*, the forms of pedagogy favoured by teachers in the schools using ability grouping were clearly quite different from those in the schools using mixed-ability teaching. We coded a significant number of students' responses to this question as 'lack of involvement' because students wrote such comments as 'lessons go on and on' or 'maths lessons are all the same'. Some 12% of responses from students in setted groups reflected a lack of involvement, compared with 4% of responses from students in mixed-ability groups. An additional 12% students from setted groups described their lessons as 'working through books', compared with 2% of students in mixed-ability groups, whilst 8% of setted students volunteered that the 'teacher talks at the board', compared with 1% of mixed-ability [grouped] students. Only 15% of students in setted groups described their mathematics lessons as either 'OK', 'fun', 'good' or 'enjoyable', compared with 34% of mixed-ability students.

In a separate open question, students were asked how mathematics lessons could be improved. This also produced differences between the students, with 19% of students taught in sets saying that there should be more open work, more variety, more group work, maths games or opportunity to think, compared to 9% of mixed-ability students. Eight per cent of setted students said that lessons should be slower or faster, compared to 4% of mixed-ability students, and 4% of setted students explicitly requested that they return to mixed-ability teaching.

The influence of ability-grouping upon teachers' pedagogy also emerged from the students' comments in interview. The following comments came from students across the spectrum of setted groups:

*I*: What are maths lessons like?

*J*: Rubbish—we just do work out of a book.

*I*: How does that compare with other lessons in years 7 and 8?

*M*: They were better. We did more fun work. (Janet and Molly, school E, set 1)

*I*: What would be your ideal maths lesson?

*L*: I would like work that is more different. Also when you can work through a chapter, but more fun.

*N*: It would have to be a bit more different.

*L*: Could do a chapter for two weeks, then the next two weeks do something else, an investigation or something—the kind of stuff we used to do. (Nelly and Lynn, school E, set 5)

*R*: Last year it was better, 'cause of the work. It was harder. In year 8 we did wall charts, bar charts etc., but we don't do anything like that. It's just from the board.

*L*: I really liked it in year 7, because we used to like do it from the books. Like at the end of the year we used to play games. But like this year it's just been like work from the board. (Ray and Lee, school E, set 5)

*D*: In year 8, sir did a lot more investigations, now you just copy off the board so you don't have to be that clever.

*S*: Before, we did investigations, like *Mystic Rose*, it was different to bookwork, 'cause books is just really short questions but those were ones sir set for himself, or posters and that, that didn't give you the answers. (David and Scott, school A, set 4)

In year 7 maths was good. We done much more stuff, like cutting out stuff, sticking in, worksheets and all stuff like that. Now, every day is copying off the board and just doing the next page, then the next page and it gets really boring. (Carol, school A, set 6)

The change in teaching approach that appeared to be initiated by setted teaching could simply reflect the increase in students' age and progression towards GCSE, but similar changes did not take place in the mixed-ability schools. The implications of such changes for students' learning of mathematics are discussed next.

# Discussion

The students interviewed from our setted schools create an image of setted mathematics lessons that reflects disaffection and polarisation, which is broadly substantiated by our observations of lessons and by questionnaire data. It seems that when students were taught in mixed-ability groups, their mathematics teachers gave them work that was at an appropriate level and pace. When the students were divided into ability groups, students in high sets came to be regarded as 'mini-mathematicians' who could work through high-level work at a sustained fast pace, whereas students in low sets came to be regarded as failures who could cope only with low-level work—or worse—copying off the board. This suggests that students are *constructed* as successes or failures by the set in which they are placed, as well as the extent to which they conform to the expectations the teachers have of their set. In particular, within top sets, students are constructed as successes and failures according to the extent to which they conform to the expectations the teachers have of their set. In particular, within top sets, students are constructed as successes and failures according to the extent to which they can cope with the highly procedural approaches adopted by teachers of those sets. Other notions of success in mathematics, such as those which emphasise depth of understanding, which are arguably much closer to the concerns of professional mathematicians (Buxton, 1981; Burton, 1997) are ruled out.

The requirement to work at an inappropriate pace is a source of real anxiety for many students, particularly girls, and is not confined to top sets:

> *M*: I get really depressed about it, and I don't want to ask, but then again like it really depressed me, the fact that everyone in the class is like really far ahead and I just don't understand.

> *L*: Yeah, 'cause like especially when everyone else understands it and you think 'Oh my God, I'm the only one in the class that doesn't understand it'. (Maggie and Linda, school C, set 3)

These students were not talking about minor feelings and peripheral details but issues that go directly to the heart of their experiences, and which have a profound impact both on their attitudes towards, and their achievement in, mathematics.

The major advantage that is claimed for ability-grouping practices is that they allow teachers to pitch work at a more appropriate level for their students. However, while ability-grouping practices can *reduce* the range of attainment in a class, within even the narrowest setting system, there will be considerable variations in attainment. Some of this will be due to the inevitable unreliability of mechanisms of allocating students to particular sets, but even if the average attainment of students in a set is reasonably similar, this will mask considerable variation in different aspects of mathematics and in different topics, as the students were well aware. Indeed, the students held strong beliefs that individuals have different strengths and weaknesses and that it is helpful to learn from each other and to learn to be supportive of each other:

> *C*: I prefer groups when we're all mixed up. There's the clever and the dumb and the dumb learn from the clever and sometimes the clever they'll be learning from the people who don't know as much. Because some things the clever are good at and some things the not so educated are good at.

> *L*: Classes should have a mixture of everyone. And then everyone could learn from everyone, because it's not like the dumb ones don't know anything, they do know it, but the atmosphere around them in lessons means they can't work.

> *C*: And they just say to themselves—what's the point? (Craig and Liam, school F, set 3)

Perhaps the most surprising finding is that setting was not perceived as accomplishing the one thing that it was designed to do—to allow teachers to match the work set to the strengths and weaknesses of individual students. When the students were asked if work they were given was at 'the right sort of level', the proportion of those taught in mixed-ability groups who said that the work set was 'usually about right' for them was actually marginally higher (81%) than that for those taught in sets (77%).

Another consequence of setting that emerged in Boaler's study, and which is beginning to emerge in our study, is the consequence of set allocation for students' entry to the GCSE. The report of the Committee of Inquiry into the Teaching of Mathematics in Schools (1982), generally known as the 'Cockcroft report', argued that it was unacceptable that the majority of students entered for the school-leaving examination would gain less than 40% of the available marks. The report recommended that school-leaving examinations in mathematics should be differentiated, so that students would take only those papers appropriate for their attainment. For the mathematics GCSE, there are currently three 'tiers' of entry, with different syllabuses. Because schools find it difficult to operate with students in the same set following different syllabuses, most schools in the country (and all the four schools using ability-grouping in our study) enter all the students in a particular set for the same tier of the examination. The effect of this is that students in the lower sets will be entered for an examination in which the highest grade they can achieve is a grade 'D', whereas the only grade that is ever specified for recruitment or for further study is a grade 'C'.

In Boaler's study, the students did not become aware of this restriction until their final year of compulsory schooling, year 11, and this discovery caused considerable resentment and disaffection. In our study, only a few students (exclusively in the top sets) are yet aware of the effects of tiering, but it is already a significant issue for those beginning to understand the implications:

> I was reading from the maths criteria sort of thing and it says if you are put in the medium group then you are aiming for a B for GCSE. But I don't think that is fair, it's like saying you can't go higher than a B sort of thing. I think they should give you the work and what you get is what you get. They shouldn't try and aim you for something, because you never know, you could get an A. (Katy, school C, set 1)

There were, of course, some students in our sample (one-sixth of those students we interviewed) who were comfortable with being taught in sets. The majority of these were those taught in intermediate groups, who did not want to move either up (interestingly) or down, and worked at a pace and level that was appropriate for them. However, none of these students was aware of any restriction of grades that they would encounter in the GCSE examinations.

As we have noted, many of the disadvantages of setting that we have described are contingent rather than necessary features of ability-grouping, but we believe that they are widespread, pervasive and difficult to avoid. The adoption of ability-grouping appears to signal to teachers that it is appropriate to use different pedagogical strategies from those that they use with mixed-ability classes. The best teachers are allocated to the ablest students, despite the evidence that high-quality teaching is more beneficial for lower-attaining students (Black & Wiliam, 1998, p. 42). Curriculum differentiation is polarised, with the top sets being ascribed qualities as mathematicians, not as a result of their individual qualities, but simply by virtue of their location in a top set. In order to ensure that the entire curriculum is covered, presumably to suit the needs of the highest-attaining students within the top set, the pace of coverage is both increased and applied to the whole class as a unit, and teachers seem to make increased use of 'transmission' pedagogies. For some students, who are able to assimilate the new material as it is covered, the experience may be satisfactory, but for the remainder, the effect is to proceduralise the curriculum until it becomes a huge task of memorisation. The curriculum polarisation results in a situation in which upward movement between sets is technically possible, but is unlikely to be successful, because a student moving up will not have covered the same material as the class he is joining. Finally, because of the perversities of the examination arrangements for mathematics GCSE, the set in which a student is taught determines the tier for which a student is entered, and thereby, the maximum grade the student can achieve. For most students, this decision will have been made 3 years or more before the examination is taken.

Because all the schools in our study make some use of mixed-ability-grouping in the earlier years, all the teachers in our sample have some experience of teaching mixed-ability classes, for which a variety of strategies are used. Some make substantial use of independent learning schemes which allow a teacher to give each student an individual programme of work. They also use within-class grouping, with students on different tables working on different materials and at different speeds. Most of the teachers in the sample also made some use of more open tasks, which can be tackled at a variety of levels. Although these more open tasks were used infrequently with setted classes, it was surprising how favourably these were regarded by the students. When the students who were taught in sets were asked for the best lesson they remembered that year, almost every student described a lesson where the whole class had worked on an investigation or a problem that could be tackled in different ways.

Within-class grouping, a system which is used by some of the teachers in one of our 'mixed-ability' schools, is much more flexible. It allows opportunities for whole classes to do the same work and allows students that are regarded as weaker to shine in some areas. One student, regarded by her teacher as the 'weakest' in her mixed-ability mathematics class, described her best lesson thus:

> It was last week, we were doing bar charts and pie charts and all that and I think I was the third person in the class who got it properly—we had to make it into a graph, it was good. (Caroline, school B, mixed-ability)

Some degree of within-class grouping also allows teachers to ensure that students are given appropriate work, and, importantly, that the level of assigned work is altered if and when this becomes appropriate:

> We have different books—high books, medium books, low books, so everyone has the right amount of work—no one's doing nothing too hard or too easy. If you think that it's too hard or too easy you just tell miss and she gives you the right level. (Ruby, school B, mixed-ability)

Of course, within-class grouping does often result in a situation in which the teacher ends up explaining the same idea to different groups at different times, but this seems a small price to pay compared to the alternative. As one boy remarked:

> It was just like, in my primary school we weren't in groups for like how good you are in certain subjects. We were just in one massive group, we did everything together. You've got some smart people and you've got some dumb people in the class, so you just blend in, sort of so you don't *have* to be that good and you don't *have* to be that bad. (David, school A, set 4, original emphasis)

Indeed, this student captures eloquently what we found to be the most important, and previously unreported feature of ability-grouping—it *creates* (McDermott, 1993) academic success and failure through a system whereby students '*have* to be that good' or they '*have* to be that bad'.

# Conclusion

Although there are substantial problems in interpreting the results of international comparisons (Brown, 1998; Wiliam, 1998), there is little doubt that, in a variety of respects, the performance of primary and secondary school students in the UK is modest by international standards (Beaton *et al.*, 1996; Mullis *et al.*, 1996). Kifer and Burstein's (1992) analysis of data from the Second International Mathematics Study (SIMS) suggests that the two factors that are most strongly associated with growth in student achievement in mathematics (indeed, the only two factors that are consistently associated with successful national education systems) are *opportunity to learn* (i.e. the proportion of students who had been taught the material contained in the tests) and the degree of *curricular homogeneity* (i.e. the extent to which students are taught in mixed-ability, rather than setted, groups).

While Bennett *et al.* (1984) found that primary teachers using within-class ability-grouping tend *to overestimate* the capabilities of weaker students, and set insufficiently challenging work to the most able, the evidence that we have found in the current study suggests very strongly that between-class ability-grouping produces the opposite effect. Indeed, the strength of the curriculum polarisation, and the diminution of the opportunity to learn that we have found in the current study, if replicated across the country, could be the single most important cause of the low levels of achievement in mathematics in the UK. The traditional British concern with ensuring that *some* of the ablest students reach the highest possible standards appears to have resulted in a situation in which the majority of students achieve well below their potential. As one student poignantly remarked:

> Obviously we're not the cleverest, we're group 5, but still— it's still maths, we're still in year 9, we've still got to learn. (Lynn, school E, set 5)

# References

Abraham, J. (1989) Testing Hargreaves' and Lacey's differentiation–polarisation theory in a setted comprehensive. *British Journal of Educational Sociology*, 40, pp. 46–81.

Abraham, J. (1994) Positivism, structurationism and the differentiation–polarisation theory: a re-consideration of Shilling's novelty and primacy thesis, *British Journal of Sociology of Education*, 15, pp. 231–241.

Ball, S. J. (1981) *Beachside Comprehensive* (Cambridge, Cambridge University Press).

Ball, S. J., Bowe, R. & Gewirtz, S. (1994) Competitive schooling: values, ethics and cultural engineering, *Journal of Curriculum and Supervision*, 9, pp. 350–367.

Barker Lunn, J. C. & Ferri, E. (1970) *Streaming in the Primary School: a longitudinal study of children in streamed and non-streamed junior schools* (Slough, National Foundation for Educational Research).

Beaton, A. E., Mullis, I. V. S., Martin, M. O., Gonzalez, E. J., Kelly, D. L. & Smith, T. A. (1996) *Mathematics Achievement in the Middle School Years: IEA's third international mathematics and science study* (Chestnut Hill, MA, Boston College).

Bennett, N., Desforges, C., Cockburn, A. & Wilkinson, B. (1984) *The Quality of Pupil Learning Experiences* (London, Lawrence Erlbaum Associates).

Black, P. J. & Wiliam, D. (1998) Assessment and classroom learning, *Assessment in Education*, 5, pp. 7–73.

Boaler, J. (1997a) Setting, social class and survival of the quickest, *British Educational Research Journal*, 23, pp. 575–595.

Boaler, J. (1997b) When even the winners are losers: evaluating the experiences of 'top set' students, *Journal of Curriculum Studies*, 29, pp. 165–182.

Boaler, J. (1997c) *Experiencing School Mathematics: teaching styles, sex and setting* (Buckingham, Open University Press).

Brown, M. L. (1998) The tyranny of the international horse race, in: R. Slee, G. Weiner & S. Tomlinson (Eds) *School Effectiveness for Whom* (London, Falmer Press).

Burton, L. (1997) *Mathematics—communities of practice?* Paper presented at *Meeting of the Research into Social Perspectives on Mathematics Education Group* held at University of London Institute of Education on 11 December (Birmingham, University of Birmingham School of Education).

Buxton, L. (1981) *Do You Panic about Maths? Coping with Maths Anxiety* (London, Heinemann).

Committee of Inquiry into the Teaching of Mathematics in Schools (1982) *Report: mathematics counts* (London, HMSO).

Dahllöf, U. (1971) *Ability Grouping, Content Validity and Curriculum Process Analysis* (New York, Teachers College Press).

Department for Education and Employment (1997) *Excellence in Schools* (London, The Stationery Office).

Epstein, D., Maw, J., Elwood, J. & Hey, V. (1998) Guest editorial, *Journal of Inclusive Education*, 2, pp. 91–94.

Gamoran, A. & Berends, M. (1987) The effects of stratification in secondary schools: synthesis of survey and ethnographic research, *Review of Educational Research*, 57, pp. 415–435.

Gewirtz, S., Ball, S. J. & Bowe, R. (1993) Values and ethics in the education market place: the case of Northwark Park, *International Studies in Sociology of Education*, 3, pp. 233–254.

Glaser, B. G. & Strauss, A. L. (1967) *The Discovery of Grounded Theory: strategies for qualitative research* (New York, Aldine).

Guardian (1996) Blair rejects mixed ability teaching, 8 June. p. 7.

Hallam, S. & Toutounji, I. (1996) *What Do We Know about the Grouping of Pupils by Ability? A research review* (London, University of London Institute of Education).

Hargreaves, D. H. (1967) *Social Relations in a Secondary School* (London, Routledge & Kegan Paul).

Harlen, W. & Malcolm, H. (1997) *Setting and Streaming: a research review* (Edinburgh, Scottish Council for Research in Education).

Jackson, B. (1964) *Streaming: an education system in miniature* (London, Routledge & Kegan Paul).

Kerchkoff, A. C. (1986) Effects of ability grouping in British secondary schools, *American Sociological Review*, 51, pp. 842–858.

Kifer, E. & Burstein, L. (1992) Concluding thoughts: what we know, what it means, in: L. Burstein (Ed.) *The IEA Study of Mathematics III: student growth and classroom processes*, pp. 329–341 (Oxford, Pergamon).

Lacey, C. (1970) *Hightown Grammar: the school as a social system* (Manchester, Manchester University Press).

McDermott, R. P. (1993) The acquisition of a child by a learning disability, in: S. Chaiklin & J. Lave (Eds) *Understanding Practice: perspectives on activity and context*, pp. 269–305 (Cambridge, Cambridge University Press).

Mullis, I. V. S., Martin, M. O., Beaton, A. E., Gonzalez, E. J., Kelly, D. L. & Smith, T. A. (1996) *Mathematics Achievement in the Primary School Years: IEA's third international mathematics and science study* (Chestnut Hill, MA, Boston College).

Oakes, J. (1985) *Keeping Track: how schools structure inequality* (New Haven, CT, Yale University Press).

Office for Standards in Education (1993) *Mathematics Key Stages 1, 2, 3 and 4, fourth year 1992–93: a report from the office of Her Majesty's Chief Inspector of Schools* (London, Her Majesty's Stationery Office).

Slavin, R. E. (1990) Achievement effects of ability grouping in secondary schools: a best evidence synthesis, *Review of Educational Research*, 60, pp. 471–499.

Sorensen, A. B. (1970) Organisational differentiation of students and their educational opportunity, *Sociology of Education*, 43, pp. 355–376.

Sukhnandan, L. & Lee, B. (1998) *Streaming, Setting and Grouping by Ability: a review of the literature* (Slough, National Foundation for Educational Research).

Tomlinson, S. (1987) Curriculum option choices in multi-ethnic schools, in: B. Troyna (Ed.) *Racial Inequality in Education* (London, Tavistock).

Whitty, G., Power, S. & Halpin, D. (1998) *Devolution and Choice in Education* (Buckingham, Open University Press).

Wiliam, D. (1998) Making international comparisons: the Third International Mathematics and Science Study, *British Journal of Curriculum and Assessment*, 8, pp. 37–42.

# Section 3

## Representations of Knowledge and Learner Identities

# 9

# Changing Pedagogy: Vocational Learning and Assessment

*David Boud, Geof Hawke and Nancy Falchikov[1]*

## Introduction

In this chapter, we will introduce some new ideas about assessment practice in vocational education and training (VET) that link with other new ideas about pedagogy in the contemporary VET environment.

The chapter briefly outlines the assessment practices that have informed VET in Australia and how these have been evolving before it explores the ways in which a changing environment for VET is creating pressures for a re-conceptualisation of assessment as a key component of pedagogy.

We then outline ways of thinking about the various functions that assessment plays within teaching and learning that suggest the shape of a new approach to assessment we call 'sustainable assessment'. The ideas of sustainable assessment are then illustrated by a practical example.

## Assessment in Australian VET pre-1990

Prior to the significant reforms of VET in Australia that began in the early 1990s, assessment in Australian VET was largely taken for granted as a second-order issue. The dominant thinking about VET as a curriculum-driven system implied that assessment was a simple matter of 'testing the curriculum'. However, it also had a character that differentiated it strongly from assessment in both secondary schooling and higher education: it was essentially criterion-referenced assessment and not norm-referenced.

This difference was rooted in VET's emphasis on preparation for the workplace and the implicit standards that defined the criteria as those of the workplace itself and drawn from the experience and expertise of the teaching workforce.

## The new emphasis on assessment

In the 1990's, however, a significant change in the basic structures and purposes of VET in Australia was implemented.

As in the many other places where a substantial reform of vocational education and training has been undertaken, Australian VET saw a shift away from a syllabus-driven assessment model to one based upon specification of outcomes. Assessment in such systems occurs according to explicitly defined standards. The exact nature of these varies, as does the terminology used, but all share a view that assessment, and the learning that precedes it, should have tangible outcomes. A number of consequences flow from this: curriculum takes on a lesser, and assessment a larger, role and learners are judged in terms of what they can do, often in realistic settings, rather than what they know. How outcomes are formulated and understood by assessors and learners becomes a dominant focus, but the result has been a reawakening of interest in assessment.

Moreover, the number of people formally engaged in assessment has grown. A key plank of the reform process was the establishment of 'workplace assessor' standards that were the minimum requirements for those who wished to provide assessments that would count towards nationally recognised qualifications. Thus, a significant number of trainers and supervisors in workplaces have become assessors within the formal VET system. Moreover, this minimum standard has also become the normal requirement, even for teachers in Technical and Further Education (TAFE) institutes.

More recently, this development has been taken a step forward with the introduction of training packages and the requirements of 'evidence-based assessment' in which the emphasis is upon the accumulation of evidence that is, subsequently, judged against predetermined standards. This has brought the role of assessment and the assessor clearly to the fore as it is assessment, with or without any associated teaching, which is the basis upon which qualifications are issued. In response to this shift in emphasis, a number of 'assessment-only' providers are now operating. These bodies issue qualifications based only on their assessment of an individual's skills and knowledge against the standards.

There have been critiques of these moves, including concerns that:

- learning processes and the role of teachers have been marginalised
- too much specification fragments learning and knowledge
- narrowly behavioural outcomes encourage minimalist responses by learners
- insufficient attention is given to adapting programmes to varying educational capacities, especially with regard to literacy.

These critiques have been accepted to a greater or lesser extent, and most systems have made some accommodations that have rarely been met with an enthusiastic response.

# The changing context of VET

These changes derived from many causes and it is not pertinent to detail them all here. However, some of the changes are especially significant and we briefly outline them.

## Changing dynamics of the workplace

There has been considerable focus on the changing nature of work and the implications of these for VET (Buchanan et al., 2001; Marginson, 2000). Of the various factors they describe, the following have significant ramifications for the thesis developed in this chapter:

- increasing labour mobility
- increasingly broad job classifications
- increasing frequency of multiple, parallel employment (through casualisation, contracted employment, etc.)
- increasing emphasis on the worker as 'free-agent', responsible for his or her own 'career progression'.

All of these create a situation in which workers are required to take a much greater share of the responsibility for their own development and for being 'employable'. They are key features of an employment context in which the knowledge base that the worker requires changes frequently, and the competitive nature of the labour market creates an increasingly individualised demand for new learning opportunities, as workers seek to find niche employment markets in which to barter their skills.

# Changing needs in VET

These changes in workplace employment arrangements and the consequent changes in the expectations of workers who wish to be employable and maintain their 'employability' have important implications for a changing approach to VET.

## The growth of knowledge-intensive learning

Firstly, knowledge is becoming an increasingly important and tradeable commodity. For many learners, this means that their 'portfolio of skills and knowledge' becomes the fundamental asset they deploy in seeking to gain and maintain employment. Moreover, as we explore below, this is no longer a static 'package' but must be constantly updated to reflect new and emerging needs. Learners, then, must be constantly reassessing their skills and knowledge and identifying how and when to modify them.

## The hollowing out of the middle

Secondly, there is now growing evidence that two, simultaneous forces are operating that are restructuring the labour force as a whole. The first derives from the growing knowledge focus of many areas of employment. This is providing an upwards force that is pushing many occupational roles that were once thought of as 'middle-level' to acquire a greater knowledge focus and, especially, to require greatly expanded analytic and conceptual skills than previously was the case.

At the same time, other forces in the economy are exerting downward forces that are resulting in the deskilling of many occupational sectors and, in particular, reducing the need for analytic and conceptual skills that were previously required. For many workers affected by this phenomenon, there is pressure to re-skill into the emerging high-skill occupations in order to ensure that they are able to maintain upward occupational mobility.

## Revitalised interest in lifelong learning

One of the main features of a lifelong learning agenda, as applied to vocational education and training, is an emphasis on equipping learners for what they require for a lifetime of learning. This has been characterised in a number of different ways: for example, key competencies, transferable skills, and learning-how-to-learn. All emphasise providing learners with the prerequisites to enable them to learn when confronted by situations not previously encountered. However, the outcomes-oriented approach has been applied in ways that privilege the immediately measured short-term, at the expense of longer-term, learning outcomes needed to equip learners for a world of changing practice. The highly desirable emphasis on recognising what learners can do, rather than what they might think, has inadvertently created an environment that tends to de-skill learners in coping with new challenges.

Some occupational groups involved in standards specification have been more open to generic learning outcomes than others. Practices in Australia, for example, range from benign neglect and optimistic assumptions that it will somehow get picked up along the way, to the incorporation of explicit competencies to be pursued in standards frameworks at each level of achievement. Generally, however, the focus on the occupationally driven formulation of outcomes has tended to emphasise immediately useful competencies, as distinct from those that might enable further learning at a later stage.

One of the issues typically overlooked in the development of standards, but implicit in the notion of learning-how-to-learn, is that of being an assessor of learning. An emphasis is frequently placed on learning and what is to be learned, but there is a common neglect of the ability to determine what has been learned and plan accordingly. Sometimes the ability to self-assess is now mentioned, but it is by no means common. This neglect in the lifelong learning literature parallels the similar neglect of assessment in the learning literature that occurred before an increasing number of studies demonstrated that assessment profoundly affects learning.

The central and inescapable process in an outcomes-based framework is the assessment of outcomes. The effect of assessing for immediate competence is to focus learners' attention on the present task and how they might address it, i.e. to satisfy assessors. The locus of control is separated from them. Learners necessarily want to complete the assessment task in ways that will meet the needs of the assessor, rather than focusing on how they make their own judgments about what constitutes satisfactory performance. In formal VET programmes, students typically do not have the opportunity to see how the process of assessment actually works. They do not see the processes of identifying appropriate standards and the criteria to be associated with each. They do not have experience of noticing features of their own work and making judgments with respect to standards and criteria. Indeed, the assessment tasks do not encourage them to do so. This would not be a problem if participants were not expected to engage in any further learning, but this is certainly not currently the case. While any given assessment activity may be terminal in the present qualification, it is an expectation that learners learn and assess throughout their lives.

In real settings, outcomes are rarely specified in explicit terms. What is required of the learner is embedded in a vocational practice or a particular context. Before learning can even commence, there is a need to identify what counts as good work from a complex set of surroundings and to develop ways of applying such an understanding to one's own work. Learners need to learn how to establish their own standards and how to judge whether they are meeting them. They will never learn this if standards are always provided and learners do not have practice in determining appropriate standards for themselves.

Acceptance of this argument does not of course imply that a framework of standards and levels is inappropriate. It does imply, however, that awareness of assessment thinking and practice must be incorporated into any programme that is part of an articulated set of qualifications. Consideration must be given to the lifelong learning agenda and to how learners move beyond the immediate requirements of any vocational task.

Our basic argument is that whatever else we do in any course in VET, we should also provide the basis for individuals to learn throughout their lives. We prepare them to be high-level learners engaged in challenging forms of work and required to solve problems and confront issues that we cannot presently imagine. We must address the challenge of how we can help learners deal with problems we have not met ourselves.

If we want to pursue the goal of equipping lifelong learners, we must take a view on what this implies, examine our current practices to see if we are doing this well, and, if not, develop ways of changing our practice to meet the challenge. Above all, we must focus on assessment practices, not just those that involve formal assessment activities, but all those elements of a programme that require learners to form judgements about their own learning. This takes us far beyond the normal assessment agenda.

In the process, we will suggest that we need to think about assessment differently. We will need to establish a new goal for assessment, that is, assessment for lifelong learning, and a new set of practices in our programmes, practices we refer to as sustainable assessment (Boud, 2000).

# The need for a new approach to VET assessment

Conventionally, it is accepted that there are two main reasons for assessment: for certification purposes and for the purpose of aiding learning. The first has typically been associated with summative assessment, that is, assessment for making judgements after a period of learning, and the second with formative assessment, that is, assessment that directly contributes to the everyday processes of learning. This conceptual distinction is often blurred in practice when intermediate assessment tasks provide both feedback to learners on their learning and record grades that contribute to certification. Experience has taught us that we cannot partition out different assessment purposes to different activities.

While the two purposes of assessment – certification and to aid learning – are necessary features of assessment, we argue that it is now necessary to add a third: assessment to promote lifelong learning. Like the first two purposes, there is also some overlap, especially with assessment to aid learning. We need a new distinction, we believe, because formative assessment is too often interpreted as assessment to aid immediate learning, for the here-and-now, not as a contribution towards the development of skills for lifelong assessment.

The starting point of this chapter is that vocational education and training has made an irreversible shift towards accountability in terms of learner outcomes and that for the foreseeable future, while there will be some practical limitations, it will be standards-based. This being so, a huge weight of responsibility is placed on those doing the specification, review and re-articulation of outcomes, since everything else flows from these. The activities of learners, teachers and assessors are necessarily oriented around a particular agenda.

Our concern is not with the principles of an outcomes-oriented approach, but with how conventional interpretation and implementation have produced, or more precisely have exacerbated, the negative effects that operate against a lifelong learning agenda.

We suggest that much of our current assessment practice inhibits the developments of lifelong assessment skills. That it, also, may not be good at fostering learning for immediate purposes simply compounds the problem. So, how do existing practices de-skill learners and distort learning? If we asked this question fifteen years ago and looked at the research then, we could have made the following list:

- Learners are assessed on those matters on which it is easy to assess them and this leads to an overemphasis on memory and lower-level skills.
- Assessment encourages learners to focus on those topics that are assessed at the expense of those which are not.
- The nature of assessment tasks influences the approaches to learning which learners adopt, often to promote surface approaches to learning.
- Learners who perform well on examinations can retain fundamental misconceptions about key concepts in the subjects they have passed. (Boud, 1990)

While, sadly, many of these may still be valid today, we must look more closely at what assessment practice often does now to undermine learners' capacity to judge themselves and thus constrain the lifelong learning agenda. A new list to supplement the old might include the following:

- Learners are encouraged to look to others (their assessors) to make judgements and don't develop their own ability to judge their own learning outcomes.
- Learners look to other learners to judge their standing rather than to appropriate standards.
- Assessment tasks often emphasise problem solution rather than problem formulation.
- Unrealistic and decontextualised settings are used to assess learning.
- Learner involvement in assessment is omitted and thus key stages in judging learning are rendered invisible, for example, establishing appropriate criteria for the completion of tasks.
- Courses often imply that all collaboration is cheating and thus de-emphasise learners working cooperatively.

Learners normally do not have the opportunity to see how the process of assessment actually works. It is something they experience as a procedure to which they submit rather than something they own.

Lest it be thought that these concerns about the negative influence of assessment practices apply only to traditional approaches, such as the test or the examination, there are new assessment traps. Strategies which have an immediate positive effect on learning now (for example, providing learners with criteria for assessment), may have unintended longer-term consequences which have yet to be identified. We have only to look at the growing use of learning outcomes and specification of standards. While in general this may be a desirable trend, it does have the unintended consequence of portraying to learners the idea that the specification of standards and outcomes is something which is a given, and that learning only proceeds following such a specification by others.

Learners need to learn how to establish their own standards and how to judge whether they are meeting them. They will never learn this if standards are always provided and they do not have practice in determining appropriate standards for themselves.

# Sustainable assessment – a new practice in assessment

When we look at any particular assessment activity, we need to ask ourselves the fundamental question: does it equip learners to be more effective in judging their own learning? This goes beyond the normal formative assessment question: does any particular assessment activity provide adequate feedback to learners on their performance? This distinction is vital and is often overlooked. Equipping learners to be lifelong assessors involves more than giving them detailed comments on their work. Sometimes rich feedback is not what is required for this purpose.

An idea we are developing is that of sustainable assessment. Sustainable assessment is defined as 'assessment that meets the needs of the present without compromising the ability of students to meet their own future learning needs' (Boud, 2000: 151). This need is emphasised by the concerns outlined above. Assessment is not just about measurement at a point in time; it is about influencing learning practices and about communicating priorities. It is through assessment that we communicate to learners what we regard as most important. It is also through assessment that learners perceive what they must do to be successful. They cannot escape from it if they want to be qualified.

Lifelong learning requires learners to be lifelong assessors of their learning. Without this, they cannot plan their own learning and identify when it is complete. There is a need to make preparation for lifelong learning such an intrinsic and necessary feature of VET practice that assessment in all contexts incorporates it as a key feature. If the priority communicated by a given assessment task is local and immediate, with no sense of future implication, it is inadequate.

The notion of sustainable assessment acts as a practical device to help us gain a grip on an issue not normally articulated in assessment talk. It focuses on learning, but it also reminds us to consider future implications and consequences. The goal is to progressively replace assessment practices that are not sustainable, that is, those practices that do not have long-term positive consequences for learning, with those that have such an influence.

While it is one thing to acknowledge the importance of assessment for lifelong learning and the need for sustainable assessment to be established, it is a major undertaking to identify what is required for practice. When we bring thinking and research about learning into the assessment arena, conceptual resources are, however, available to help us begin to sketch what might be required.

This initial investigation has lead to the identification of a set of features of tasks that can help promote a capacity for lifelong learning. These tasks focus on what have traditionally been regarded as learning activities, as well as those considered part of formal assessment activities.

While we are still developing this idea, we believe that some features of tasks promoting capacity for lifelong learning are:

- engages with standards and criteria and problem analysis
- emphasises the importance of context
- involves working in association with others
- involves authentic representations and productions

- promotes transparency of knowledge
- fosters reflexivity
- builds learner agency and constructs active learners
- considers risk and confidence of judgement
- promotes seeking appropriate feedback
- requires portrayal of outcomes for different purposes.

Some of these are elaborated on below.

## Engages with standards and criteria and problem analysis

- provides practice in discernment to identify critical aspects of problems and issues and the knowledge required to address them
- involves finding appropriate assistance to scaffold understanding from existing knowledge base
- gives learners practice in identifying, developing and engaging with criteria and standards.

## Emphasises importance of context

- locates issues in a context that must be taken into account
- identifies aspects of context that must be considered
- decides on what aspects of work require feedback from others
- recognises that solutions vary according to context.

## Involves working in association with others

- participates in giving and receiving feedback
- utilises practitioners and other parties external to the educational institution
- involves engagement with communities of practice and ways in which their knowledge is represented
- involves working collaboratively with others (not necessarily involving group assessment), including parties external to the educational institution
- identifies and uses communities of practice to assist in developing criteria for good work and peer feedback
- tasks directly reflect forms of activity in professional practice commensurate with the level of skill possessed (i.e. high level of authenticity).

## Promotes transparency of knowledge

- invites analysis of task structure and purpose
- fosters consideration of the epistemology of learning embedded in tasks
- tasks draw attention to how they are constructed and seek to make this transparent.

## Fosters reflexivity

- fosters the linking of new knowledge to what is already known
- not all the information required for the solution of problems is given
- prompts self-monitoring and judging progression towards goals (testing new knowledge).

## Builds learner agency and constructs active learners

- involves learners in creating assessment tasks
- assumes learners construct their own knowledge in the light of what works in the world around them
- focuses on producing rather than reproducing knowledge (fosters systematic inquiry)
- provides opportunities for learners to appropriate assessment activities to their own ends.

## Considers risk and confidence of judgement

- provides scope for taking the initiative (e.g. always taking the safe option is not encouraged)
- elements of the task are not fully determined
- confidence in the outcomes is built and sought (e.g. tasks encourage students to be confident of what they know and don't know).

## Promotes seeking appropriate feedback

- involves seeking and utilising feedback
- feedback is used from a variety of sources (e.g. from teacher, peer, and practitioner)
- grades and marks are subordinated to qualitative feedback.

## Requires the portrayal of outcomes for different purposes

- identifiably leaves students better equipped to complete future tasks
- involves portraying achievements to others (e.g. portfolio or patchwork text construction).

The item 'identifies and uses communities of practice to assist in developing criteria for good work and peer feedback' (part of 'Involves working in association with others') provides a good illustration of what a sustainable assessment activity might involve. In vocational practice, learners have to identify what counts as good work and often this requires an appreciation of who the appropriate groups that influence standards are and of what criteria they use. In highly regulated occupations, there may be some codification of this knowledge, but in many others it is the informal communities of practice that influence what counts as appropriate. Learners need to understand this and be able to access the knowledge that exists in such communities, so one assessment activity in a programme of study might involve practice in accessing such knowledge and applying it to one's own work.

Some who may know Boud's earlier work may be thinking that we are making an argument to support the idea of student self-assessment (Boud, 1995). While it is true that self-assessment is part of what we are considering here, it is far from all of it. To focus merely on self-assessment is to ignore the wider changes that are necessary. It is not just a matter of adding self-assessment to the learning and assessment repertoire, but of rethinking learning and assessment from a new point of view and examining the consequences for practice.

In the same way that assessment to promote lifelong learning cannot be reduced to learner self-assessment, neither can it be collapsed into formative assessment. It is a separate purpose. It simultaneously involves both more and less. There are features that involve more than is commonly included in assessment for learning – the development of frameworks for approaching a range of tasks – and some features of formative assessment may be less significant for longer-term goals. For example, some categories and styles of feedback from teachers may encourage an over-dependency on being 'corrected'.

Some potentially useful sources of ideas are as follows. Some of these are explicitly concerned with assessment practice, but others are more generally about learning and judgement.

- Formative assessment (e.g. Black and Wiliam, 1998; Hounsell, 2003) – ideas about types and sources of feedback.
- Discernment of variation (e.g. Bowden and Marton, 1998) – about the importance of learners noticing key features of concepts being learned.
- Generative ideas of learning (e.g. Jonassen et al., 1999) – about the need for testing learning through resorting to evidence.
- Situated learning and communities of practice (e.g. Lave and Wenger, 1991) – for the significance of knowledge being located in local practice.
- Identity and learners and the construction of tasks as learning (e.g. Boud and Solomon, 2003) – for the notion that learners need to identify as such and construct their activities to render learning visible.
- Risk and risk society (e.g. Beck, 1992; Einhorn and Hogarth, 1978) – for the pervasiveness of risk and because confidence in judgement is often as important as correct knowledge.
- Judgement and decision-making (e.g. Tversky and Kahneman, 1981) – for the idea that judgements can be easily compromised by the surrounding circumstances.
- Apprentices in judgement (Sadler, 1998) – for recognition that judgement does not come fully formed and staging is needed to develop expertise.
- Scaffolding of knowledge (Vygotsky and the neo-Vygotskians; also see Bliss et al., 1996) – to focus on the importance of learners finding ways of scaffolding for themselves from what they do know to what they don't know.
- Social construction of assessments (e.g. Kvale, 1996) – for drawing attention to the fact that assessments actually construct socially valued knowledge. [...]

If the new agenda involves problematising this boundary, which we believe it does, then we will need to question many of our normal processes, not least of which are quality assurance procedures.

This is a substantial agenda. However, there are many issues we need to face and explore.

# Linking assessment to pedagogy

Current assessment practice has characteristics that undermine the ability of learners to equip themselves for a lifetime of continuing learning that is a necessary feature of most contemporary work. Therefore, a new link needs to be formed between assessment and lifelong learning. This takes the form of sustainable assessment in which preparation for future learning and assessment are incorporated into assessment practices at all levels.

Many of the assessment activities being considered are not new, but when they are placed in a new framework they take on a new character. Of course, it is not just assessment practices that need to be modified, but learning outcomes and teaching and learning practices as well (Shepard, 2000). It has been convenient to maintain a separation between teaching/learning activities and assessment activities and many of our institutional practices reinforce this distinction.

We should not underestimate the difficulty of linking assessment with learning in practice, despite an extensive literature on the subject. Ecclestone's (2002) study, set in the context of GNVQs with progressive assessment practices such as self- and peer-assessment and learning portfolios, disappointingly showed that 'none of the teachers saw assessment explicitly shaping or affecting learning' (p. 155). We have to reshape our thinking if we are to prepare learners to be lifelong assessors as well as lifelong learners. We need to use the two lenses of assessment and pedagogy in examining our practices, and sustainable assessment appears to provide a useful bridge between the uneasy tension that currently exists between them. To achieve this, we'll need to reconsider the existing distinction between assessment and pedagogy. We need to rethink our assessment practices from the perspective of lifelong learning while, at the same time, using that perspective to rethink pedagogy more broadly.

# Implications for VET

As we've noted, the changing emphasis being proposed involves significant shifts in both thinking and practice. However, for VET, it appears that the greatest changes may be required in the current policy settings and the assumptions on which they're based.

The current policy framework has created a complete separation between assessment and the learning process. However, we argue that assessment alone is incapable of supporting the changes in learning outcomes that a lifelong learning perspective requires. In future work, we will explore these issues more thoroughly, but our thinking suggests that there are immediate questions that policy-makers need to consider.[2] These include:

- How must the standards for judgement that are currently set out in training packages change, if lifelong learning capacity is a core goal?
- Can an assessment-only mode support lifelong learning? Is it inherently a counter-productive approach or is there a problem with our current practice?
- What skills and knowledge must an assessor have to support the approach we propose? Do the revised assessor standards ensure these?

# Notes

1. This chapter was prepared for this collection and is based on Boud and Hawke (2003) and supplemented with material from Boud and Falchikov (2006).
2. We have done some of this in the context of higher education (Boud and Falchikov, 2007).

# References

Beck. U. (1992) *Risk Society*. London: Sage.

Black, P. and Wiliam, D. (1998) 'Assessment and classroom learning', *Assessment in Education*, 5(1): 7–74.

Bliss, J., Askew, M. and Macrae, S. (1996) 'Effective teaching and learning: scaffolding revisited', *Oxford Review of Education*, 22(1): 37–61.

Boud, D. (1990) 'Assessment and the promotion of academic values', *Studies in Higher Education*, 15(1): 101–11.

Boud, D. (1995) *Enhancing Learning through Self Assessment*. London: Kogan Page.

Boud, D. (2000) 'Sustainable assessment: rethinking assessment for the learning society', *Studies in Continuing Education*, 22(2): 151–67.

Boud, D. and Falchikov, N. (2006) 'Aligning assessment with long-term learning', *Assessment and Evaluation in Higher Education*, 31(4): 399–413.

Boud, D. and Falchikov, N. (2007) 'Developing assessment for informing judgement.' In D. Boud and N. Falchikov (eds), *Rethinking Assessment for Higher Education: Learning for the Longer Term*. London: Routledge.

Boud, D. and Hawke, G. (2003) Changing Pedagogy: Vocational Learning and Assessment. OVAL Research Working Paper 03–17. Sydney: The Australian Centre for Organisational, Vocational and Adult Learning, University of Technology.

Boud, D. and Solomon, N. (2003) '"I don't think I am a learner": acts of naming learners at work', *Journal of Workplace Learning*, 15(7–8): 326–31.

Bowden, J. and Marton, F. (1998) *The University of Learning: Beyond Quality and Competence in Higher Education*. London: Kogan Page.

Buchanan, J., Schofield, K., Briggs, C., Considine, G., Hager, P., Hawke, G., Kitay, J., McIntyre, J., Mounier, A. and Ryan, S. (2001) *Beyond Flexibility: Skills and the Future of Work*. Sydney: NSW Board of Vocational Education and Training.

Ecclestone, K. (2002) *Learning Autonomy in Post-16 Education: The Politics and Practice of Formative Assessment*. London: RoutledgeFalmer.

Einhorn, H. J. and Hogarth, R. M. (1978) 'Confidence in judgement: persistence of the illusion of validity', *Psychological Review*, 85: 395–416.

Hounsell, D. (2003) 'Student feedback, learning and development.' In M. Slowey and D. Watson (eds), *Higher Education and the Lifecourse*, pp. 67–78. Buckingham: SRHE & Open University Press.

Jonassen, D. H., Peck, K. L. and Wilson, B. G. (1999) *Learning with Technology: A Constructivist Perspective*. Upper Saddle River, NJ: Merrill.

Kvale, S. (1996) 'Examinations re-examined: certification of students or certification of knowledge?' In S. Chaiklin and J. Lave (eds), *Understanding Practice: Perspectives on Activity and Context*. Cambridge: Cambridge University Press.

Lave, J. and Wenger, E. (1991) *Situated Learning: Legitimate Peripheral Participation*. Cambridge: Cambridge University Press.

Marginson, S. (2000) 'The changing nature and organisation of work and the implications for vocational education and training in Australia', Issues paper, National Centre for Vocational Education Research, Leabrook, South Australia.

Sadler, D. R. (1998) 'Formative assessment: revisiting the territory', *Assessment in Education*, 5(1): 77–84.

Shepard, L. A. (2000) 'The role of assessment in a learning culture', *Educational Researcher*, 29(7): 4–14.

Tversky, A. and Kahneman, D. (1981) 'The framing of decisions and the psychology of choice', *Science*, 211(4481): 453–58.

# 10

# Mapping the Transformation of Understanding

*Marilyn Fleer and Carmel Richardson*

## Introduction

Approaches to teaching in early childhood education have moved towards a socio-cultural approach (Berk and Winsler, 1995; Cullen, 1994, 1996; Fleer, 1992; MacNaughton, 1995; Smith, 1993, 1996), while assessment and evaluation have generally stayed within a Piagetian framework or, at best, as a 'social influence approach' (see Rogoff, 1998). However, how practical is it to work within a socio-cultural perspective when considering evaluation and assessment? What sorts of tools would be needed to gather data, and how might practitioners frame their observations when following a socio-cultural approach?

The study reported in this chapter sought to determine ways of documenting how young children participate in socio-cultural activity and to record how their participation changes from being relatively peripheral participants to assuming responsible roles in the management or transformation of such activities. Teacher observations framed from a socio-cultural perspective (Rogoff, 1998) are presented alongside diary records documenting the transition from a traditional to a socio-cultural approach. These data demonstrate both the theoretical and practical implications of following a socio-cultural approach to assessment and evaluation.

## Socio-cultural perspectives on learning

> *Child development* is represented as a process subject to natural laws and taking place as a kind of maturation, whereas education is seen as some purely external use of the capacities that emerge during the process of development ... *education* is the tail behind child development, guided not by tomorrow, but by yesterday, by the child's weakness, not his [sic] strength. (Vygotsky, 1982–84, vol. 2: 225, cited in Davydov and Zinchenko, 1993: 100; my emphasis)

Vygotsky wrote about the need to develop pedagogy which looked forward (toward tomorrow) in child development rather than being situated always in the past. In these arguments

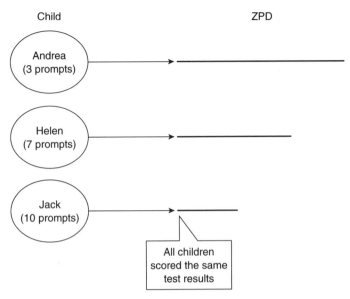

**Figure 10.1   Assessing beyond the actual and into the potential (Fleer, 2002)**

he spoke of working with children within their zone of proximal development (ZPD). Although this term and the learning processes of inter-psychological and intra-psychological functioning have been fully addressed in the literature (see Berk and Winsler, 1995; Wertsch, 1985) and need not be reproduced here, the implications for assessment are enormous.

Western assessment has predominantly focused on the individual, usually in contexts in which the child is unsupported. Vygotsky argued that this approach to assessment only ever tapped into a child's present and unsupported development and understanding. An individualistic orientation does not allow the assessor to determine children's potential capabilities. It has been argued elsewhere (Fleer, 2002) that mapping a child's potential is far more valuable for programme planning. Figure 10.1 models the assessment of both unsupported and supported learning. Although all children can be viewed as achieving at the same level, assessment within the ZPD measures more accurately the potential capacity of the children.

> To gain a complete picture of assessment, it is necessary to assess the child at the second level, i.e. the zone of proximal development. Such assessment by definition involves a dynamic interaction and focuses on the child's processes of learning or ability to interact with a more competent adult. (Lunt, 1993: 160)

Western approaches to assessment are less likely to examine what children do when supported by others, and are therefore unlikely to map the potential capabilities of children. The assessment for tomorrow (the ZPD) examines the children's strengths rather than their weaknesses. Measuring the children's potential level of development allows early childhood teachers to plan more thoughtfully. Socio-cultural assessment moves the focus from a deficit view of assessment to a much more powerful and useful assessment practice for informing teaching and learning practices. Carr has used the term 'credit' to describe this orientation to assessment (Carr, 1998a, 1998b). Yet a socio-cultural view of assessment has generally not been taken up in assessment practices.

A socio-cultural approach to assessment is also influenced by the image we have of the child. Although educators' views are diverse and constantly changing, there is at any time a predominant view which dictates our understanding of how children learn and develop and also of how we assess this development. Our most recent assessment practice in the field of early childhood education has been influenced by developmental psychologists whose image of the child can be expressed as 'the scientific child of biological stages'. In this construction:

> ... the focus is on the individual child who, irrespective of context, follows a standard of biological stages. Despite frequent talk about a holistic perspective ... the child is frequently reduced to separate and measurable categories, such as social development, intellectual development, motor development. Consequently, processes which are very complex and interrelated in everyday life are isolated from one another and viewed dichotomously, instead of viewing them as intrinsically interrelated functions that all work together in the production of change. (Dahlberg et al., 1999: 46)

Assessment following this developmental approach can be seen to be fragmented. Observational data are collected and then separated into discrete areas of attainment. A desire to be 'objective' in the collection of this information necessarily denies recording details of the observer or others who may influence the behaviour of the child being observed.

However, Loris Malaguzzi, founder of the innovative early childhood educational programme in Reggio Emilia, has presented us with an alternative image which foregrounds the competence and complexity of children and also the deep embeddedness they have in the community to which they belong. Dahlberg et al. cite the seminal paragraph in which Malaguzzi defined the Reggio Emilia version of children as:

> rich in potential, strong, powerful, competent and, most of all, connected to adults and other children (Malaguzzi, 1993, cited in Dahlberg et al., 1999: 50)

This image of the 'rich' child is reflected in the work undertaken in the Reggio Emilia centres. While this work and the relationship that exists between the centres and the communities they serve are unique to the cultural context of the Reggio Emilia region in Italy, there are elements that are equally transmutable to the Australian context. Foremost of these is the notion of the 'rich' child. If we adopt this construction of children and childhood, then we equally adopt the notion of 'rich' teachers, 'rich' families, 'rich' learning experiences and consequently 'rich' assessment that recognises 'that the young child as learner is an active *co*-constructor' (Dahlberg et al., 1999: 50). Dahlberg et al. argue that 'constructions of childhood are *productive* of practice; in other words, pedagogical work is the product of who we think the child is' (1999: 52).

This 'pedagogical work' necessarily includes assessment. A socio-cultural approach to assessment within this framework moves beyond being objective and exclusive to being subjective and inclusive. Documentation of interactions becomes the focus of study and the collection of rich observational data is made possible. 'What we document represents a choice ... in which pedagogues themselves are participating' (Dahlberg et al., 1999: 147).

Assessment approaches have developed from the traditional practice of norm-referenced, criterion-referenced and curriculum-based assessment (see Losardo and Notari-Syverson, 2001) with some researchers beginning to embrace approaches which link more closely with socio-cultural theory. Research by Margaret Carr and her colleagues in New Zealand (Carr, 2001a, 2001b), although concentrating upon individuals, provides a richer image of the child as a result of mapping children's learning journeys which includes recording evidence of other children's behaviours and cultural artifacts valued by the community. Similarly, alternative assessment as proposed by Losardo and Notari-Syverson (2001) begins to articulate the ways in which assessment practices can be embedded, authentic or mediated. Further, work undertaken by Feurestein and his colleagues (see Kozulin, 1998) documents the intentionality/reciprocity of interactions, the transcendence of learning and interactions which are transfused with meaning.

In socio-cultural approaches to teaching and learning, we foreground the notion that learning is more than an individual construction. Meaning occurs in the context of participation in the real world. Ideas are socially mediated and reside not in individuals but are constituted in collectives, such as a particular community of practice (Wenger, 1998). Since meaning and therefore understanding are enacted in social contexts, assessment of this understanding must be viewed as transient and fluid (see Rogoff, 1998; Wenger, 1998). Using this approach, assessment does not simply focus on the 'end product' but rather documents the whole learning journey (see Carr, 2001a) of the groups of children, rather than individuals, in order to document the achievements of the whole community of practice (Wenger, 1998). That is:

> ...cognitive development (must be seen) as a process, as people move *through* understanding rather than *to* understanding. (Rogoff, 1998: 690; original emphasis)

Consequently, assessment practices that follow a socio-cultural perspective are framed to map the transformation of understanding and not some end point. Rogoff (1998) explains this idea within the field of research:

> What is key is transformation in the process of participation in community activities, not acquisition of competences defined independently of the socio-cultural activities in which people participate. (Rogoff, 1998: 691)

Rogoff (1998) articulates this perspective further through her thoughtful questioning of how this transformation can be adequately mapped:

> How do people participate in socio-cultural activity and how does their participation change from being relatively peripheral participants (cf. Lave and Wenger, 1991), observing and carrying out secondary roles, to assuming various responsible roles in the management or transformation of such activities? (Rogoff, 1998: 695)

Yet very little research has been undertaken to investigate and record the benefits of a socio-cultural approach to the assessment of young children in early childhood education. The study reported below is an attempt to do so.

# The study

The study sought to determine whether early childhood teachers can document how young children participate in socio-cultural activity and how their participation may change from being relatively peripheral participants to assuming responsible roles in the management or transformation of such activities. Teacher observations framed from a socio-cultural perspective (Rogoff, 1998) were gathered over twelve months alongside of the diary records which documented the teachers' transition from a traditional to a socio-cultural approach. Over 200 child observations were recorded by the staff.

A total of 25 diary entries were made between February and November. Six staff members were involved in the study. Only the pre-school teacher kept a diary. Five of the six staff were all student teachers in their third year of their Bachelor of Early Childhood Education. The Centre was a University Child Care Centre with 30 children between the ages of 2.5 years and 5.4 years.

The analysis of the diary entries was undertaken using Rogoff's (1998) three planes of analysis. Rogoff (1998) has identified these lenses at three planes, closely mirroring the Vygotskian idea of inter-psychological and intra-psychological functioning (see Figures 10.2 to 10.4):

> Using personal interpersonal and community/institutional planes of analysis involves focusing on one plane, but still using background information from the other planes, as if with different lenses. (Rogoff, 1998: 688)

In Figure 10.2, the traditional focus on the individual in research contexts is shown. In this study, the individual perspective present in the diary entries was examined for patterns or changes over time.

In Figure 10.3, the lens is on the interaction between the individual, the teacher and other children. The diary entries were examined for evidence of comments on interactions between teacher and child, and teacher and teacher. The social context was featured.

Finally, in Figure 10.4, we note that the focus is on the whole cultural or institutional context. This is symbolically represented by the artifacts being used in the context. However, the discourse of schooling, the codes of behaviour and ways of learning are all part of this third lens. For instance, the taken-for-granted practices of the staff and the centre, as well as the policies, are all considered when the third lens is applied to the context. The habits or habitus (see Bourdieu on habitas, discussed in Grenfell et al., 1998) assumed as normal practice are critically examined in order to provide a broader and richer analysis of the early childhood context.

What is interesting about this approach to assessment is that the adult's participation in the lived teaching-learning, and the cultural tools that are being used, are considered as part of the assessment. The diary entries were analysed for references to documentation, charts, techniques for gathering data and other cultural or institutional tools.

# The findings – case study

A predominant theme that emerged over the course of the journal entries was an expression of discomfort in the way that the socio-cultural observations were to be recorded and

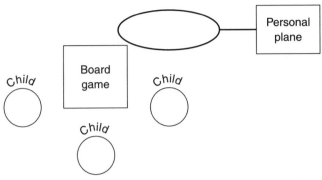

**Figure 10.2   Using a personal plane of analysis (Rogoff, 1998: 688)**

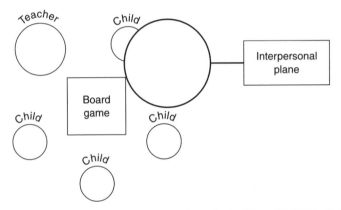

**Figure 10.3   Using an interpersonal plane of analysis (Rogoff, 1998: 688)**

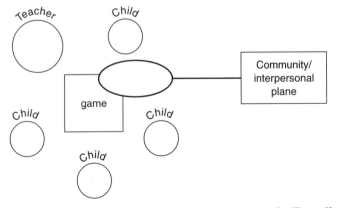

**Figure 10.4   Using a community/institutional plane of analysis (Rogoff, 1998: 688)**

collected. Staff at the centre had previously assessed children by collecting observational data based on a developmental approach. Over several years, the technology for collecting these observations had varied and the success of different methods had been questioned. At the outset of the research it was decided to collect observations, still based on a developmental approach, on small sticky Post-it labels and to then affix these to an observation chart. These would in turn be transferred to an observation folder. When the decision was made to attempt a socio-cultural approach to assessment it was decided to continue with the sticky label method and, in addition, staff were asked to place their observations on a new 'Interactions Chart' that would indicate and map whether interactions were *modelled, shared* or *independent.*

Staff were reluctant to use the new interactions chart. What did the terms *modelled, shared* and *independent* mean? How could observations, still firmly entrenched in a traditional individualistic developmental approach, fit with this continuum? Two charts remained in the staff room: the original observation chart and the new Interactions chart. It soon became obvious that staff were having difficulties using the Interactions chart. A note in the research diary recorded:

> We are observing children and their socio-cultural interactions constantly and yet we seem to be reluctant? resistant? to recording them. Why? Is it the time and effort involved or the fact that it's difficult to capture in words some of the rather intangible things that we see or are part of? ... difficult to record? (7 June 2001)

There is a feeling of not really knowing or understanding what is meant by the term 'socio-cultural'. Could a socio-cultural interaction be the obvious event that is witnessed or is it a rather more intangible event demanding a greater depth of understanding than is otherwise required? Or is it the fact that recording an interaction requires more time and effort than just recording a brief 'objective' observation of what has happened? Early childhood educators have long held the belief that observations are to be made from an objective 'distance' that did not include themselves or their subjective interpretations of what they were witnessing. Again a research diary entry records the dilemma:

> Recording interactions is problematic because they are often done after the event/learning experience interaction and can become vague post-event recollections. (18 June 2001)

If we are to record an interaction that we are involved in, or one that involves a group of children, how are we to do this and still remain true to the interaction itself? Is accuracy in documentation important or is the essence of the interaction recorded at a later time enough to capture the true meaning of what has happened? How can educators collect meaningful data that are not just a 'vague post-event recollection'? Using electronic technology could offer solutions to this dilemma but the presence of a video camera or an audio recording device may also impact on the dynamics of the interaction and also on the element of spontaneity. If we are committed to recording these interactional observations using the current technology (sticky labels and interaction charts), how will this be achieved?

> One of the student teachers said to me today that she was happy to do observations but really didn't know what to record. Later she informed me that she had recorded an observation of a child writing [see Figure 10.5] (21 July 2001)

Bronte: attempted to write name: Wrote B R O – then asked how to do the E. (R) handed – good pencil grip. Using invented letter forms to write her name. (21 July 2001).

**Figure 10.5    Domains-based observation**

Why was she comfortable recording this observation? Was it because she had observed a child involved in an activity that was valued and easily identified? How else could this have been recorded? What other information would have informed this observation?

As I look on this journal I realize that I have asked these same questions many times. Perhaps the answer lies in the fact that we need to record more about each day –What happened? What did children say and do? What did I say and do? (7 August 2001)

This journal entry typifies the general concerns expressed by staff with regard to any observation that is made and then recorded. How do you determine just what to record? Why do we choose to record some things while choosing not to record others? Our observations are always subjective and reflect those things that we value. Dahlberg argued: 'When we document we are co-constructors of children's lives, and we also embody our implied thoughts of what we think are valuable actions in a pedagogical practice' (Dahlberg et al., 1999: 147). For instance, the observation recorded in Figure 10.6, taken much later in the project, documents evidence of staff and children co-constructing meaning. It highlights how difficult it is to isolate learning simply to an individual.

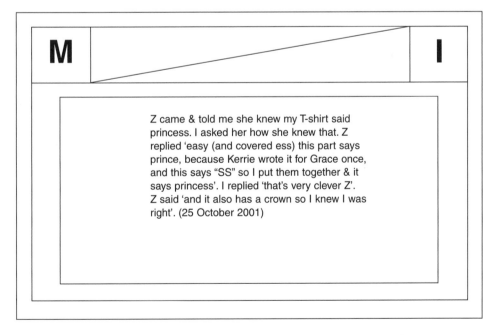

**Figure 10.6    Socio-cultural observation (M: modelled; I: independent)**

Observations recorded in Figures 10.5 and 10.6 reflect the value that is placed on early literacy attempts at the centre. The first example is deeply influenced by a developmental approach to assessment. The observer makes no reference to any scaffolding that may have been offered to the child. The child is seen to be acting in isolation. The information provided is important but lacks a socio-cultural context. Yet in the second observation staff begin to document the socio-cultural context in which literacy understanding is being co-constructed between teachers and children.

In an attempt to better understand the socio-cultural context of an interaction, it was decided that more information needed to be recorded about each day's activities. This occurred within the context of the journal. The journal entries themselves provided a context for daily activities that added another dimension to the brief observations collected by staff members. However, this was problematic because the journal was only accessed by the pre-school teacher. A further problem was that the journal was not addressed on a daily basis. *Another busy day! Too busy to write lengthy observations'* (7 August 2001). Although acknowledging the importance of the journal and the contributions it could offer to a socio-cultural approach to assessment, it was obvious that anything that required lengthy observations was destined to be unsuccessful. Another way of recording observations that would provide this contextual information in a succinct, yet meaningful, way was needed.

> Noticed more observations on the daily Obs. Chart but no new observations on the Interactions Chart. Perhaps a different method of recording should be employed? Perhaps a sticker system to identify whether interactions are modeled/shared/independent would be useful? (8 August 2001)

At this point in the year, staff were recording more observations that contained socio-cultural information. The voice of the observer was occasionally heard and the interactions were more fully explored. However, there was still a tendency to place these on the observational chart rather than on the interactions chart. It was felt at this stage that perhaps another method of identifying whether an interaction was modelled, shared or independent could be employed. Perhaps a sticker or colour-coded system would be useful? Observations could then be moved from the chart to the observation folder with this piece of information intact. However, there was still the problem of identifying the degree of interaction. The staff still expressed a reluctance to use the terms *modelled, shared* or *independent* when describing an interaction.

> Recording daily in journal but not transferring this to Interactions Chart. Still not entirely sure how do this. (22 September 2001)
>
> This afternoon I attempted to place some of the observations on the Interactions Chart. The chart has many limitations. It doesn't really have enough breadth in the shared area. Some of the children are barely in this zone while others have reached far beyond this, only needing occasional support. How can this be illustrated so that it is meaningful? (23 September 2001)

Towards the end of September, a two-week unit of work was undertaken in the centre that had a distinct literacy theme. Work revolved around a book that had been written for this express purpose. The children had collaborated in some of the design elements of the book and they were exposed to all stages of its production. It was felt that this would be an ideal time to concentrate on the socio-cultural assessment project. Perhaps a concentrated effort to collect assessment data related to this one specific unit of work would reveal more about the possibilities of socio-cultural assessment and also expose a better way of recording the gathered assessment data.

Daily entries were made in the journal and these provided a great deal of contextual detail about the activities that were taking place in the centre. At the same time, brief observational notes were collected on a small group of children with the intention of placing these on the interactions chart. At the conclusion of the two-week period, these collected observations were placed on the original interactions chart and it was at this time that it became obvious that the chart had many limitations that had not been previously noted.

Most significant of these was the fact the most interactions fell in the area identified as *shared interaction* and yet identifying an interaction as *shared* did not fully allow an expression of the degree of participation being observed. Rogoff (1998) talks about specialised as well as asymmetrical roles in collaboration:

> Collaboration also includes interactions in which participants' roles are complementary or with some leading and others following, supporting or actively observing. Under varying circumstances, different partners may be more responsible for initiating and managing shared endeavours. (Rogoff, 1998: 723)

It was felt that these shared interactions were of great significance because they often contained evidence of scaffolded assistance. An understanding of 'scaffolding' as being 'qualitatively different from "help" in that it is aimed at supporting students to tackle *future* tasks in new contexts' was important.

We were attempting to map interactions and wanted to see if it was possible to record movement from one designated area to another. Using the terms *modelled, shared* and *independent* increasingly appeared to be too simplistic as there seemed to be a wide range of possibilities for interactions within the *'shared'* zone. For example, a child's shared behaviour recorded on one day may influence that witnessed on a subsequent occasion that may still fall within the *'shared'* zone. What may change is the child's degree of participation in the interaction or the degree of scaffolding required to support the child. This movement from an area of significant support to an area of less support could not be demonstrated. This was also true of the differences to be seen in a group of children participating in a shared activity. In other words, children could take on different roles in a shared interaction or need differing degrees of scaffolding to reach a desired endpoint but this could not be easily shown. If we were to adopt Rogff's definition of learning and development as *'transformation in participation* in socio-cultural activity' (Rogoff, 1998: 687), then we needed some way to document these dynamic processes and this included movement within the area of *shared* interaction.

Although there was frustration caused by the constraints imposed by the interactions chart there was a sense that a minor change to the current method of recording interactions could overcome these shortcomings. The value of socio-cultural assessment had become more evident and it was felt that recording these interactions, including the scaffolding efforts of the more capable other *and* any movement that may occur within the shared zone, was valuable. Information gathered not only indicated what was said or done in the interaction that could be used to inform future action, but the information also suggested

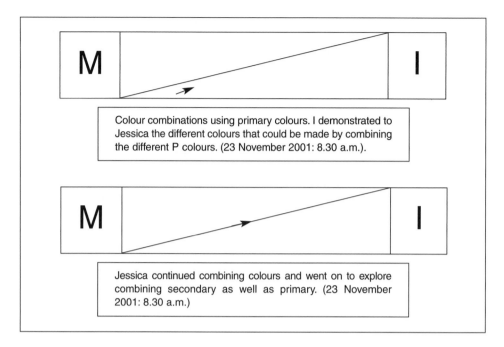

**Figure 10.7   Mediated assessment (two linked observations – M: modelled; I: independent)**

a competence in the scaffolded child that may not have been otherwise appreciated. Figure 10.7 provides an example which demonstrates one way that the staff attempted to record the movement (note the arrows) within a zone alongside of the adult input.

Although the majority of the observations made of children tended to focus on individual children, it was possible to see some examples early in the study, as shown in Figure 10.6, of interactions between children and staff being documented. Towards the end of the study period, observations were made and work samples gathered, along with their corresponding assessment, and it was evident that the teachers had begun to demonstrate a 'collective' mediated orientation, as shown in Figure 10.8.

It should be noted that moving from an individualistic orientation to a collective perspective was one of the difficult aspects of the teachers' work during the study. Although the staff felt comfortable noting informally what collectively was taking place, they found it much more difficult to document formally 'collective activity' – preferring to focus more on what an individual was doing and gaining from the experience. However, as they gathered more evidence of learning through work samples and observations of what was taking place as groups of children worked together, they found at these times it was very difficult to 'pull the children apart' in order to make individual assessments. In fact, by focusing their assessment on the performance of an individual they found that their judgments were no longer accurate – since what the child could do alone would be very different to what the child could do when working with more capable peers or with adult support or mediation (depending upon the context). Figure 10.8 demonstrates the collective nature of the children's learning. An assessment of each child that was independent of the teacher or the other children would render the assessment inappropriate for this approach. The complexity

Once the children were settled in the writing centre (after hearing a story about the Aussie Postie) they began to work on the problem of writing the word 'motorbike'. The children worked together to identify the main phonemes and sounded out and wrote the letters MTOBIC. I suggested that they attempt to write 'postie' and once again the children worked together to write POSD. I asked the children to decide what they should write next and the suggestion was made to attempt the word 'mailbox'.

In the writing sample (not included here) it can be seen that while two children (C, G) wrote MALBC, the other (F) sounded out and wrote the letters LBC to represent the word, letterbox. The children's work was further embellished with their own names and other known names, such as 'Mama', 'Silvia' and 'Zoe'. Drawings of mailboxes completed these impressive pieces of group work (not included here).

E had not participated in the initial discussion that had so engaged the first three children but she was interested in the writing activity in which they were presently occupied. While C, G and F worked on a joint project, E was on the periphery. E's work (not shown here) shows a collection of known and invented letters. While there is evidence to show that she is working at a different level to that demonstrated by the others, she can still be seen to be acting in collaboration with them. E's peripheral participation was not passive. Everything she observed was preparing her for future participation in related enterprises.

**Figure 10.8   Collective mediated assessment (writing postbox/mailbox)**

arises in documenting collective mediated assessment. In much the same way as teachers identify the 'teachable moment', the staff needed to determine the 'assessable moment' (Fleer, 2003) in order to document and assess children's learning collectively.

# Conclusion

Over the twelve months, the staff at the centre moved from being relatively peripheral participants of socio-cultural assessment through to assuming responsibility for documenting socio-cultural observations. In particular, the staff began to consider the whole socio-cultural context when they made their assessments. The voice of the teacher in the observations emerged over time, as demonstrated in Figure 10.6. The teachers had positioned themselves, rather than rendering themselves 'invisible', in the observations. They also began recording the scaffolding and other deliberate or intentional interactions in learning episodes, as demonstrated in Figure 10.7. Similarly, the teachers included records of reciprocity between the child and themselves, but also began to include peer interactions. Towards the end of the year, the observations were of collective mediated interaction, as in Figure 10.8. Teacher observations depicted interactions that were infused with meaning and contexts. The dynamics in thinking during the interactional sequences were recorded through the use of arrows and notes – thus mapping movement in cognition. Finally, observations of staff also identified and recorded evidence of teacher modelling. Prior to the commencement of the study, modelled interactions were never recorded in child-observations. However, as Vygotsky notes, assessment must record not only those cognitive processes of the child that are fully developed, but also those that are in a state of being developed at the time of assessment and that:

This development, according to Vygotsky, depends on a co-operative interaction between the child and the adult, who represents the culture and assists the child in acquiring the necessary symbolic tools of learning. (Kozulin, 1998: 69)

As such, what the adult does is a highly significant component of mapping children's cognitive competence. Yet this is rarely done in observations made by most early childhood teachers. The findings of this study indicate that when staff take a socio-cultural approach to assessment, they record their intentional interactions, their modelling and use of cultural tools, and child–teacher and child–child (depicted as reciprocity) interactions in their observational notes. In the process of moving from an individualistic orientation to a socio-cultural perspective, assessment practices shift from being an analysis of observations which 'carve up the individual child' into domains of competence, such as physical, social and cognitive attainments, to viewing assessment practice as part of a mediated process residing within the collective rather than the individual. This orientation to assessment represents a significant paradigm shift in early childhood practice. In taking a socio-cultural approach to assessment, early childhood educators will be able to record broader, richer and culturally embedded data on the groups of children they interact with each day in their centres. This will allow for more meaningful assessments to be made about learning and teaching. Teachers will find the 'assessable moments' (Fleer, 2003) when the majority of observations should take place.

But it should be noted that the transformation in participation by the staff detailed in this chapter took place over a twelve-month period. The time needed for staff to move from an individualistic approach to a socio-cultural approach was extensive. It demonstrates the challenge that lies ahead for early childhood professionals, as we reflect upon and begin to move away from decades of training in observational techniques and related individualistic and reductionist assessment practices.

# References

Berk, L. and Winsler, A. (1995) *Scaffolding Children's Learning: Vygotsky and Early Childhood Education.* Washington, DC: National Association for the Education of Young Children.

Carr, M. (1998a) *Assessing Children's Experiences in Early Childhood: Final Report to the Ministry of Education. Part One.* Wellington: Research Division, Ministry of Education.

Carr, M. (1998b) *Project for Assessing Children's Experiences: Final Report to the Ministry of Education. Part Two: Five Case Studies.* Hamilton: University of Waikato.

Carr, M. (2001a) *Assessment in Early Childhood Settings: Learning Stories.* London: Paul Chapman.

Carr, M. (2001b) 'Let me count the ways. Analysing the relationship between the learner and everyday technology in early childhood', *Research in Science Education,* 31: 29–47.

Cullen, J. (1994) 'Why retain a development focus in early education?', in E. Mellor and K. Coombe (eds), *Issues in Early in Childhood Services: Australian Perspectives.* Dubuque, IA: Wm C. Brown, pp. 53–64.

Cullen, J. (1996) 'The challenge of *Te Whāriki* for future development in early childhood education', *Delta,* 48(1): 113–25.

Dahlberg, G., Moss, P. and Pence, A. (1999) *Beyond Quality in Early Childhood Education and Care: Postmodern Perspectives.* London: Falmer Press.

Davydov, V. V. and Zinchenko. V. P. (1993) 'Vygotsky's contribution to the development of psychology', in H. Daniels (ed.), *Charting the Agenda: Educational Activity after Vygotsky*. London: Routledge, pp. 93–106.

Fleer, M. (1992) 'From Piaget to Vygotsky: moving into a new era of early childhood education', in B. Lambert (ed.), *The Changing Face of Early Childhood*. Canberra: Australian Early Childhood Association, pp. 134–49.

Fleer, M. (2002) 'Sociocultural assessment in early years education – myth or reality?', *International Journal of Early Years Education,* 10(2): 105–20.

Fleer, M. (2003) '"The assessable moment": a sociocultural perspective on assessing young children', unpublished paper, Monash University.

Grenfell, M. and James, D. with Hodkinson, P., Reay, D. and Robbins, D. (1998) *Bourdieu and Education: Acts of Practical Theory*. London: Falmer Press.

Kozulin, A. (1998) *Psychological Tools: A Sociological Approach to Education*. Cambridge, MA: Harvard University Press.

Lave, J. and Wenger, E. (1991) *Situated Learning: Legitimate Peripheral Participation*. Cambridge: Cambridge University Press.

Losardo, A. and Notari-Syverson, A. (2001) *Alternative Approaches to Assessing Young Children*. Baltimore, MD: Paul H. Brookes.

Lunt, I. (1993) 'The practice of assessment', in H. Daniels (ed.), *Charting the Agenda: Educational Activity after Vygotsky*. London: Routledge.

MacNaughton, G. (1995) 'A post-structuralist analysis of learning in early childhood setting', in M. Fleer (ed.), *DAPcentrism: Challenging Developmentally Appropriate Practice*. Canberra: Australian Early Childhood Association, pp. 35–54.

Rogoff, B. (1998) 'Cognition as a collaborative process', in D. Kuhn and R. S. Siegler (eds), *Handbook of Child Psychology, Vol. 2*, 5th edn. New York: John Wiley, pp. 679–744.

Smith, A. B. (1993) 'Early childhood educare: seeking a theoretical framework in Vygotsky's work', *International Journal of Early Years Education,* 1(1): 47–61.

Smith, A. B. (1996) 'The early childhood curriculum from a sociocultural perspective', *Early Child Development and Care,* 115: 51–64.

Wenger, E. (1998) *Communities of Practice: Learning, Meaning and Identity*. Cambridge: Cambridge University Press.

Wertsch, J. V. (1985) *Vygotsky and the Social Formation of Mind*. Cambridge, MA: Harvard University Press.

# 11

# Learning to be Engineers: How Engineer Identity Embodied Expertise, Gender, and Power

*Karen L. Tonso*

As had become common for this senior engineering design team, Pam arrived with work in progress, but no one else had anything to share. Almost immediately, Carson began to grill her about what she had done, calling himself the devil's advocate; after months of this, she became irritated and asked him where his work was. Other team members lowered their heads and studied something—anything—on the table, but soon began to talk about how they spent the weekend, topics they expected on an upcoming test, or other course-work completed instead of work promised to the team. Pam turned to Samuel to go over key chemical engineering concepts and equations that fell outside Carson's mechanical engineering expertise. When their faculty advisor arrived, Pete—who never participated in technical discussion or paid them much attention—took it upon himself to be the team's voice, to present Pam's work as his own, to miscast Samuel as someone not committed to teamwork, and on one occasion to announce that he had "found the problem" that had stymied the team, something he had only moments before been unable to describe to team-mates, and in other ways gave the appearance that he was central to the team's everyday engineering work and an accomplished engineer, the opposite impression he created during teamwork. Student engineers "recognized" these students' behaviors—and a wide range of other ways to be engineers—via an array of engineer-identity terms, referring to Pete as a brown-noser or sometimes as anal, to Carson as a hard-core over-achiever, and thinking of Samuel as a nerd. Yet, they had no term for Pam, though someone mentioned she was a "unique individual," clearly marking her as someone not *recognizable* as an engineer on this campus. Evidently, since none of the students on freshman teams used or could explain these terms, but seniors gave long lists of terms and spoke at length about them during interviews, student engineers learned these ways to be an engineer on campus as a routine part of their engineering education. But how did this occur and what did student engineers' sense of the organization of these terms into engineer-identity categories [imply] about the campus culture's underpinnings? And, ultimately, did campus-preferred ways of life become embodied in individual students, and if so, how were these embodiments expressed in face-to-face, everyday social interactions on campus; and simultaneously, did

From: Roth, W.F. & Tobin, K. (eds.) *Science, Learning, Identity: Sociocultural and Cultural-Historical Perspectives*. (Rotterdam, Netherlands: Sense Publishers, 2007). Reproduced by kind permission of the publisher.

the actions and interactions of individuals construct everyday life on campus? Articulating answers to these questions is the central purpose of this chapter.

The approach taken here aligns with that of critical cultural anthropology, which gives pride of place to the knowledge, beliefs, and productions of local communities, while it looks carefully at the ways relations of power play out within communities. [...] And, though such communities have historical persistence and seeming stability, they are by no means static but are instead capable of generating themselves into the future in ways that are sensible to their pasts. However, though local, such communities are not isolable from larger societal forces, but are contexts where ideologies of power and prestige seep in and become taken for granted, even as they are taken up in context- or community-dependent ways. Thus, rather than beginning—as many researchers grounded in psychological perspectives seem to do—by asking "What do people make of themselves?," the research reported here asks "What do cultures, communities, and institutions make of people?," and goes on to examine identity productions as a complex process of personas shaped in context, as simultaneously persons shape context. Ultimately, the results here will not suggest absolutes applicable to all sites of engineering education practice, but will instead strive to describe complex, contextual, identity-development processes at play on this campus and illustrate how these are linked not only to campus culture, but also how campus culture took up societal frames of reference (or ideologies) for academic science expertise and gender status. Thus, in time, this chapter will suggest the importance of studying power relations as a way to follow how societal ideologies are taken up in learning cultures, and then how learning cultures reach into face-to-face interactions among individuals, arguing that community-developed identity linked culture to person, that personas embodied relations of power, and persons acting in context through cultural identity produced and reproduced community.

# Public engineering school

Public Engineering School is a well-recognized, stand-alone campus devoted to educating engineers in the U.S. mid-continent. At the time of the study in the early to mid-1990s, women comprised 20–25 percent of 2,300 undergraduates and 11 percent of faculty, representations higher than national levels. Its commitment to reform in engineering education and to women's full inclusion, and its full support of my research project, made it an attractive site.

Reform at PES came primarily in one curricular change. In the 1980s, PES began offering explicit instruction in engineering design—a set of courses intended to mimic real-world engineering work. Students took one-semester courses at the first- and second-year levels, and then completed a one- or two-semester capstone design course as seniors. Design courses organized students into teams who completed an everyday project for industry or government clients, and along the way presented (individual and team) oral and written reports for feedback and grades from faculty. At the time of the research in the early to mid-1990s, design teamwork was touted as almost a panacea for changing women's negative experiences in engineering education (e.g., Felder et al., 1995). Teams seemed well suited as a palliative because of women's perceived organization, writing, and interaction strengths, and because of women's perceived need for more hands-on activities (McIlwee & Robinson, 1992). Earlier research also suggested that peer groups played a key role in women's loss of motivation to study challenging mathematics and science fields, but I was skeptical of an additional finding that classrooms played a less central role

(Holland & Eisenhart, 1990). And, much of this research failed to carefully examine men's experiences, which gave the impression that there was a uniformity of experience, and that studying "gender" meant studying women (here Seymour and Hewitt [1997] constitute a notable exception). Thus, student design teamwork at PES provided an entrée to peer group culture that was connected to curricular goals, but was somewhat out of sight of faculty members. Such a study would require carefully organizing the research project to study interactions among student engineers directly, something not possible in earlier research.

The research method aligned with cultural anthropology ethnographic practices: join the community and become a trusted person there; collect field notes grounded in one's participation—paying attention to who is present, what they say, do, and produce; talk to insiders about what is going on and what events mean to them. [...]

Ultimately, in this large-scale cultural study, engineer identity became a central pivot through which societal norms reached into campus culture, and campus culture moved into teamwork via individuals who learned to *embody* engineering practices. To understand engineer identity at PES requires an appreciation of cultural frames of reference for being recognized as an engineer on campus, and an awareness of how student engineers learned and performed engineer selves, as well as how engineer identities and performances of engineer selves interacted to produce belonging (or not) on campus, which here reinforced campus culture.

## Cultural frames of reference for identity

Student engineers used an array of terms to refer to one another as people thought of as engineers on campus. When asked explicitly "what are all the terms you use to refer to one another as engineers here?," seniors usually began with "Well, we're all nerds here." But, they went on to not only list a large set of terms, but also to describe each term in detail, especially answering the question "How would I [the researcher] know a [kind of engineer] if one were on our team?" First-year students, by comparison, gave many fewer terms and only limited explanations of them. At a second interview, as part of the larger ethnographic project, students returned to the issue of engineer identity to sort the 36 most frequently occurring terms into categories and explain their sorting.

Students' understandings of the organization of terms provided a look inside campus culture, the way the world of appropriate engineer-identity was "imagined" or "supposed" to be. The engineer-identity terrain made apparent not only the ways they thought of engineer types, but also which ideologies from the wider society were taken up by campus culture. First, terms coalesced around three central identity categories: Nerds, Greeks, and Academic-Achievers (Figure 11.1). Students thought of Greeks (Social-Achievers) and Academic-Achievers as comprising a super-category, Over-Achievers, signaling the prominence of those who affiliated here, and conversely the lower status of Nerds. Though detailed elsewhere (Tonso, 2006), space limitations in this chapter preclude descriptions of these terms, but suffice it to say that in students' minds these were living, breathing personas that they could identify based on how a person behaved. Each of the categories contained desirable and undesirable terms, or in the words of student engineers, "People who are normal and people who go too far." Undesirable identities included those willing to exploit others, cheat, and otherwise cut corners to maintain their standing on campus shown up and to the right among Academic-Achievers: hard-core over-achievers, anal, curve-breaker, and brown-noser. Those who party too much for success in an engineering

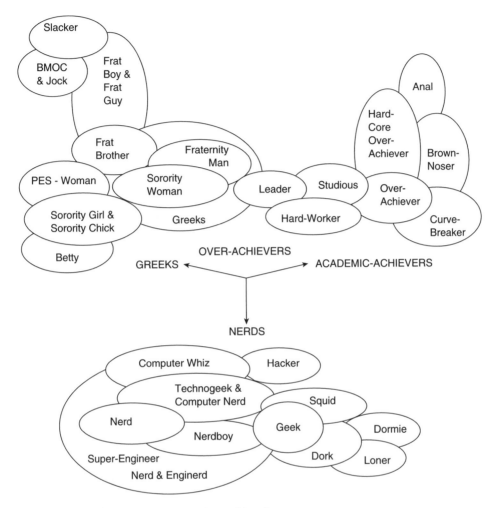

**Figure 11.1   Organization of engineer-identity terms**

education exist up and to the left for men among Greeks—BMOC (big man on campus), jocks, frat boy, frat guy, and slacker—and down and to the left for women among Greeks—PES-woman, sorority girl, sorority chick, and betty. Likewise, among Nerds, up and to the right are those whose thoroughly asocial behaviors set them apart from other Nerds: hacker, squid, geek, dork, dormie, and loner.

Second, the two strata among engineer identities—Over-Achievers and Nerds—practiced different forms of engineering expertise. Over-Achievers practiced the form of engineering given prominence on campus, answering rapid-fire, one-right-answer, decontextualized, "textbook" problems represented in mathematical equations, using "givens" to seek an unknown quantity. Good grades depended on not only completing long homework assignments comprised almost entirely of these kinds of items, but also on taking hour exams throughout the semester and a comprehensive final exam at the end of the term with more of these items. Though it was common to study with other students, some students openly cheated by either sharing homework problems that each had completed, or copying outright from another student without doing any of the items. Students thought this was more common among Greeks than others. And, Greeks had another advantage—the storied "fraternity files." Here, fraternity members accumulated exams from every course, taught by every professor and, to study for an exam, some students only learned the solutions to the narrow set of items used on exams.

Nerds, on the other hand, developed a set of engineering expertise more akin to design engineering. Thus, in one of the more lopsided logics of this campus, Nerd students who understood both the mathematical and scientific principles from their classes *and* could put these ideas to use in specific situations for their clients (the kind of expertise industry urges engineering schools to develop in graduates) did not come to the attention of campus authorities and remained below the prestige "radar" on campus. Thus, in a campus culture that organized the evaluation of student work to focus on the easier-to-assess, one-right-answer solutions of textbook problems, instead of developing careful ways to assess the more difficult to evaluate—but genuine—engineering products associated with design classes, Over-Achievers gained prestige and status on campus and rose above Nerds. While these two forms of engineering expertise are widely acknowledged (e.g., Bucciarelli, 1994) and the former is criticized as inadequate for preparing engineers for industry careers (Dutson, Todd, Magleby, & Sorenson, 1997), rarely is the structure of engineering education directly implicated. But, clearly, campus culture—especially taken for granted sets of ideas about the "right" way to teach engineering, how to assess students' work, and what knowledge counts—should be under scrutiny.

Third, the engineer-identity terrain encoded gender—different forms of masculinity and femininity made salient on campus. Over-Achiever masculinities valorized men who took charge (often described with militaristic code-phrases like "divide and conquer," and "forming, storming, and norming"), took advantage of others, and made a show of themselves through public performances that depended on the work of others and bragging about high-grade points and campus standing. Nerds took great care not to reveal any of these markers of over-achievement, treated their colleagues with respect, and practiced egalitarian relations. This "nice-guy" form of masculinity was subordinate to the domineering man of went-too-far Over-Achievers. Some forms of masculinity, however, could not be expressed on campus. For instance, many students told me that the campus was aggressively homophobic, further suggesting that campus culture elevated a prototypic masculinity associated with dominance over others, especially eschewing becoming "feminized." Categories also demonstrated the ascendance of masculine ways of life over feminine in campus culture. Heightened concern about women's intrusion into men's ways of life came from two portions of the engineer-identity terrain. Went-too-far Greeks talked about women in disparaging ways, especially referring to women as sex objects and detailing their physical deficiencies when compared to some men's "ideal" woman. Went-too-far Academic-Achievers described gender relations using expansive stories about reverse discrimination. Respectable Over-Achievers and Nerds did not relate to their women colleagues or talk about them in these ways, but treated them with respect, incorporated women's ideas in the team's work, and gave them credit for their contributions.

But, and this is more telling, terms for women were absent among students known for their engineering work (among Nerds and Academic-Achievers), so woman-terms existed only among students known for their social prowess, only one of which—sorority woman—was a desirable engineer identity (for some, but hardly for all women who study engineering). Sorority woman encoded a femininity associated with social service, being men's normatively heterosexual partners at social events, and being "good" girls. Three other terms—sorority chick, sorority girl, and betty—marked women who only partied on campus and were thought of as promiscuous, an unacceptable sort of femininity, not potential engineers. And the final term—PES-woman (where PES stands in for the campus nickname) encoded the rest of women as "other": "big, easy sluts, who go out too much and flunk out of school, so the women who stay here are ugly." Ultimately, in the student engineer imagination or suppositions about the kinds of people recognizable as engineers, PES-woman constrained the possibility of femininity becoming attached to engineering expertise on campus, and women known for doing engineering that put classroom ideas to work in design projects seemed to fit in only to the extent they eschewed all vestiges of femininity; that is, became indistinguishable from men, or conversely invisible *as* women.

Thus, student engineers used a complicated *cultural* set of terms and orderings to talk about engineer identity and to interpret events and people on campus, that is, to make sense of daily life. Engineer identities were framed by campus cultures having taken up the pre-eminence of academic-science (mathematized abstractions of the real world) over more mundane approaches typical of work in an engineering career and gender status—some forms of men (masculinities) above others, and some forms of women ahead of others (femininities), and within each strata (Over-Achievers or Nerds), men ahead of women. When these ideologies intersected, Over-Achiever and Greek men had more power on campus, sorority women and Nerd men had intermediate amounts, and women not recognizable among, or identifying with, sorority women had the least. These orderings came not from a vacuum but from the way campus practices outside the reach of students framed *becoming an engineer*—especially decisions made about organizing and delivering the curriculum, and about distributing awards and recognition for "excellence." By calling the tune for the piper to which all students danced, campus organizational practices connected a certain kind of domineering masculinity to an academic-science form of engineering expertise and these practitioners ascended.

Student engineers spoke *as if* these terms referred to living, breathing persons, in effect acting as if these crystallized engineer identities, albeit with considerably more variety and complexity than captured in the term "engineer," or expected by some researchers. For instance, in the case of situated learning theorists, a leading identity is conjectured, such as a tailor, and this identity is seen as motivating people to learn the practices of tailoring (Lave & Wenger, 1991). But, identity trajectories are spoken of as if they are somehow linear and lead to the same end result for everyone who can perform the tasks required of tailors. Varieties of tailors, for instance, are not envisioned. Engineer identity variety suggests that science, technology, engineering, and mathematics educational tracks, especially at the post-secondary level, are considerably more complex than a linear trajectory can accommodate. Likewise, research about professional identity in post-secondary education programs (Nespor, 1994) suggests curricular structures—the ordering of coursework, the kinds of choices given to students about programs of study, and expectations about appropriate social behaviors to fit into their field—play a key role in producing among graduates a professional identity. But, Nespor, like Lave and Wenger, took for granted that "physicist" or "manager" held the same meaning across graduates, and that being a graduate conferred on all graduates the same kinds of power and standing in their respective fields. Clearly for engineer identity, this was not the case, further suggesting that curricular structures, while they are important to framing the production of engineer identities, may not be sufficient to explain how professional identities operate in day-to-day campus life.

That a set of cultural expectations about acceptable ways to belong as an engineer on campus exists is all good and fine, but several questions about them require answers to understand how they operate. In particular, how did student engineers learn engineer identities, how did they deploy them, and to what extent did the terms capture the performances of engineer selves given by student engineers?

## Learning and performing engineer selves

As in other communities where members learn tacit cultural knowledge, student engineers learned engineer identities by participating in a community where others used the terms and implied their taken-for-granted meanings. For instance, one of the students explained that *enginerds* turn ordinary conversation into an engineering analysis, engaging a kind of engineering wordplay. This student told of his hearing the term during a conversation he had with his older brother, a practicing engineer and alumnus of PES, and went on to recall another instance of its use:

> We're talking about gum right, and my sister-in-law said something about [him, that] he chews his gum in about five minutes. And then we started talking about half-life and then we were talking about when half the flavor is gone from the gum, natural log of two over tau, [something like the half-life formula]. And we were watching baseball one day, me and my roommate, and I said that [the pitcher's] ERA is pi over two [about 1.57]. We just do it to be funny. We know we're all nerds. We might as well not worry about it.

Thus, the term "enginerd" named a certain kind of behavior that he and his brother engaged in, and then was used to mark his banter with his roommate. People who exhibited this kind of behavior most of the time came to be thought of as enginerds. But, this form of engineering wordplay also connoted that "we're all nerds"—we belong here and share something that makes us a community. Thus, deploying the terms, and being marked with one of them, meant that a student engineer belonged.

Such terms liberally sprinkled the field notes, and student engineers used them to police the boundaries of acceptable and unacceptable behaviors. For example, a student entered a classroom and a colleague asked, "What did you get on the test?" He replied, "A 93." His teammate grunted, "Curve-breaker." Used pejoratively, curve-breakers did too well on tests, which made others look bad. As I stood in the library waiting for a team to gather, chatting with one of the students, we watched a student from our class, but on another team, roller blade down the asphalt pavement hesitantly, knee pads, elbow pads, wrist braces, and helmet in place. The student commented: "He's a dork, but he provides an endless source of amusement." Being termed a dork implied social deficiencies, here a lack of athletic skill. On another occasion, a student asked a teammate if he wanted to go for a beer after the team meeting. When the other student declined because he needed to study, the first commented, "Nerdboy," implying that he had just stepped over the line between studying enough and studying too much. I heard students cautioned not to be "such a geek," heard others referred to as slackers, jocks, BMOCs (self-important individuals associated with sports teams but not excelling athletically), and so on. Study too much and risk being characterized as a nerdboy. Do so in a part of the library where anyone looking in could see you and where no talking, eating, or drinking are allowed and become a squid. Toady up to a professor by asking questions after class or walking to the faculty member's office for a conversation and be chastised as a brown-noser. Those whose behaviors settled into these facile grooves came to be thought of as characterizing particular engineer identities. Thus, becoming a certain kind of engineer was a complex interplay of individual action and group recognition of those actions, and it took time to be "recognized" on campus as fitting a certain form.

In addition, student engineers used the terms to characterize other people's fit among the categories, as a way to explain another's actions or predict how they might act in a given situation. For instance, Pam expected her team's climate to be precisely what she experienced (glimpsed in the vignette opening this chapter), because she thought of Pete and Carson in terms of their being went-too-far Academic-Achievers who would either exploit the work of others, in Pete's case, or presume to double-check what others did to protect his standing on campus, in the case of Carson. When a student thought of a teammate as a went-too-far Academic-Achiever, for instance, the student expected that teammate to lobby for a certain interpretation of events and to push for the kind of teamwork that protected their place on campus. Pete's masterful lobbying for meeting as a team as little as possible, for his taking on the least time-intensive tasks, and for his giving public oral presentations (and being seen as a leader by faculty) "since Pam had done so much already," confirmed her interpretation of Pete's engineer identity and influenced how she interacted with him. Likewise, for Samuel on this team, even though his careful explanation of a major dilemma completing their project possessed a wealth of engineering expertise and should have guided the team's changing their approach, Pete's standing on campus gave him the cachet to promote waiting until the last minute before altering their course of action.

Samuel and Pam both told me that it would "not change anything" to confront Pete on this issue, and that Pete would probably retaliate if they did. Samuel had experienced Pete's not-so-subtle controlling behaviors when Pete diminished Samuel's reputation with their faculty advisor. For instance, as Pete, the faculty advisor, and others waited for their team meeting time to arrive, Samuel walked in as the carillon began to chime the hour. Pete commented, for their advisor's benefit, "Finally, here's Samuel, late as usual," miscasting Samuel as a slacker who was not committed to the team's work. These power-deploying events played out on a regular basis—Pete lording it over Pam and Samuel, and Carson grilling Pam about her calculations, but doing none of their own work in their assigned areas. Yet, none of the other team members confronted either Pete or Carson, even though they told me that both sets of behaviors were unacceptable engineering practices, justifying inaction by saying: "It wouldn't change anything." And, if (as I argue) Pete or Carson is the way he is because of campus culture, not because of any innate exploitation proclivity, then student engineers are probably right. Confronting Pete or Carson will not address the campus culture, which grew out of campus practices completely outside the reach of student engineers.

In addition to being used for deciding how to act in this field of power relations, the terms became filters for reducing complex human behaviors to understandable tropes on this campus and these neither provided accurate predictions about unseen behaviors nor captured all behaviors. For instance, Pete's being seen as a star in conventional classes, because of his stratospheric grade-point average, brought with it faculty's assumption that he was capable of figuring out the team's dilemma, though he offered no bona fide explanation of it, or any other technical aspects of the project, during their two semesters together. In fact, at the team's final presentation to their client, Pete's description of the condenser he purported to design was all but vacuous, which a company engineer subtly critiqued by asking, "Shell and tube? Cold water running through it?" In effect: "The most basic kind of condenser imaginable took you two semesters to develop?" Because their faculty advisor's expertise lay in electrical engineering, he missed the company engineer's skepticism of Pete's expertise. Pete's conventional-course successes, grounded in academic-science expertise, gave him "star" status, which carried with it the presumption of his being a key player on his team. It seemed that little he did to demonstrate his considerable ignorance during teamwork and oral presentations undercut his image. Ultimately, he had several lucrative job offers, suggesting that on-campus job-search practices further reinforced campus-preferred ways of life and undercut industry desires.

Likewise, aspects of students engineer behaviors that fell outside norms assumed by engineer-identity terms could not be noticed, and might have been penalized had they become known. For instance, though as a computer whiz Martin was considered the team's expert programmer, he insisted on receiving everyone's feedback on his ideas for software to monitor equipment. Here, Martin practiced a form of leadership that systematically took his teammates' contributions into account, but never took credit for another person's work or coerced them to do work—countering the "normal" kind of leader on campus. Some faculty would have found this unacceptable and berated Martin for needing "hand-holding." Also, Martin facilitated making the team a welcoming place where everyone was included via snack choices (keeping each person's favorite kind of potato chips at his apartment where we met), conversations about rock music, and engineering work. He enacted the role of social hostess, someone who made others comfortable and saw to their needs, a role associated with women in U.S. society. This, too, could not be "seen" by engineer identities, and some faculty and students would find his "acting like a girl" inappropriate. Finally, he actively kept his relatively high grade-point average quiet and gave no impression that he knew more than they did, though his expertise in mathematics and computer science engineering was quite deep. Ultimately, his counter-hegemonic leadership practices, his prototypically feminine social hostess activities, and his deep understanding of scientific and engineering principles learned in conventional classes and his ability to "see" the world in terms of these principles, never came to the attention of faculty and fell below campus prestige radar. Lacking markers of affiliation with campus culture's Over-Achiever ways of life, Martin was assumed to fit among Nerds, which meant he had less access to job-searches than student engineers like Carson and Pete, and fewer, and less attractive, job offers in spite of the industry's claim to prefer this kind of graduate.

But, women such as Pam and Marianne—whose skills trumped the engineering expertise demonstrated by Pete and Carson and who were every bit as capable as Nerd colleagues like Martin and Samuel, student engineers able not only to understand, but also to deploy, scientific and engineering principles learned in their conventional classes—had few on-campus interviews and no jobs at the time of graduation. They simply could not be recognized *as* engineers on campus and became invisible there. To be thought of as women, which both very clearly were, meant not being thought of as engineers. Why did their in-team demonstrations of engineering expertise fail to garner recognition as engineers? The best explanation seems to be that the cultural terrain for belonging—engineer-identity terms—filtered them out, much like a polarizing lens filters out glare from the surface of the water. For instance, Martin talked about whether a woman could be considered a Nerd—the sort of engineering self that Marianne performed:

> You don't think of women as that [fitting among Nerds], I guess. 'Cause, at least at this school, I think guys here so much appreciate that a girl chose to come to this campus that you're just like, "Great!" There are so many guys that you can say "this guy's a nerd," the pocket-protector-wearing guy. [But he couldn't say that of a "girl."]

Martin knew Marianne better than almost any other student engineer and was among the most open-minded student engineers when it came to overt thoughts about women's place on campus. Though he recognized, and deeply appreciated, her skill as an engineer, when asked about women being Nerds, he deployed taken-for-granted forms of belonging (cultural knowledge about campus engineer identities) and was unable to place her *as an engineer*: "You don't think of women as [Nerds]." Also, the contradiction between his acceptance of her as an excellent engineer and his inability to see her as fitting among Nerds failed to register; he could not see her as counter-evidence to the way campus culture was *supposed* to work. This is, of course, the dilemma of the engineer identity terms: as cultural knowledge, they are taken for granted, and are rarely open to reflection or conscious thought.

Thus, a campus status hierarchy emerged that was inversely proportional to design engineering expertise; those with the most power demonstrated the least expertise. Women with the best sets of engineering skills—those who could really *do* engineering, who made good use of their opportunities for hands-on experiences, who understood how to recontextualize decontextualixed scientific and engineering principles—were made invisible through campus cultural routines and this was encoded in the identity terrain. Men with extraordinary design engineering expertise, such as Samuel and Martin, never received their due, while watching men like Carson and Pete receive premier job offers and on-campus awards. This thoroughly illogical state of affairs suggests the power of historically salient campus cultural practices to constrain change. And, I argue that the production of a domineering masculinity seemed to be required to achieve at the highest levels on the arcane academic-science tasks that comprised the bulk of the curriculum, and that this concurrently minimized the impact that otherwise progressive men on the inside might have changing such a campus.

# Identity development

Though there is certainly an engineer stereotype in the US, it fell by the wayside when student engineers thought about being an engineer in PES campus culture. In fact, developing an engineer identity occurred through a complex cultural process for learning to be an engineer. As student engineers went about their everyday lives, they made decisions about how to act relative to affiliating with campus-preferred ways of life. In time, student engineers came to think of engineer types in terms of students being Greeks, Academic-Achievers, or Nerds, and to think of specific people as fitting among these engineer identities. Social control routines used the terms to police behaviors consistent with Over-Achievers versus Nerds, such as a Nerd-affiliate calling a colleague a curve-breaker for his high grade on a test when the average was much lower, or a fraternity man cautioning a frat brother not to be a geek. And through these interactions, student engineers actively modified their behaviors and came to be thought of as fitting into niches with which they *identified*.

Each student who ultimately persisted through graduation thought of her/himself as an engineer. Such statements as "we're all nerds" set students apart from the general population and conveyed being a member of the campus community, which student engineers expanded into the larger set of terms for engineer identity. Also, students performed themselves as engineers, whether through persistent shirking of teamwork duties and displaying affiliations with Over-Achiever ways of life, or through demonstrations of design engineering expertise. But, as the cases of the Nerds (Martin and Samuel) and women with design engineering expertise (Pam and Marianne) on the senior teams made clear, being recognized via engineer-identity terms played a critically important role in the extent to which one's development as an engineer counted in this campus culture. For Nerds, recognition meant being thought of as second class; for women design engineers, recognition *as an engineer* could not occur sans terms for women among Nerds. To have an engineer identity, it was not enough to *identify* as an engineer, but one must also *be identified* as an engineer. Thus, developing an engineer identity was a dialectic process through which members of the community *did* engineering: demonstrated (a) engineering expertise (of two dominant forms), (b) gender norms, and (c) positions of relative power, as simultaneously they made sense of their student engineer colleagues based on understandings about the kinds of engineers who fit on this campus. A woman might think she was an engineer, might demonstrate extraordinary design engineering expertise, but still not have an engineer identity because she failed to gain recognition—to be *identified*—as an engineer. This flies in the face of wisdom advocating increasing women's numbers in engineering by giving them opportunities to demonstrate their communication and interpersonal skills, and gain hands-on experiences, and deepens the call for cultural change in engineering education (Tonso, 1999).

Engineer identity developed over time through participating in the everyday activities of PES, and encoded ideologies of power aligned with the pre-eminence of academic science and of a domineering masculinity relative to others, as well as of men relative to women. Thus, campus life set the stage for contestations about what it meant to be a "real" engineer. Rather than engineer identity being a prototypic "mature practitioner," as envisioned by Lave and Wenger's situated learning theory, terms students used and their organization of them into three related categories provided ample evidence of contestations about what being a "real" engineer meant on this campus. Rather than students moving along a trajectory toward some shared notion of "engineer," students went about their everyday lives deciding whether to affiliate with Greek life or not, to devote themselves completely to their studies or take a more relaxed approach, to align with an academic-science form of engineering, or adopt the more expansive engineering form promoted in design classes. In other words, student engineers *differentiated* themselves from one another, but not in open-ended, anything-goes ways, but in culturally salient dimensions. And, for most students, some facets of student behaviors came to be thought of as indicating an engineer type, while some actions and behaviors fell outside institutionalized recognition processes. In time, students assumed these terms (and other things) as cultural fact and deployed them to make sense of how their world was *supposed* or *imagined* to work, even when there was considerable empirical evidence that the world did not in fact work in the way presumed.

Thus, at PES identity emerged from, or developed in response to, campus culture, "[t]his collective ability to take imaginary worlds seriously ... [which] is the magic that anthropologists have tried to capture in the concept of culture" (Holland et al., 1998, p. 280).

At PES in particular, categories of engineer identities served as a refined set of cultural pivots for belonging, and being *recognized* as an engineer seemed to trump either thinking of oneself as an engineer or performing an engineering self. Understanding how academic-science prestige and gender-status ideologies framed belonging proved central to understanding identity productions. Thus, because of the specificity of the knowledge base built into the intended curriculum and of the salience of becoming an engineer to each student engineer's future, one cannot help but wonder about the extent to which the identity-development process that occurred at PES might occur in K–12 settings.

In what we know of high school peer group productions from anthropological studies, a wide range of student identities can exist: Jocks who associated with their school's middle-class-affiliated "corporate" culture and Burnouts who opposed it (Eckert, 1989); jocks, vatos, cheerleaders, band fags, "good" girls, cow-boys, and others representing affiliations with ethnic-, gender-, social class-, and school-aligned strata (Foley, 1990); and working-class lads who resisted being made into middle-class ear'oles who accepted school practices (Willis, 1977). Among these are nerds, a term implying those thought of as out of step with the popular crowd—not as attractive, lacking social skills, and overly interested in mathematics, science, and technology courses, which are notoriously more difficult, time-consuming, and likely to interfere with high grade-point averages and with extracurricular social activities central to being thought of as a popular student. Thus, high schools, unlike PES, produced peer group cultures that encompassed a much wider range of knowledge and of attendant personas, communities not focused explicitly on producing scientist or engineer identities. But, without further study, one cannot rule out a scientist sub-culture being produced among students affiliated with scientific ways of life, and the PES research suggests studying to what extent high school science-learning settings begin the process of students learning academic-science prestige and gender status norms present in U.S. society and given prominence at PES.

When studied in K–12, students' scientist identity appears to emerge relative to a stereotypic "scientist," which the PES research suggests will be inadequate for understanding the next phase of identity development as a scientist. In particular, based on the way that student engineers understood "engineer" in considerably more complexity than an engineer stereotype presages, one wonders if emerging scientists in particular college science majors—student biologists, student chemists, student geologists, student physicists, and so on—eschew becoming a "scientist" of the sort presumed in a scientist stereotype and instead have discipline-specific (cultural) identities produced in similar ways to that at PES. Some evidence exists that this may be the case and that different scientific disciplines take up societal ideologies in different ways. For instance, a pecking order similar to student engineers exists among physicists, which sets particle physicists ahead of others (Traweek, 1988). Their way of life valorizes practices associated with removing oneself as far as possible from the mundane and a masculinity grounded in something akin to a competitive aesthete who aggressively goes after linear accelerator time for conducting tightly controlled experiments harnessing the world of atoms and particles (an academic-science form of practice), and ignores bodily functions like sleeping, eating, and socializing outside one's colleagues (a certain form of masculinity). However, among environmental biologists, a much more collaborative sort of scientist who is connected to the world emerges, even though being a bit too pie-in-the-sky can be pejoratively termed acting like a "flowery bonehead" (Eisenhart, 1996). Here, esteemed practices align with considerable stewardship of, not dominion over, the mundane world and being able to connect with the world, and not distance oneself from it, is valued (Eisenhart & Finkel, 1998). These are prototypically feminine ways of life practiced in out-of-the-lab sites, where experimental methods are possible only to a limited extent, practices clearly not aligned with academic science.

In the main, then, identity development at PES aligned most closely with a process approach peculiar to a cultural understanding of identity:

> [Identities] are social forms of organization, [bridging] public and intimate, that mediate this development of human agency ... But the cultural figurings of selves, identities, and figured worlds [cultures] that constitute the horizons of their meaning against which they operate, are collective products ... One can never inhabit a world without at least the figural presence of others, of a social history of person[as]. The space of authoring, of self-fashioning, remains a social and cultural space, no matter how intimately held it may become. And, it remains, more often than not, a contested space, a space of struggle. (Holland et al., 1998, p. 282)
>
> The social and political work of identification, in brief, reveals two closely held inter-related lessons. First, identities and the acts attributed to them are always forming and re-forming in relation to historically specific contexts ... The second lesson is that identities form on intimate and social landscapes through time. The distinction of particular acts as indexical of an identity, and the expansion of identities to include broader or different ranges of acts, depend upon the work of their allies and opponents. ... [And, this identity production work] cannot simply be dictated by the discourse, the cultural form itself. (pp. 284–285)

Having an engineer identity connoted being recognized through engineer-identity cultural frames of reference produced and re-produced in everyday life. Also, in spite of considerable evidence that the PES campus culture was quite obdurate, it could have been otherwise. Campus could have taken up different societal ideologies and given more credence to design-engineering expertise suited to industry's needs. But, the PES academic community promoted the way of life most familiar to its faculty (who were in an earlier time likely Academic-Achievers going on to graduate studies) and maintained engineering's standing relative to other academic sites of science practice. Taking a critical cultural anthropologic approach to understanding identity made clear that persons could be made to seem more than they are (as when Pete's standing as a star conveyed on him design-engineering expertise he clearly lacked) or less than they are (as exemplified by the lack of recognition given Martin's counter-hegemonic leadership, prototypically feminine social skills, and markers of achievement, or by Marianne and Pam's invisibility as engineers because there was no way to think of them as fitting among Nerds).

Contextualizing individuals not just in the social situation of the moment, but also in the flow of history and imagined reality that was campus culture, illuminated a historically persistent process involving living together as engineers and through this process making the future of engineering. These young adults, actively producing and re-producing science practice through their everyday social interactions, held considerable power because those deemed to belong acted *as engineering practitioners*, and this power made them more than simply students of engineering; it also made them producers of engineering. As such, I am left wondering if it is possible to possess the power that flows with engineer (or scientist) identities (albeit differentially distributed among practitioners) before one achieves an undergraduate degree. Might this power conferred via being recognized—identified—as an engineer be something that sets identity productions of the sort apparent at PES apart from those in K–12 sites of science learning?

# References

Bucciarelli, L. L. (1994). *Designing engineers*. Cambridge, MA: MIT Press.

Dutson, A. J., Todd, R. H., Magleby, S. P., & Sorenson, C. D. (1997). A review of literature on teaching engineering design through project-oriented capstone courses. *Journal of Engineering Education*, 86, 17–28.

Eckert, P. (1989). *Jocks and burnouts: Social categories and identity in the high school*. New York: Teachers College Press.

Eisenhart, M. A. (1996). The production of biologists at school and work: Making scientists, conservationists, or flowery bone-heads? In B. A. Levinson, D. E. Foley, & D. C. Holland (Eds.), *The cultural production of the educated person: Critical ethnographies of schooling and local practice* (pp. 169–185). Albany: State University of New York Press.

Eisenhart, M. A., & Finkel, E. (1998). *Women's science: Learning and succeeding from the margins*. Chicago: University of Chicago Press.

Felder, R. M., Felder, G. N., Mauney, M., Hamrin, C. E., Jr., & Dietz, E. J. (1995). A longitudinal study of engineering student performance and retention III: Gender differences in student performance and attitudes. *Journal of Engineering Education*, 84, 151–163.

Foley, D. E. (1990). *Learning capitalist culture: Deep in the heart of Tejas*. Philadelphia: University of Pennsylvania Press.

Holland, D. C., & Eisenhart, M. A. (1990). *Educated in romance: Women, achievement, and college culture*. Chicago: University of Chicago Press.

Holland, D. C., Lachicotte, W., Jr., Skinner, D., & Cain, C. (1998). *Identity and agency in cultural worlds*. Cambridge, MA: Harvard University Press.

Lave, J., & Wenger, E. (1991). *Situated learning: Legitimate peripheral participation*. Cambridge: Cambridge University Pres..

McIlwee, J. S., & Robinson, J. G. (1992). *Women in engineering: Gender, power, and workplace culture*. Albany: State University of New York.

Nespor, J. (1994). *Knowledge in motion: Space, time, and curriculum in undergraduate physics and management*. London: Falmer.

Seymour, E., & Hewitt, N. M. (1997). *Talking about leaving: Why undergraduates leave the sciences*. Boulder, CO: Westview.

Tonso, K. L. (1999). Engineering gender—gendering engineering: A cultural model for belonging. *Journal of Women and Minorities in Science and Engineering*, 5, 365–404.

Tonso, K. L. (2006). Student engineers and engineer identity: Campus engineer identities as figured world. *Cultural Studies of Science Education*, 1, 273–307.

Traweek, S. (1988). *Beamtimes and lifetimes: The world of high energy physics*. Cambridge, MA: Harvard University Press.

Willis, P. (1977). *Learning to labor: How working class kids get working class jobs*. New York: Columbia University Press.

# 12

# Expanding Our Understandings of Urban Science Education by Expanding the Roles of Students as Researchers

*Rowhea Elmesky and Kenneth Tobin*

All students deserve and must have the opportunity to become scientifically literate. (National Research Council, 1996, p. ix)
Randy: Ain't my fault they ain't teach me nothin'.
Ivory: In that school, nobody's teaching nobody nothin'…. Next year, I betchya' I ain't learnin' nothin' either. (research meeting, 7/01)

Nine years ago, the National Science Education Standards (National Research Council, 1996) articulated a goal of scientific literacy for all students. Despite widespread acceptance of this goal we, as a nation, struggle to achieve it, especially in inner city schools. For example, in classrooms throughout Philadelphia, one of the nation's largest school districts with more than 50,000 high school students, contradictions to this objective are evident in the observations of student researchers like Randy and Ivory and in the statistics of high failure and low graduation rates in the school they attend. In an effort to improve science teaching and learning such that education is a transformative force in urban youths' lives, initiatives are continuously introduced and implemented (National Research Council, 1996). However, in a recent report, *Looking Inside the Classroom: A Study of K–12 Mathematics and Science Education in the United States* (Weiss, Pasley, Smith, Banilower, & Heck, 2003), there is evidence to suggest that, despite reform initiatives, the quality of science instruction remains well below the ideal. Research undertaken in a national sample of science and math classrooms indicates that:

> …only about a third of lessons nationally are likely to have a positive impact on student understanding of mathematics/science concepts, and 16% are likely to have a negative effect on their understanding; the remaining lessons would likely have no effect, or both positive and negative effects. (p. 42)

With 75% of the population residing in urban centers and the majority of the nation's students attending urban public schools (Barton & Tobin, 2001), improving the quality of science education for all students places a premium on obtaining insights from research in urban science classrooms.

From: *Journal of Research in Science Teaching*, 42 (7), pp. 807–828. © 2005 Wiley Periodicals, Inc. Reprinted with permission of John Wiley & Sons, Inc.

In this chapter, we present a blend of salient findings that have emerged over the past 5 years as multiple studies of urban science education have been undertaken in conjunction with one comprehensive neighborhood high school (City High) in Philadelphia. Although the findings are expansive because these studies are ongoing, for the purpose of this chapter, we focus on sharing what we have learned regarding the role of varying forms of capital, youth identity, and embodied dispositions (Bourdieu, 1992) in science teaching and learning, through our deployment of student researchers as part of an evolving methodological approach aimed to build insider perspectives on the participation and learning of urban youth. Thus, our purpose in this study is not to present findings limited to one particular study but rather to benefit the literature by contributing a summary of findings (in relation to three research questions) emerging from years of urban studies that are deeply intertwined and inform one another. The questions driving the research presented here are as follows:

1.  How do teachers build capital with students (e.g., earn respect and build rapport) and thereby afford the learning of students?
2.  How does the formation/(re)formation of student identity in fields outside of school affect youth practices in the science classroom?
3.  What components of the students' cultural capital are conducive to their learning of science?

In the initial portion of this chapter, we address the first question through an historical look at how the involvement of student researchers began, focusing predominantly upon sharing data from early studies at City High (1998–2000) in which Ken was re-learning to teach in urban settings. The remainder of the paper provides insights into Questions 2 and 3; we focus on studies conducted during the summers of 2001 and 2002 when four City High students joined our research team in expanded researcher capacities. These students remained central to our team and continued to participate in subsequent and ongoing studies.

# The need for different theoretical lenses

## Nondeficit conceptions of culture and marginalized communities

Although the challenges facing urban schools and the science achievement of marginalized communities continue to be cited, the development of educational policies aimed to remedy the situation are far from effective. We contend that the trends of science education in urban settings will continue if theoretical frameworks of cultural poverty, deprivation, and social reproduction continue to inform research. We find these theories to be hegemonic—laden with deficit views of marginalized youth and with a static view of culture. Moreover, these theories reinforce the cycles of oppression experienced by the urban poor by asking us to focus upon understanding academic failure in terms of finding out what is wrong internally with a child or externally, in his/her home and neighborhood surroundings (McDermott & Varenne, 1995). Not only do these lenses tend to place the blame on the youth, or in the best case on his/her immediate home surroundings, they limit conversations from addressing the complexities of social life and understanding that students' academic failures are "a product of our own activities" as a society (McDermott & Varenne, 1995, p. 331). Culture then can no longer be viewed as being created in isolation, bound to particular settings, nor as being deterministic in nature. Rather, we argue that, in addition to new methodological approaches to urban science education research, we need expanded theoretical lenses for understanding culture and the dialectical relationship between structure and human agency.

In our research, culture is dialectically conceptualized as a system of symbols, the associated meanings, and practices; such a system is loosely bounded so that symbols, practices, and associated meanings originating in one field may appear within another (Sewell, 1999). Fields, places where culture is enacted (Swartz, 1997), are structured by the human and material resources available to support the agency of participants and are weakly bounded (Sewell, 1992), thereby allowing culture that "belongs elsewhere" (i.e., predominantly associated with other fields) to be enacted in a given field. Building from Sewell's critique of and departure from Geertz's (1973) long-standing traditional view of culture, we regard the culture of urban youth as a resource to afford their learning of mainstream discourses such as science, and their appropriation of science to meet goals in multiple fields in and out of school. In doing so, we move beyond traditional notions of science as products and processes, science as argument, and science as products and intentions to the studying of science as culture and the learning of science as cultural production, reproduction, and transformation. Thus, a major focus of our research lies in recognizing, from the practices of urban youth, those aspects of their capital (Bourdieu, 1992) that connect to the learning of science in ways that are potentially transformative to them. We look for ways in which cultural practices from other fields are enacted in science classrooms and afford student learning. Moreover, through investigations of the enactment of culture, we focus on identifying patterns and contradictions to those patterns.

# Methodology

Issues of civil rights—indeed issues of equity and social justice in the urban place—are central threads in a diverse fabric that comprises the core of urban science education studies. (Barton, 2002, p. 3)

Urban schooling in its current form is limited in its potential to afford social transformation for its students (e.g., Haberman, 1991; Knapp & Plecki, 2001; Songer, Lee, & Kam, 2002); schooling, in fact, contributes significantly to the "stratification" of society (Barton & McLaren, 2001). Understanding that educational practices are oppressive, particularly for urban youth from marginalized communities experiencing severe poverty (Freire, 1993), and considering that critical theory encourages participatory critique, empowerment, transformation, and social justice (Kincheloe, 1998; Lather, 1986; Pizarro, 1998), we like others (e.g., Barton, 2001; Seiler, 2002) have found critical ethnography to be an ideal methodological approach to studying science teaching and learning in urban settings. A critical research process invokes a goal of determining the existence of injustice, finding methods for altering it, and identifying the sites for transformation (Kincheloe, 1998). Specifically, critical ethnography is a form of critical research that goes beyond interpretive and naturalist research and is ultimately concerned with the structural transformation of society and the emancipation of individuals through the revealing of dominant social ideology. Thus, in engaging critical ethnography, we are committed to studying science classrooms with the goal of transforming them. In addition, because such a methodology calls for the affordance of the agency of those involved in the research, we have developed and are using research methods that do more than describe and interpret as we plan and enact research. Specifically, over the course of 5 years, we have worked to restructure traditional researcher roles as well as to expand our notion of whom is central to the research process within our studies of the teaching and learning of science.

## When students become researchers

Although it is becoming common to include teachers as central participants in qualitative educational research (Doerr & Tinto, 2000), the involvement of student researchers is much more limited. Typically, students' roles are restricted to the inclusion of their voices in others' stories and providing member checks on the interpretations of adult researchers. However, evident through our work and that of others (e.g., Barton, 2001; La Van, 2004; Wassell, 2004), there is growing progress toward involving students in more empowering research capacities, which is rooted within Freire's (1970) call for both teachers and students to function as critical agents and problem-solvers through expanding their ways of knowing and questioning and by taking ownership of their ideas. Steinberg and Kincheloe (1998), in their edited book addressing multiple education disciplines, *Students as Researchers: Creating Classrooms that Matter*, further Freire's notion and advocate student researcher roles that are clearly political and challenge "dominant forms of ideology (constructs that maintain status quo and its unequal power relations by producing particular meanings and interpretations of reality), and conventional purposes of education" (p. 3).

Through our work, we argue that the need for student researchers is profound within urban settings, especially as traditional methods of engaging students in research reinforce unequal power hierarchies between the researcher and the researched. Such power differentials are particularly acute across boundaries of age, race, and class, and these borders are pronounced in urban settings that are characterized by a majority of people from minority populations and conditions of severe poverty on both individual and neighborhood levels. Moreover, because "knowledge generation within research is understood as an active, context-based process influenced by the values, histories, and practices of the researcher and the community in which the research gets done" (Barton, 2001, pp. 905–906), there exists great danger in perpetuating schooling inequities and reinforcing hegemonic structures shaping accepted schooling practices when researchers may be "other" in regard to those they seek to understand. In fact, more often than not, research findings emerging from urban settings are saturated with a middle-class ideology that can further hegemonic structures of urban schooling. In accordance with a critical ethnographic methodology, then, we have developed new windows into the lives of urban youth, to contest the privileging of our voices as the adult, university-based researchers and so as not to put forth claims rooted in our own experiences of research, teacher education, and teaching and learning of science in institutions where the teachers and students may have shared social and cultural histories similar to our own.[1]

Consequently, we contend that students in urban settings must be involved in urban science education research in ways that allow them to help us to "challenge the common sense views of reality with which most individuals have grown so comfortable" (Steinberg & Kincheloe,

1998, p. 2). This chapter challenges traditional views as we share the emergence and development of student researcher roles within our program of research and the ways their involvement has allowed our understandings of urban science education to expand along new pathways. Specifically, we address the community from which we recruited student researchers, the roles and associated tasks in which they engaged, the resources they utilized, and the methods by which we gradually included them more substantively in data collection and analyses.

## Methods for data collection, analysis, and interpretation

We have worked with student researchers over a wide variety of researcher roles (e.g., teacher educators, interviewers/interviewees, ethnographers, and science learners/curriculum developers) across social fields, including the workplace, neighborhood, and the science classroom. Although these roles have varied across time and context, what has remained consistent is our endeavor to include students as central members of our research team, our resolve to learn from them in deeply meaningful ways, and our willingness to alter our approaches to research and the roles and practices of participants. The major question that then arises to the reader may be regarding what methods for data collection/production, analysis, and interpretation were utilized to remain consistent with our methodological commitments to conducting empowering, educative, and catalytic research. This question becomes even more important because we hold our research practices to Guba and Lincoln's (1989) four authenticity criteria in which authentic research requires researchers to change their constructions as a result of doing the research; is educative to all of the participants; catalyzes changes that afford the goals of the participants; and creates opportunities for all members of a community to benefit from being involved in the research, especially those who could not easily help themselves (Guba & Lincoln, 1989; Tobin, 2000).

We have worked with numerous student researchers at City High for varying periods of time over the years; however, the data and interpretations presented in this chapter have emerged from longitudinal work with specific students. We highlight research conducted with one of the first youth members of our research team, Tyrone, as well as share data connected with 4 years of work with a group of four students.[2] The methods we have engaged include traditional and atypical types of data collection as we attended the science classes of these student researchers, particularly in their ninth, tenth, and eleventh grade years, and as we participated as senior members of the research team during three summer sessions.[3] We video- and audiotaped their science classrooms as well as recorded their work with us at the University of Pennsylvania during the summer sessions. In addition, we obtained formal interviews (audio-and/or videotaped formats) spanning the 4 years, with each of the students. As discussed later, the interviews were conducted mostly by the students. We also recorded informal conversations with student researchers as well as cogenerative dialogues (Roth & Tobin, 2002). In addition, the students kept reflective journals describing lived experiences and interactions within the research setting during each summer. We saw journaling as a powerful tool for contemplating upon one's feelings and reactions to incidents within a research environment. Across the summers, we worked with students on ethnography projects, gradually introducing and encouraging the incorporation of theoretical frameworks into their work, In addition, throughout our presence in the various research environments, we wrote field notes—to remember what occurred during science lessons or following interviews, the viewing of videotapes, and listening to audiotaped research sessions.

While we invoked these traditional data-gathering techniques, we also worked with students to produce more unique artifacts—which included, but were not limited to: transcriptions; self-authored raps; data from internet research; video analyses; ethnographies; independently designed interviews; the production of a science-related movie and rap videos through video-editing software, such as *Imovie* and *Final Cut Pro*; and presentation materials associated with dissemination activities, such as seminars and professional conferences. To produce such artifacts, the student researchers needed preparation and training in both technical and theoretical areas. For instance, they learned to utilize transcribers and video-editing equipment/software. In addition, for curriculum development roles, the students had to understand content-specific knowledge (e.g., concepts of frequency, amplitude, standing waves). Moreover, to assist us in the analysis and interpretation of artifacts they produced, we introduced them to theoretical constructs that inform our research, particularly sociocultural concepts such as culture, structure, agency, schema/ideology, hegemony, different forms of capital (social, cultural, symbolic), and dispositions. In this manner, it became possible to actively engage their assistance in the interpretation of data being generated. They were able to apply understandings of sociocultural theory to select patterned actions of themselves and others. For example, students watched hours of tapes from a variety of contexts (i.e., neighborhood streets, homes, classrooms, research work place) to identify segments that they found to illustrate the building and/or loss of social, cultural, and symbolic capital (Bourdieu, 1992). In some cases, they identified salient vignettes of student–student interactions or teacher–student(s) interactions: we also asked them to focus on their own interactions and to help themselves and us become more aware of their dispositions (Bourdieu, 1992). Because dispositional resources are mostly unconscious, in addition to theory, we introduced the concept of microanalysis as a method for analysis and interpretation for the extensive video footage collected. We explained and engaged in activities to emphasize the importance of slowing down or speeding up video to recognize patterned actions. For instance, Rowhea shared some of her microanalytical work with students to provide them with examples of the process through which subtle movements (e.g., the slight gesture of a finger) can be identified and why that could be salient in a science classroom. In addition, we studied relationships of agency and structure through conversations and writing activities around actual footage from their science classrooms, select readings (e.g., *Bad Boys, Code of the Street,* and *Flyy Girl*), and instructional movies (e.g., *Dangerous Minds* and *Stand by Me*). With time, students were able to engage in video analysis to identify and create edited vignettes that illustrated student agency (i.e., access and appropriation of material and/or human resources [Sewell, 1992]). Each of the roles and tasks the students engaged in helped us to obtain further insights into their interests, dispositions, and the conscious and unconscious aspects of their identities that impact their learning of science and would have otherwise been inaccessible to us. Thus, here we exemplify how some of these artifacts and, more importantly, the processes through which they were produced, proved to be significant interpretive resources for understanding how science might be enacted differently in comprehensive neighborhood high schools.

# Pathways to insider interpretations

The present studies of scientific literacy and the extent to which it can be accessed and appropriated by urban youth began in 1997. At that time, Ken was convinced of the benefits of including high school students as teacher educators, to assist teachers "to better teach kids like us." When Ken began to teach science in an inner-city high school, to afford his roles as teacher educator and researcher, he quickly realized that he needed insider perspectives to inform his practices and further learning (Tobin, 2001). His teaching practices were in constant breakdown and most of what he believed to be good teaching did not appear to work when he taught urban youth, most of whom were African American and from home circumstances of economic hardship. Ken had to learn to use interpretive frameworks and associated practices that were culturally appropriate for the youth he was teaching, to adopt ways of teaching to enable his students to take advantage of what they knew and could do.

We first began to work with urban high school students as researchers in a low-track, small learning community[4] (SLC). The opportunity to employ Tyrone[5] as a student researcher arose from Ken's search for a student who could critically review his teaching and provide suggestions on how to create and sustain more productive learning environments:

> Ken: I first met Tyrone on a day when he was victim of unfair treatment from a teacher who had seen Tyrone violate a school rule at an assembly and had stepped in to reprimand him. Tyrone was removing his jacket because he was hot and his actions were somehow misinterpreted. Soon the problem became not only the initial violation but also Tyrone's aggressive verbal retaliation against what he considered to be an unfair and unwarranted attack from the teacher. I watched much of the unfolding drama with another teacher, and as soon as possible, after the event, I spoke to Tyrone about the incident. He was rational and bright, as well as very "street" [Anderson, 1999] in the way he spoke and presented himself. He wore his hair in dread locks at a time when not many students styled their hair in that way and he had a front tooth missing. He maintained that he was always experiencing unfair treatment from those in authority because they anticipated that he would cause trouble and did what they could to get him expelled. Whether or not that was their strategy, Tyrone was suspended often. So much so, in fact, that he repeated grade 9 for the third time before dropping out of high school.[6] When Tyrone explained to me that he could not get a job at MacDonald's due to his physical appearance, I decided to hire him as a researcher[7] in a study of learning to teach in urban high schools.

# Students as teacher educators

One of the initial roles we developed for student researchers involved their active participation as teacher educators. They acted as consultants, advisors for prospective teachers, and they also produced artifacts that were utilized within the university teacher education program to improve the practices of teaching within their urban school:

Ken: Tyrone was available as a consultant to my graduate students and participated willingly, to the extent that he adopted the practice of dropping by for my classes. In the process he learned some of the theory we used in our teacher education program and he also began to browse though some of the texts that I used as references for the course. Tyrone began to prepare himself for his work by reading texts about urban education, minorities, and social theory back in my office.[8] Initially I was amused by this practice but soon came to realize just how useful it would be to our research. We also deployed the student researchers as experts on learning in an urban comprehensive neighborhood high school. As such they presented a symposium to teacher education students seeking high school certification. Their responses during an associated question/answer session with professors, graduate students, and high school science teachers provided greater insights than would have been possible from the artifacts alone or a presentation involving their use.

It quickly became apparent that Tyrone made an excellent student researcher/teacher educator as his perspective was always strong and articulate. His arguments were internally consistent, and he typically spoke on issues with passion and conviction. We included him on many panels, with his peers, to speak to prospective teachers because he fitted the role of expert with aplomb and his wisdom provided food for thought. Incidentally, we found that some of our most interesting artifacts, interpretations and insights have come from those students who have been labeled as "at risk," "resistant," or possessing dispositions that are counter to the traditional school culture, as defined by middle- and upper-middle-class Eurocentric values. Students like Tyrone can provide voice to the population of students typically marginalized in school.

## Learning about respect

We regard the counsel that student researchers, like Tyrone, have provided concerning respect in classrooms as a breakthrough for urban teaching, for it is starkly contrary to the culture enacted in their comprehensive neighborhood school where strict discipline and "in your face" techniques are practiced by teachers, nonteaching assistants, and even the principal:

Ken: Early on, Tyrone had me wondering about whether or not to take his advice on "Don't teach 'em if they ain't gonna learn. They'll come to you when they wanna learn." There were many reasons why this advice seemed not to make sense. However, when you consider that respect is the currency of the inner-city street realm (Anderson, 1999), then Tyrone's advice made perfect sense. As a basic concept, if students did not want to learn, and I tried to make them engage, it provided them with opportunities to earn their peers' respect by disrespecting me. Yet, Tyrone's analogy was even blunter and more vivid. "You go to them when they ain't wanna learn they gonna treat yo' like a ho." As hard as it might seem, that was exactly what I was experiencing, although putting Tyrone's advice into action ended up being no easy matter.

Mediating social interactions is the accumulation and appropriation of various forms of embodied and material capital (Bourdieu, 1992). Respect, then, can be conceptualized as a form of symbolic capital or a means by which one's status or the identity others attribute to you can be built, lost or exchanged for other forms of capital (e.g., social and/or cultural). On neighborhood streets among the youth, status may emerge through objectified symbols of culture (e.g., particular clothing or shoes) or through embodied dispositions (e.g., movement—dance and orality—rap or playin'). This symbolic capital can be exchanged for social capital; for example, group membership, and contributing to the safety youth can experience in their neighborhoods (Elmesky, 2003). In addition to understanding the centrality of respect in inner-city neighborhoods (Anderson, 1999), through developing teacher educator roles for student researchers, we have gained deep insights into understanding respect as a highly valued form of currency in inner-city classrooms. Moreover, due to the porous boundaries of fields, this symbolic capital is often built in similar manners inside classrooms among peers for the purposes of exchange outside of school.

Following Tyrone's successes as a researcher and a consultant to urban science teachers, we continued to involve several urban youth in much the same ways; then, during the summer of 2001, we embarked on new waters by employing five student researchers to participate in our research on teaching and learning science in urban high schools for 4 hours a day for several months. Within the summer research context, we continued to engage the students' skills as teacher educators, and although these researchers collaborated with us several years after Tyrone, there were stark similarities in their perspectives regarding teaching and learning, and coherent patterns emerged that reemphasized the significance of respect in urban classrooms:

Ms. Rana: What makes a good teacher?

Shakeem: Now, if you one of them people where you feel as though you got put out a strong image, ya' know, a straight image to gain respect and to gain attention in your classroom because that's how it's been in the past. Well I think you should just see who you workin' with. First be yourself…I think they should start out bein' theyself. If you are naturally a person who wants stuff done at a certain time cuz you think that's how you supposed to do it…hey, stay that way because you try to be somebody else is what screws your class up…

Ms. Rana: How does a teacher build up a relationship with a student?

Shakeem: You got to keep your eyes open, man. Pay attention to 'em and stuff…don't be all up in his grill. I mean, damn, don't be "Hey, what you do this weekend…Oh, really, did you do this?" …It's cool but not all up in his face everyday, you should…I think you should just sit back and observe your students for a little while and then when you can—like pick up on a change in attitude. You know.

In the above interchange that occurred between Shakeem, in a "teacher educator" role, and Ms. Rana, his new ninth grade teacher,[9] his evaluation of teachers and teaching was similar in many ways to Tyrone's. Interestingly, both young men recommended teaching practices that are nonintrusive and sincere—Tyrone warning against acting "like a ho" and Shakeem cautioning against being "all up in his grill." Moreover, what these student researchers have communicated to us is supported by studies (e.g., La Van, 2004) on creating classrooms characterized by cultural "fluency" in urban high schools. La Van also found that students possess clear images of teaching practices that communicate respect and disrespect, and they need spaces within the research process for their voices to be heard:

> I hated her in the beginning. She was boring and I thought she disrespected me every opportunity she got. Instead of asking me what was wrong she yelled at me, was very disrespectful, which made me mad a lot of times so I resisted, didn't do work in class, talked to my friends, and tried to just slide by…. (Ace, student electronic journal, reflection of his teacher, 2003; cited in La Van [2004], p. 2)

Unconsciously and/or consciously, teachers can engage in practices that are culturally incongruent with their students, and this contributes to their struggle to establish respect in the classroom and gain the symbolic capital of "teacher." When teachers engage in practices that communicate disrespect, their classrooms tend to be characterized by failed, non-synchronous interactions and the generation of negative emotional energy (Collins, 2004), and they find their practices in constant breakdown and/or reactive (rather than in-time) to the unfolding events. Culturally incongruent practices contribute to the lack of solidarity between teachers and students within urban science classrooms, especially when teachers and students are culturally and socially "other" (e.g., La Van, 2004; Wassell, 2004). Hence, although we had identified the importance of both teachers and students building and maintaining respect, we had much to learn to be able to fully comprehend the semiotic meanings associated with the concept of "respect" for urban youth. We needed to be able to understand the structure of cultural fields, outside of school, in which they participated. We needed images of the practices, symbols, and meanings that exist therein, the human and material resources that are accessible to young people and impact the formation of their dispositions, as well as ideas of how student agency and identity are shaped consciously and unconsciously. Ethnography projects undertaken by student researchers across three summers have been a significant tool for opening dynamic doorways into such understandings.

## Students as ethnographers

Although we wanted to learn more about student researchers' homes and neighborhoods, and the aspects of those fields (i.e., cultural symbols, practices, and underlying/associated meanings) that they regarded as salient to their learning of science, we could not ignore the fact that we would be outsiders in those fields and unable to accurately represent culture and develop useful understandings for research purposes. As we tried to overcome these obstacles to building authentic understandings, we first engaged students as interviewers and interviewees, and then expanded student researcher roles to include that of ethnographer. That is, we created opportunities for the youth to select and capture data resources (e.g., via videotaped raw footage) and then to create edited representations or narratives of their experiences in fields outside of school. Rather than traditional ethnography, using approaches that typically involve the written description of the cultural experiences of others, we encouraged the youth to engage in self-ethnography across three summers to, in some cases, reflect on earlier life events to communicate values, interests, and goals, and in other cases to identify the forms of capital and cultural resources that they possess. The term "self" is utilized to emphasize that these were not external studies of spaces that the students participated within; rather, self-ethnography empowered the insider perspective—student researchers' voices—as it was their choice of which stories they wanted to share from their life-worlds.

## Students as interviewers and interviewees

The initial way that we found "insider" knowledge of "outside" spaces could be accessed was when student researchers conducted interviews with peers as well as being interviewed by other student researchers. In fact, we realized that our learning trajectory increased dramatically when students spoke to each other rather than exclusively to adult researchers:

> Ken: One of the most useful roles I envisioned for Tyrone was that of interviewer, and we were not let down. In fact, during the 2 years in which he worked with us as a researcher, interviews were perhaps Tyrone's greatest contribution. He carefully planned structured interviews and then identified students from throughout the school to ask about life at school and at home. We soon noticed that students were more comfortable speaking to Tyrone about their lives at home, in the streets, and at school. He asked questions that we may have asked if we were to do the interview, but the students were more relaxed with Tyrone and seemed less likely to try to figure out what sort of answer he was looking for. Accordingly, the interviews seemed authentic and we had access to data that we normally would not get.

Thus, one of the research tasks we utilized to expand students' roles as researchers is the activity of interviewing. In some cases, we wrote out a list of questions or discussion topics to guide their interviews of fellow students or of other student researchers; in other cases, the youth were asked to independently devise interview questions. During the summer researcher sessions, we began to make a shift toward student-generated ethnography to provide varying descriptors of social life in a variety of fields. In addition to interviewing one another, their family members, neighbors, and friends, the student researchers also captured video footage; in this manner, they were able to chart their life events over the years and provide practical and theoretical insights into the ways they participated in their neighborhoods. In preparation, some of the student researchers would develop specific questions, so that, through a video interview format, they could provide more information regarding the events, people, and locations that they chose to record. Typically, the student researchers chose to produce edited movies of their neighborhoods and interviews with residents and PowerPoint presentations to represent aspects of their lives out of school. However, rap and poetry were genres that were also used. For example, each summer Ivory chose to write, memorize, and perform a rap capturing her life experiences. She would also transcribe the rap and provide an explanation of the lyrics.

## Learning about urban students' identities

We perceive identity as constantly being formed and (re)formed (Roth, Tobin, Elmesky, Carambo, McKnight, & Beers, 2004). More than simply a way of defining your own sense of self, the making and (re)making of identity is a social and cultural process. Thus, identity is the dialectical interplay between how one defines him/herself and the way that others in the community define him or her. Identity and respect, then, are recursively interconnected because identity develops differently depending upon the capital (e.g., symbolic capital in the form of respect) that an individual holds and upon whether or not others see him or her as having access and power to appropriate the resources in a field. Through student researchers' work as ethnographers, represented in artefacts using video, PowerPoint, poetry, and rap, we are able to learn about daily practices engaged by youth on the streets and in their homes as well as to begin to obtain insight into students' identities in various fields and the ways in which those identities affect their participation in science classrooms. For example, in one of her ethnography raps, Ivory provides salient insights into her identity and her life experience. In so doing she provides clues as to what we might expect of her as a student of science and what she might expect from her science teacher:

1. I'm going to tenth [grade]
2. Been headed towards college
3. I see my young bulls walking the streets like they got it
4. On the corners 20 deep selling drugs like the cops forgot it
5. And get a hold of these 9s and 22s
6. Then talk like they got the runs
7. Still don't know what a thug is about
8. First to talk about spraying guns
9. People say I rap hardcore sometimes real
10. I'm a ghost writer
11. Ain't no other cat that's hotter …
12. I broke my finger playing football
13. Still will play any day
14. I play sports with injuries
15. But ball all the way
16. Life I think is really weak and dead in a way
17. You got crimes suicides and murders each day
18. Any night I get down and pray
19. It's really nothing more I can say
20. I'm spitting from the da bridge life is hard to survive
21. And that's a triple threat if you step against I.

With her rap name of EB Marvelous, Ivory depicts pride in her excellence as a rapper and rap author. The rap expresses Ivory's goal of attending college and projects a competitive spirit and determination to succeed in the fields of academe and sports (lines 2 and 12–15). Ivory regards herself as a triple threat and formidable opponent should anyone choose to oppose her (line 21).

These attributes of identity suggest that in her science class Ivory will be a determined learner who is proactive in accessing human and material resources and, in situations in which there is shortage, she would be expected to compete with her peers. The rap also suggests she is unlikely to give up if the demands are high or to allow frustration and obstacles to divert her from her determination to succeed. The rap provides a caution for teachers to be aware that Ivory may project herself into a situation that she perceives as advantageous for learning through (what could be perceived as) aggressive modes of participation. For example, Ivory has been observed as being loud in her efforts to be heard and gain attention during science lessons (e.g., "Where'd that come from, though? You can't do that!"), and she might willingly leave her seat to make a point or to access and appropriate resources that are not proximate. Moreover, Ivory has identified such practices as evidence of her agency as a science learner during our data analysis sessions.

Much of Ivory's rap provides insights into life in her neighborhood. She makes specific reference to the overconfidence of "big-talking" male youth (line 6) on downward trajectories, the prevalence of drug dealing, and a tendency to act as if they are immune from prosecution and harm (lines 3–8). Ivory alludes to the fragility of life and her experience with violence and murder (lines 16–20). These insights provide a contrast to our experiences and Ivory's science teacher because we have not encountered murder and rarely experience violence or drug-associated activities. The rap is informative in that we can be aware that Ivory and urban youth generally have succeeded in surviving and navigating dangerous circumstances and, in so doing, they have knowledge, skills, and dispositions that have served them well and are resources on which the learning of science might build. For example, Ivory helps us to understand how the "big" talk of urban youth, which is useful in establishing respect and warding off danger on the street, might find its way into the science classroom as students strive to make sense of the curriculum (e.g., Elmesky, 2003) as well as to gain or maintain respect or symbolic capital with peers. Thus, Ivory facilitates our recognition of the necessity for science teachers in urban schools to find ways in which students can maintain respect within their youth subculture and, at the same time, participate in science.

In Shakeem's ethnographic work, he has shown us that navigating fields that are structured differently requires African American male youth, like himself, to develop and maintain multiple and sometimes contradictory identities. He introduces the dichotomy of "gangsta" and "gentleman," and emphasizes the importance of being "both/and" rather than "either/or." He presents us with alternating images of Shakeem as a caring young teen who appreciates hard work, good friends, and family, and Shakeem as a young man who aggressively demands respect from peers through freestyle rap, slag talk, and "bustin' strategies" or practices that earn respect by disrespecting others (Sterba, 2003). For example, in his video ethnography, we watch Shakeem playfully demeaning and threatening his friend so as to coerce him into rapping on camera. "We got this 'ho' down here. Yo rap, man before I…Yo rap, dog!" Shakeem also shares images of different interactions with family and friends in his grandmother's neighborhood where he was living at the time. His fondness for his cousin and her two young daughters is evident as he teases her about what costume she'll wear for Halloween and marvels over the intelligence of the older daughter. Shakeem's strong sense of loyalty and caring for younger youth in the neighborhood is apparent later in the tape as we listen to him introduce and speak with his "adopted son" who is working in a garden:

Shakeem:    This my young boy, Steve, ya mean, helpin' out the community. Makin' a home for these plants. Tryin' to make the world a better place?
Steve:       Yup.
Shakeem:    He a rapper too!! You can tell he's gonna look out when get older. You gonna come an' support the community when yous a rapper, Steve?
Steve:       Yes.
Shakeem:    You better look out.
Steve:       I am.

Shakeem's grandmother provides a home for him when things become unstable with his mother. As his temporary caretaker, the grandmother struggles to make sure he has enough shirts and pants for his school uniform and new shoes to start off the school year. Shakeem cuts her grass, reads her the mail, buys groceries for her when he has money, as well as warmly pokes fun at her age and associated aches and pains. In addition to caring for his grandmother, he financially and emotionally supports family members going through difficult times. For example, he called from work to console a relative when her van got repossessed and discreetly leaves cash at her house to help pay late utility bills.

In a school in which poverty is widespread, Shakeem has fewer economic resources to access than most of his peers and even fewer following his assistance with those who need among his family and friends. Shakeem has learned to ignore the sarcasm directed by some peers toward the signs of his poverty that are part of his being, such as few and soiled clothes or reliance on free meals and free tokens to travel on public transport to and from school. The lack of money to pay for laundry more than once a week combined with a limited number of shirts, for example, detracts from the symbolic capital he holds and can result in what could be interpreted as resistance if a teacher were to call on a student like Shakeem to go to the chalkboard to display some work. Understandably, Shakeem would avoid humiliation in front of his peers by refusing to go. Hence, it is important that teachers be on the lookout for indicators of poverty so as to not inadvertently place students like Shakeem in places where peers can use their oral skills to disrespect him due to his poverty.

Although some males choose to build financial resources by engaging in illegal activities, including the drug trade, Shakeem is determined to earn money to support himself and his extended family without having to sell drugs. Thus, even though drugs and violence are parts of Shakeem's life, his adamancy against building such an identity is clearly expressed on one of his slides of a PowerPoint presentation developed in conjunction with his video ethnography:

> It's so many drug dealers on da 5th it's a shame. The average person would think a poor black kid would see the drugs and sell it because of their financial problems, but I'm just the opposite. I go to school and learn so I don't have to sit out in the rain, sell that sh*t and duck from the law. F**K THAT!

Without the social and symbolic capital afforded by dealing drugs or at least owning particular clothing and sneakers, Shakeem pays close attention to other ways of building social capital that will afford a "gangsta" persona and respect among peers. In a recent presentation at an international meeting of ethnographers, Shakeem described how at school he works the hallways and lunchroom to talk to peers and socially interact with them depending on their status and the respect he affords them. This creation and maintenance of social networks is important for Shakeem, more so for his life out of school than for his academic performance. Yet, because the boundaries that separate school from the other fields in which he participates are porous, practices from those fields are enacted by Shakeem, frequently without conscious awareness, as he builds social capital in school. So, inside school, he interacts with youth in manners common to the street field—for example, he may fight to defend himself, rap, smoke weed, and use profanities.

Due to the porous boundaries between those fields from outside of school and those in school, Shakeem is continually required to resolve contradictions between his "gangsta" – motivated identity and the identity expected by school norms. He means well and wants to succeed in school, yet some of his practices make success less likely than he or we would like. As part of catalytic authenticity, we have constantly intervened on behalf of Shakeem to reverse decisions to suspend him and even expel him from school. Shakeem has many attributes that would guarantee his success if only teachers would encourage him to use what he knows, can do, is interested in doing, and is disposed to do. Shakeem, and his peers, need regular encouragement to get involved and stay involved in activities associated with the learning of science. Recognizing what Shakeem knows and can do as resources he can use to learn is an important requirement. However, it is also important to realize that earning and maintaining respect is central to Shakeem's identity, and he will do what he has to do to retain his status among his peers. Teachers might have to accommodate and align activity systems in which students like Shakeem can sustain their identities associated with maintaining and earning respect while learning science.

# Forming deeper understandings of how urban youth learn science

By expanding the roles of student researchers to include interviewing and ethnography, we have become more attentive to the unconscious enactment of culture as well as more capable of understanding how identity is reinforced by the structures of fields outside of science classrooms, and the internal turmoil and contradictions that can arise as youth attend school. This is particularly important as we rethink scientific literacy and look for different images of how science learning can successfully occur in urban classrooms.

## Students as science learners and curriculum developers

In order to gain deeper understandings of how urban youth learn science, during our summer research sessions we also asked the student researchers to participate in capacities that included the roles of science learner and curriculum developer in addition to teacher educator, ethnographer, and interviewer/interviewee. Our principal interest was to have our group of researchers involved in science-related activities that were "school-like" so as to: (1) study the extent to which different instructional approaches afforded their learning; (2) assist us in selecting relevant activities that could mediate between their cultural capital and canonical science; and (3) develop culturally appropriate curriculum resources. For instance, during the first summer, we focused on presenting the student researchers with opportunities to learn general physics concepts related to sound and we gained deep insights into the teaching and learning of science through their successful development of a curriculum enhancer—a movie entitled *Sound in the City*. By asking the student researchers to produce such a movie, we expected the youth to learn physical science concepts regarding sound such as frequency, velocity, wave properties, period, wavelength, amplitude, standing waves, and wave reflection. As they engaged as learners, we looked for the ways in which they utilized human and material resources to make sense of and represent scientific concepts. We expected that such an artifact would sharpen our understandings of how urban youth's cultural resources, and specifically unconscious dispositions, could help them both reproduce and produce the culture of science. Although a certain amount of science culture was reproduced in the form of terminology, diagrams, and definitions of concepts related to sound, such as when May explained amplitude through a universally recognized wave diagram, the movie as a whole also presented evidence of cultural production.

In creating the movie, May, Ivory, Shakeem, Randy, and Tim were able to utilize their researcher roles to share their embodied knowledge and practices associated with other fields within a context of learning science. In addition, the youth were more than passive participants; they were actively expanding their own physics understandings of sound and developing methods by which they could represent the science to engage students in lower grades. They were encouraged to "be themselves" so that the dispositions they unconsciously invoked on a daily basis could emerge through skits, rap, dance, posters, and their use of simple props as they made sense of conceptual ideas associated with sound. In the remaining portion of this article, we focus upon two of nine dispositions ("movement" and "verve"), which are described by Boykin (1986) as central dimensions of the Afro-cultural experience. Movement, refers to "an emphasis on the interweaving of movement, rhythm, percussiveness, music, and dance, which are taken as central to psychological health" (p. 61). A second disposition, verve, is "a propensity for relatively high levels of stimulation, to action that is energetic and lively" (p. 61). While we selected this theoretical lens for making sense of students' dispositions, we identified these as highly salient through our work with student researchers. For example, in interview data, student researchers spoke about "living life to a soundtrack" and music being "part" of them. They also described how these ways of being (i.e., beating a tempo on a desk, rapping aloud, or wearing headphones) consistently resulted in negative consequences in school because they are considered inappropriate and/or a distraction to the curriculum. In addition, during theoretical sessions where we focused upon understanding different forms of capital, the students identified video footage in which they or others were invoking dispositions of movement and verve (e.g., rap performances or dance) as examples of cultural resources for peers' building of social and symbolic capital with each other. Even when the researchers were asked to select a series of video vignettes of effective teaching, they chose ones that revealed teachers incorporating high energy, motion, and rhythmic ways of being in the classroom. Moreover, throughout the artefacts produced as part of the research, the majority of student researchers incorporated movement and verve to demonstrate originality and creativity and to build social and symbolic capital with their research peers. The *Sound in the City* movie represents an artifact that is replete with examples of movement and verve, and it was during its production that we became acutely aware of the ways in which these dispositions contribute to the teaching and learning of science.

## The wave dance: learning about verve and movement

One of the numerous examples of how *Sound in the City* revealed the student researchers' embodied dispositions within a context of science learning was their decision to include, as an "intermission," video footage that had been captured when dance practices, in the form of "battle,"[10] spontaneously erupted within the research space as the youth participated in science activities:

Rowhea: The "wave dance" began the day I brought in a plastic multicolored slinky as a resource to engage the students in experimenting with translational and longitudinal wave movement, standing waves, and wave reflection. I had just finished taping the slinky to the wall when, suddenly, I found Randy grasping the slinky with one hand and holding Ivory's hand with the other. Shakeem was playing some "beats" on the computer. They started to dance to a beat that seemed so perfect, yet what was so profound was the manner in which they moved to give the illusion that a translational wave of energy was passing through their bodies, through the slinky, and then reflecting back in the opposite direction. Without discussion or deliberation, the two researchers began to utilize dispositions of verve and movement to demonstrate the movement of sound wave energy. Later, following the spontaneous outburst, I asked them consciously to verbalize what had occurred. Anticipating that the segment would later become part of the movie, Ivory explained to the camera: "Today, we're going to show you how—by usin' this slinky, as you see, how the wave can travel as the energy goes through us an' the slinky—our body an' the slinky using well, it's called battle from where we come from."

Slowing down the video of their dance to frame-by-frame speed, we could follow the pattern of movement in remarkable detail. Ivory began the dance with her head turned in the direction of her left arm. As she arched her left arm downward, her head turned to Randy who then began to arch his left arm upward, drawing Ivory's right arm upward simultaneously. For a thirtieth of a second, Randy and Ivory's heads were turned to each other as their arms were both extended fully upward, mimicking a wave crest. Then, with Randy initiating the descent, both lowered their arms. Just as they had reached a rest, Randy turned his head to face the wall while simultaneously arching his right arm to "pass" the wave of energy to the plastic slinky. As the wave reflected off the wall, the reverse order of movement then occurred. Through this fluid, coordinated movement of hands, arms, head, and body, the student researchers were unconsciously invoking dispositions from a different field within the research and science learning context (Figure 12.1).

## Dispositions and structural resonances[11]

By working with student researchers as curriculum developers, we were learning how to identify and begin to understand the significance and unconscious nature of two dispositions that were common to the researchers and have been widely observed in urban classrooms. Moreover, we were able to observe how particular structural conditions produce resonances in individuals and allow cultural capital such as verve and movement to unconsciously emerge. The subtleties of field structure became increasingly clear as we observed the student researchers within different spaces. Of particular interest was video footage of their time spent within a university lab interacting with undergraduate physics lab setups. During one portion of the day when Randy and Ivory were working together on a lab that involved an oscilloscope and a microphone, we were able to study, in additional depth, these same dispositions enacted in association with the science curriculum:

Rowhea: Randy was interested, right from the start, in the effects his own voice had on the wave patterns produced on the oscilloscope. He held the microphone to his mouth and imitated a car revving up and later hummed loudly. He also placed the microphone inside the part of the apparatus that consisted of a tube of air and moved it quickly back and forth and observed the monitor keenly. However, he soon gravitated towards Ivory's headphones and CD player and picked them up. "This got a radio on here, Ivory?" For a while, Randy was satisfied with placing the microphone on top of the headphones and quietly watching the wave pattern on the oscilloscope

1: Ivory began the wave pattern with her left arm. Randy's head turned toward her in anticipation of her next move.

2: As Ivory's head turned toward him. Randy began to arch his left arm upwards, drawing Ivory's right arm upwards simultaneously.

3: Randy and Ivory's heads were turned to each other as their arms were both extended fully upwards mimicking a wave crest.

4: Randy turned his head to face the wall while simultaneously arching his right arm to "pass" the wave of energy to the plastic slinky.

**Figure 12.1    Randy and Ivory shared embodied dispositions of how to perform the wave dance. These verve and movement dispositions unconsciously emerged as the researchers engaged in activities to further their understandings of sound waves so as to develop the curriculum enhancer, *Sound in the City***

screen. However, about 15 minutes later, lively music suddenly flooded the room when Randy decided to remove the earphones from the CD player to experiment further. That was when Ivory became involved. As if on cue, she stood and began to rap into the microphone, "kik, kik, kik, kik." She moved her shoulders and feet to the beat of the music. Both she and Randy watched the monitor as she sang/rapped into the microphone in synchrony with the CD. Then, a section consisting only of "beats," rather than lyrics, played and Ivory began to really dance—switching the microphone from hand to hand—as she moved in perfect rhythm to the fast beat.

Although there was a seemingly contrasting structure from the informal learning environment of the research space just a week earlier, utilizing microanalysis techniques, dispositions of verve and movement were emergent in this physics laboratory. Despite being different fields there were common human and material resources, rule systems, and ideology that

Ivory engaged in "battle" as she observed the oscilloscope screen showing sound wave patterns associated with the music she was playing aloud. Her arm and head movements were coordinated and resemble those that emerged while developing the *Sound in the City* movie.

**Figure 12.2   Randy and Ivory engaging similar dispositions of verve and movement within a different field (university physics lab)**

allowed "structural resonances" to arise and particular unconscious dispositions to be enacted. More specifically, three structural consistencies were evident: (1) human resources remained the same as Randy and Ivory worked together and had access to each other's dispositions; (2) auditory resources corresponded as lively music consisting of sections of "beats" was playing in each space; and (3) similar visual resources illustrated the wave pattern and motion—the oscilloscope screen in the lab and the slinky in the research office. As a result, Randy and Ivory's practices closely resembled those enacted previously, although this was difficult to identify while playing the videotape in real time. For example, facing the oscilloscope monitor, Ivory's left arm began to move to the music in the shape of a wave—she arched it upward mimicking a crest and then nose-dived her fingers to signify movement; the wave passed through her body and then "appeared" in her other arm's upward motion (Figure 12.2).

The level of understandings that became possible regarding the teaching and learning of urban youth underwent marked growth as the student researchers helped us learn more about their unconscious practices and the structure of fields. With a research design that included student researchers within capacities that extended well beyond those of the traditional "member checker," the result was a curriculum resource, which, in Ivory's view, was "about urban science—how science is related to your everyday life. How you're learning." Shakeem further explained: "Basically learnin' science before ya'll, ya mean? So ya'll can better understand how to do things in ya'll classroom." As expressed by May, the movie was about "helping younger children to look at science in a different way."

## Implication for urban science education

The very nature of the educational practice—its necessary directive nature, the objectives, the dreams that follow in the practice—do not allow education to be neutral as it is always political. …The question before us is to know what type of politics it is, in favor of whom and what, and against what and for whom it is realized. (Freire, 1993, p. 22)

Considering the political context of urban education with oppressive structures informing teaching and learning practices, we contend that, for research of urban settings to make a difference in the manner in which science is taught, we must engage a methodological approach that provides real voice to the primary stakeholders—our urban youth. In this study, we have shared how our involvement of student researchers, within a variety of research roles that extend beyond traditionally passive ones, has allowed for the formation of deeper meso[12]-level understandings of the importance of respect in urban youths' lives, and the ways in which practices and student identities, emerging from other fields, may impact their participation in science classrooms. In addition, we have been able to take micro looks at students learning science and have begun to recognize patterned practices that can then be identified as helping them as science learners. Moreover, we are now increasingly interested in understanding the structural components that allow resonance to occur such that particular dispositions associated with various identities are afforded in science classrooms.

These understandings have much to add to the current literature regarding urban science education. For instance, Delpit (2002) argued that there is a "culture of power" in school that serves to privilege mainly white, middle-class students by allocating rewards to the students most familiar with its rules and norms. Findings from our research studies indicate the ease by which classroom-based practices communicate and further reinforce this culture of power, especially when teachers do not have insight into what gains or loses them respect with their students. Furthermore, viewing respect as a form of symbolic capital and recognizing the potential it carries for exchange into other forms of capital, such as science cultural capital, makes it a top priority for teachers and administrators to form deep understandings of the practices that students engage to build respect. Hence, rather than enacting practices that may afford students' disrespect, teachers may work with students to restructure curriculum and classroom actives to afford the building and exchange of symbolic capital (i.e., respect) in other ways. As shown here, the involvement of student researchers as curriculum developers has allowed us insights into other ways in which respect can be earned. Peers of the student researchers who have watched the student-produced sound movie, for example, remark excitedly and in awe of their counterparts who are engaging in practices that are valued in the neighborhood and home (e.g., dance, rap, and verbal playin') in conjunction with the doing of science. More often than not, the enactment of dispositions such as these position students to be "at odds with larger mainstream ideals" (Allen & Boykin, 1992, p. 589) rather than assisting the youth in the building of any forms of capital that will be useful in transforming their positions in social space. This is because, traditionally, in science classrooms, including those in urban settings, gaining symbolic capital with one's teacher may be tied to engaging practices that reinforce the culture of power, especially as middle-class language and methods of argumentation are privileged in science classes (Lemke, 1990), rather than the enriching discursive and embodied dispositional resources (e.g., movement and verve) of youth. In fact, their cultural capital, knowledge, and dispositions are often not valued and teachers have difficulty designing a curriculum that recognizes, understands, and draws upon the resources of low-income and minority students. When dispositions are afforded, it is accidental, fleeting, or through a concerted effort of student(s), teacher, or both (e.g., Elmesky,

2003). The sense of exclusion that students therefore experience is compounded by cultural differences between them and their teachers, many of whom are white and middle class and may base their teaching practices on deficit views (Nieto, 2002). Recent urban science education research (e.g., LaVan, 2004; Wassell, 2004) has revealed that, when conscious techniques are engaged to afford the use of students' capital within a science learning context to meet science-related goals, culturally congruent teaching arises, which is often unconscious, synchronous, fluid, and replete with positive emotional energy (Collins, 2004). Moreover, teachers and students are found to develop similar practices, experience high levels of positive emotional energy during interactions, and have a productive exchange of varying forms of capital.

If "science for all" is a goal for public education, our findings and a body of supporting literature indicate a real need for better understandings of how supportive, culturally fluid science learning communities can be formed within science classrooms to foster positive identities associated with science and greater accessibility of the subject matter. Moreover, our findings suggest that, with the assistance of urban youth, preservice and in-service teachers can come to understand the practices and structures that promote solidarity and a sense of community. Thus, science classrooms may be transformed from sites where the cultural capital of minority and low-income students are sometimes not valued or are actively discouraged and where students are often expected to wholly adopt the language and symbols associated with the dominant culture, to sites where students' contributions are valued resources and successful interactions can enable new symbols associated with science to become invested with positive emotional energy.

# Notes

1. The first author is from a mixed racial background, yet has been enculturated to some extent with white, middle-class value systems. The second author is white.
2. May, Ivory, Shakeem, and Randal. They referred to our research group as DUS, or Discovering Urban Science.
3. Average length of time was 20 hours/week for 8 weeks.
4. A small learning community is often referred to as a school within a school.
5. All student researcher names are pseudonyms.
6. Eventually, Tyrone attended a charter school for at-risk students and in 1 year earned the credits to successfully graduate from high school.
7. Supported with a grant from the Spencer Foundation.
8. Dr. Gale Seiler, who was a graduate student at the time, is credited with having the insight that Tyrone could benefit from reading these texts and use them in his roles as a student researcher. […]
9. We use the phrase new teacher rather than student teacher because of the roles they enact in urban high schools. […]
10. "Battle" refers to instances when youth engage in competitions requiring movement and verve prowess. Often two youths, well versed in synchronous movement and sharing an embodied understanding of specific sets of dance moves, "perform" for other peers who may or may not choose to counter the performance with a performance of their own.
11. The metaphor of resonance was developed by Ken and Wolff-Michael Roth during the course of theoretical discussions in the spring of 2002.
12. Intermediate between micro and macro; concerns unfolding events in actual (experienced) time.

# References

Allen, B. & Boykin, A. W. (1992). African American children and the educational process: Alleviating cultural discontinuity through prescriptive pedagogy. School Psychology Review, 21, 586–596.

Anderson, E. (1999). Code of the street: Decency, violence, and the moral life of the inner city. New York: W. W. Norton & Co.

Barton, A. C. (2001). Science education in urban settings: Seeking new ways of praxis through critical ethnography. Journal of Research on Science Teaching, 38, 899–917.

Barton, A. C. (2002). Urban science education studies: A commitment to equity, social justice and a sense of place. Studies in Science Education, 38, 1–38.

Barton, A. C. & McLaren, P. (2001). Capitalism, critical pedagogy, and urban science education: An interview with Peter McLaren. Journal of Research on Science Teaching, 38, 847–859.

Barton, A. C. & Tobin, K. (2001). Editorial: Urban science education. Journal of Research on Science Teaching, 38, 843–846.

Bourdieu, P. (1992). The practice of reflexive sociology (The Paris workshop). In P. Bourdieu & L. J. D. Wacquant (Eds.), An invitation to reflexive sociology (pp. 216–260). Chicago: University of Chicago Press.

Boykin, A.W. (1986). The triple quandary and the schooling of Afro-American children. In U. Neisser (Ed.), The school achievement of minority children: New perspectives (pp. 57–92). Hillsdale, NJ: Erlbaum.

Collins, R. (2004). Interaction ritual chains. Princeton, NJ: Princeton University Press.

Delpit, L. (2002). No kinda sense. In L. Delpit & J. K. Dowdy (Eds.), The skin we speak (pp. 31–38). New York: The New Press.

Doerr, H. & Tinto, P. P. (2000). Paradigms for teacher-centered, classroom-based research. In A. E. Kelly & R. A. Lesh (Eds.), Handbook of research design in mathematics and science education (pp. 403–427). Mahwah, NJ: Erlbaum.

Elmesky, R. (2003). Crossfire on the streets and into the classroom: Meso–micro understandings of weak cultural boundaries, strategies of action and a sense of the game in an inner-city chemistry classroom. Cybernetics and Human Knowing, 10, 29–50.

Freire, P. (1970). Pedagogy of the oppressed. New York: Continuum Press.

Freire, P. (1993). Pedagogy of the city. New York: Continuum Press.

Geertz, C. (1973). The interpretation of cultures. New York: Basic Books.

Guba, E. & Lincoln, Y. (1989). Fourth generation evaluation. Newbury Park, CA: Sage.

Haberman, M. (1991). The pedagogy of poverty versus good teaching. Phi Delta Kappan, 73, 290–294.

Kincheloe, J. L. (1998). Critical research in science education. In B. J. Fraser & K. G. Tobin (Eds.), International handbook of science education (pp. 1191–1205). Dordrecht: Kluwer.

Knapp, M. S. & Plecki, M. (2001). Investing in the renewal of urban science teaching. Journal of Research in Science Teaching, 38, 1089–1100.

Lather, P. (1986). Research as praxis. Harvard Educational Review, 56, 257–277.

LaVan, S. K. (2004). Cogenerating fluency in urban science classrooms. Unpublished doctoral dissertation, University of Pennsylvania, Philadelphia.

Lemke, J. L. (1990). Talking science: Language, learning and values. Norwood, NJ: Ablex.

McDermott, R. & Varenne, H. (1995). Culture as disability. Anthropology & Education Quarterly, 26, 324–348.

National Research Council. (1996). National science education standards. Washington, DC: National Academy Press.

Nieto, S. (2002). The light in their eyes: Creating multicultural learning communities. New York: Teachers College Press.

Pizarro, M. (1998). Chicano/a power! Epistemology and methodology for social justice and empowerment in Chicano/a communities. Qualitative Studies in Education, 1, 57–80.

Roth, W. -M. & Tobin, K. (2002). At the elbows of another: Learning to teach through coteaching. New York: Peter Lang.

Roth, W. -M., Tobin, K., Elmesky, R., Carambo, C., McKnight, Y., & Beers, J. (2004). Re/making identities in the praxis of urban schooling: A cultural historical perspective. Mind, Culture, & Activity, 11, 48–69.

Seiler, G. (2002). Understanding social reproduction: The recursive nature of coherence and contradiction within a science class. Unpublished doctoral dissertation, University of Pennsylvania, Philadelphia, PA.

Sewell, W. H. (1992). A theory of structure: Duality, agency, and transformation. American Journal of Sociology, 98, 1–29.

Sewell, W. H. (1999). The concept(s) of culture. In V. E. Bonnell & L. Hunt (Eds.), Beyond the cultural turn: New directions in the story of society and culture (pp. 35–61). Berkeley, CA: University of California Press.

Songer, N. B., Lee, H. S., & Kam, R. (2002). Technology-rich inquiry science in urban classrooms: What are the barriers to inquiry pedagogy? Journal of Research in Science Teaching, 39, 128–150.

Steinberg, S. R. & Kincheloe, J.L. (1998). Students as researchers: Creating classrooms that matter. Bristol, PA: Falmer Press, Taylor & Francis.

Sterba, M. (2003). Respect, struggle and change: Examining the agency of African American female adolescents in city schools. Unpublished doctoral dissertation, University of Pennsylvania, Philadelphia, PA.

Swartz, D. (1997). Culture & Power: The sociology of Pierre Bourdieu. Chicago: University of Chicago Press.

Tobin, K. (2000). Interpretive research in science education. In A. E. Kelly & R. Lesh (Eds.), Handbook of research design in mathematics and science education (pp. 487–512). Mahwah, NJ: Erlbaum.

Tobin, K. (2001). Learning/knowing how to teach science in urban high schools. Educational Horizons, 80, 41–45.

Wassell, B. (2004). On becoming an urban teacher: Exploring agency through the journey from student to first year practitioner. Unpublished doctoral dissertation, University of Pennsylvania, Philadelphia, PA.

Weiss, I. R., Pasley, J. D., Smith, P. S., Banilower, E. R., & Heck, D. J. (2003). Looking inside the classroom: A study of K–12 mathematics and science education in the United States. Chapel Hill, NC: Horizon Research.

# 13

# Schooled Mathematics and Cultural Knowledge

*Guida de Abreu and Tony Cline*

## Cultural nature of mathematical practices

Since the 1980s, research with school children and adults engaged in mathematical activities in and out of school has highlighted the cultural nature of these practices. This research has been the product of a multidisciplinary enterprise with key contributions from anthropologists (Lave, 1988; Pinxten, 1994), sociologists (Restivo, 1998), mathematics educators (D'Ambrosio, 1985; Bishop, 1988) and developmental psychologists (Cole, 1989; Saxe, 1991; Nunes, 1992). A shared view unifying the work of these authors was their understanding of mathematics as a cultural phenomenon. As summarised by Bishop (1988), mathematics needs to be understood 'as a kind of cultural knowledge, which all cultures generate but which need not necessarily "look" the same from one cultural group to another. Just as all human cultures generate language, religious beliefs, rituals, food-producing techniques, etc., so it seems do all human cultures generate mathematics' (p. 180).

Several distinct approaches to conceptualise and investigate the influences of the cultural nature of mathematical knowledge in its learning and uses have emerged. For instance, developmental psychologists drawing on Vygotsky's (1978) ideas have focused on the relationships between culture and mathematical cognition. Their analysis covers two planes:

- the personal plane – addressing the influences of the mathematical tools of different cultures on cognition;
- the interactional plane – addressing the mediating role of experts or old-timers in the transformation of cultural into psychological knowledge.

Mathematics educators and ethno-mathematicians following a 'critical science' tradition focus their analysis on the societal plane. Together, this research addresses Rogoff's (1995) three planes of sociocultural activity covering community, interpersonal and personal processes (see Ivinson & Murphy, 2003 and Gulbrandsen, 2003), but we will argue in this chapter that the aspects of the societal plane foregrounded by psychologists for analysis at the personal and interactional planes need to be expanded.

From: *Pedagogy, Culture and Society*, 11 (1), 2003, pp. 11–30. Reprinted by permission of the publisher (Taylor & Francis Ltd, http://www.informaworld.com).

Developmental psychological research into mathematics learning in specific sociocultural contexts has shown that mathematical activities are both culturally and socially organised. The cultural organisation is seen in the way communities select specific mathematical resources drawing upon specific cultural traditions. Thus, for instance, in the Brazilan sugar-cane-farming community studied by Abreu (1993, 1999), children at school were taught the metric system of measurement and in their family's farming practices they still used an indigenous system based on '*braças*'. Analysis on the personal plane has demonstrated that distinct cultural tools, such as the farmers' measurement system, act as mediators of the psychological activity shaping thinking. Vygotsky's main claim that mental tools shape psychological functioning in the same way as physical tools shape physical interaction with the environment was applied to the area of schooled mathematics.

The cultural organisation is also seen in the way each community of practice defines criteria for knowing. For instance, Abreu found that Brazilian children in school were usually expected to find exact answers to their sums. By contrast, in farming practices most of the time estimated answers were the norm (e.g. in calculating averages, decimals tended to be discounted). In the same vein, when farmers engaged in mathematical practices to solve everyday problems in their farming, such as calculating amounts of fertiliser per area, they used estimations, but they were aware of the need to do exact sums when dealing with banks or with buyers of their harvest. It was also apparent that, although most of the time these norms were implicit, there was a tendency for learning and uses of mathematics to reflect the situated nature of the practices. Thus, for instance, schooled farmers will explain to the researcher that at school they learned to calculate areas using a specific procedure, but in farming they used a different one.

Similar findings were observed within the context of schooled mathematical practices. When in the mathematics classroom, school children tend to select resources they believed to be linked to this practice. Säljö and Wyndhamn (1993) found that Swedish students, when asked to solve postage problems, called on different strategies according to the context in which the task was presented. In a mathematics lesson, most of the students attempted some type of calculation. In a social studies lesson, most of the students found the solution by reading the postage table. Research findings such as those were interpreted as evidence of the situated nature of mathematical cognition. This research, however, says little that is useful about how mathematical cognition becomes socially situated during development. We cannot answer the question – what exactly happens to create influential ideas in children's minds about the social positioning of certain mathematical practices? Anyone involved in human learning will know that very often people bring understanding from previous experiences to make sense of new experiences (for examples in mathematical cognition, see Saxe, 1982, 1991). So, it is puzzling to observe that children who have acquired ways of dealing with mathematical problems in one practice keep this apart from another practice. This is particularly puzzling in circumstances where the mathematics of one practice is functionally equivalent to the other, e.g. when a school child competent in mental arithmetic does not call on this knowledge to support their learning of school written arithmetic (Nunes et al., 1993).

Scholars following the 'critical science' perspective attribute the apparent lack of connection between mathematical knowledge of distinct social practices to the relationship between the social-political order and individual learning. They claim that the value social groups attribute to certain forms of mathematics mediates its ' transmission' and 'appropriation' (D'Ambrosio, 1985; Bishop, 1988). In this perspective, the 'exclusion' of the mathematical knowledge of minority groups, at a societal plane, has a consequence in the personal plane, the building of negative self-esteem and negative cultural identity, which may block access to constructions of mathematical meanings.

To sum up, until recently many authors concentrated their social analysis on the mediating role of the expert in the social structuring of interactions, which will facilitate the reconstruction of cultural tools by individuals. The aim was to provide detailed accounts of how cultural tools, part of the community social plane, are reconstructed by learners, becoming part of their internal psychological plane (Saxe, 1991; Guberman, 1996). This trend again reflects Vygotsky's general law of cultural development. The processes analysed were the growing of mathematical cognitive competence at interpersonal and personal levels. However, it can be argued that it is not enough to focus on 'cultural knowledge as tools for knowing' (or physical and mental artefacts). Next, we wish to explore the complementary notion of 'cultural knowledge as *socially valued* tools or ways of knowing'. This will make it possible to consider in more detail how exactly the social positioning of mathematical practices within a social-political order may influence personal development (and, for example, the formation of children's social identities as users of mathematics).

# Social nature of mathematical practices

From a social representations view (Moscovici, 1998) each mathematical tool/artefact can be seen as having two aspects. One aspect relates to the technological characteristic of mathematics as historically developed tools/artefacts (e.g. counting systems, measuring systems, calculators, etc.). The other aspect relates to the value communities of practice associate with these tools or their valorisation. The value one community attributes to its tools may vary from the value that outside communities attribute to them. This value can also vary between individuals, who have different types of engagement in the practice.

Analytically separating knowing from valuing, however, seems to be very important. Like thought and language one is connected to the other, but at the same time they may follow distinct patterns in their development. Thus, differences in valuing do not necessarily reflect differences in the tools mediating knowing. One tool can be valued in the context of one practice and de-valued in the context of another. The valuing can also change historically because of changes in the needs of societies or social-political pressures. In England, helping children to learn their multiplication tables by heart was at the core of primary mathematics teaching some decades ago, then it went out of fashion, and currently the demands of the National Numeracy Strategy may turn it again into a highly valued tool. If one follows a social representations perspective, the multiplication tables can be seen as a mathematical tool, providing means for action. At the same time, knowing multiplication tables by heart or teaching someone to learn them by heart is not only a means to develop tools for action. The tool is invested with a symbolic value, and therefore mastering or not mastering it also reflects evaluation of the relevance of that particular form of knowing in the context of schooled practices.

Thus, employing the notion of social representation makes it possible to conceive the learning of mathematics at the societal plane in a way that takes account of how the social-political order may influence cultural constructions. An account that highlights social representations addresses the dimension stressed by the critical mathematics educators.

However, that tells only one part of the story. If we are to understand the psychology of mathematical development in full, it is necessary, in addition, to show how the social valorisation of mathematical practices may have an impact on the personal and interactional planes.

# Impact of social representation on the personal and interactional planes

Very few studies have addressed the reconstruction of social representations at the personal level. One exception to this has been the work of Duveen (1997, 2001). Based on their empirical studies on gender development in young children, Lloyd and Duveen (1992) argued that similar social representations can support distinct patterns of personal development. For young children in Western society, representations of gender are objectified in specific cultural artefacts, such as clothes and toys. Lloyd and Duveen found that both boys and girls were equally aware of the gender marking of toys. However, a girl might play with cars knowing that cars are 'male toys' or, vice-versa, a boy may play with dolls knowing that they are 'female toys'. By this stage, children have developed ways of 'identifying the other', knowledge of the given gender identities in their community. However, in addition, their behaviour also shows that they have been engaged in developing 'self-identification'. Thus, when a child resists the pressure to conform to the dominant social representation of her or his gender group, this may not be a reflection of her/his knowledge of gender marking, but the assertion of an identity.

A similar account of development seems to be useful to understand mathematical learning when the mathematics practices at school are different from those at home. When studying the school children in Brazil, Abreu found that most of them knew that sugar-cane farmers used indigenous mathematics in their everyday practices. They were aware of the existence of mathematical practices in the farming community. Indeed, some of them had personal engagement in these practices. However, when asked to categorise practices in terms of use and non-use of mathematics, sugar-cane farming tended to be classified as a setting in which people did not use mathematics. Conforming to the dominant social representation, they attributed no knowledge of mathematics to their home 'illiterate' community. What at first glance could be interpreted as not knowing was in fact a reflection of a deeper social representation that denies the status of knowledge to the mathematical practices of a socially and economically marginalised group. Following on Tajfel (Mosvovici & Paicheler, 1978; Tajfel, 1978), these findings can be taken as evidence that these school children have learned to categorise common social practices of co-existing communities as mathematical and non-mathematical. This categorisation was based on a comparison of the positions occupied by these communities in the overall social structure, rather than on their actual use of mathematical artefacts. Farming mathematics was not seen as mathematics because it was associated with low status. Children's understanding of how communities of practice were identified was, however, just one part of the process. The other part was the evidence that processes of self-identification were also at work and were visible in the school children's different patterns of participation in their home and school practices.

In parallel with the example of the gender identification process described by Lloyd and Duveen, the school children in the farming community, first, had clear markers for 'identifying the other' in relation to the communities of practice co-existing in their social world. Secondly, as in gender identity development, most children from the farming community minimised the differences by not showing preferences for the mathematics associated with the low-status identity (farming mathematics) when interviewed. In doing this, some children were engaging in processes of 'self-identification', which by excluding their home identity could be a potential source of conflicts. This seemed to be particularly relevant for children whose lives required them to engage in both practices. That is, although they denied the status of knowledge to farming mathematics, in their everyday lives they had to work in farming to help their families survive. It follows that children in this situation were more likely to develop mathematical knowledge that could conflict with school mathematics. In the communities studied, out-of-school mathematics was not legitimated by school practices, and children were aware of that.

# Complementary processes of identity formation: an empirical approach

After the publication of Lave and Wenger (1991) and Wenger's (1998) accounts of learning as participation in communities of practice, the interest in the notion of mathematical learning as a process that includes identity development has been growing (Boaler et al., 2000). Wenger justified the introduction of the identity component in his approach to a theory of learning on the basis that it provides 'a way of talking about how learning changes who we are and creates personal histories in the context of our communities' (p. 5). He also argued that a focus on identity extends the social practice accounts in two directions. First, 'it narrows the focus onto the person, but from a social perspective' and, secondly, 'it expands the focus beyond communities of practice, calling attention to broader processes of identification and social structures' (p. 145). These claims are certainly very much in agreement with concerns raised by several scholars about the dominant theories of situated learning as formulated in the last decade (Forman et al., 1993; Goodnow, 1993; Duveen, 1997). Both Wenger and post-Vygotskian scholars share the view that identity formation needs to be conceptualised as located in practice.

Thus, we combined two notions: first, the idea that the development of identities in learning is associated with specific practices and, secondly, the view that social identity formation involves access to social representations. On this basis we developed a framework to study these processes considering:

*The societal plane* – investigation of the social representations of identities associated with mathematical practices ('given identities'). Following Tajfel (1978), this analysis explores social categorisation and social comparison of mathematical practices in terms of the position a community of practice occupies in a wide social structure (institutional or societal).

*The personal plane* – investigation of emerging identities associated with participation in home and school mathematical practices. This analysis is based on children's accounts of their experiences of participation in mathematical practices at school and at home. These accounts cover both their personal elaboration (intrapersonal) and their interactions with teachers, parents and other relatives (interpersonal).

An analysis of social representations is thus combined with an analysis of accounts of how these are reconstructed in individual children's experiences. In our studies with school children in multiethnic primary schools in England, these processes have been explored in the following ways:

*'Identifying the other'* – how children categorise and compare uses of mathematics by other people involved in different practices in their society (such as office workers, children playing, etc.).

*'Being identified'* – how children come to understand the way other people who play a significant role in their lives view their participation in specific mathematical practices (e.g. on what basis a parent thinks they are good or bad at school mathematics).

*'Self-identification'*– how children develop preferences and come to identify themselves as suited to (or the kind of person who does best with) particular mathematical practices.

# 'Identifying the other': investigation of the social representations of identities associated with mathematical practices

In order to illustrate the processes described above, we will draw selectively from findings obtained in studies with school children in multiethnic primary schools (Abreu & Cline, 1998; Abreu et al., 1999, 2002). The studies involved children from British-South-Asian (Bangladeshi and Pakistani) and white-British backgrounds, aged 7–11.

In these studies, we have used sorting tasks to investigate how children categorise and compare uses of mathematics by other people involved in different practices in their society. These tasks involved sorting a set of pictures that represent common practices in the child's society. The set of pictures used in England was planned to include adults (in jobs of different status, e.g. office worker, taxi driver) and children (at home and at school). Taking the pictures as a stimulus, the children were then asked to complete the sequence of tasks detailed in Table 13.1.

The 'Maths Sort' task required classification of the set of pictures into 'mathematical practices' and 'non-mathematical practices'. The choice of 'best–worst' pupil when at school task was designed to explore children's understanding of processes of social comparison.

These tasks were originally developed by Abreu (1993) in order to investigate whether children recognise the use of mathematics outside school and in what circumstances. Her findings suggested that besides providing answers to the initial question, the tasks shed light on children's understanding of the valorisation of mathematical practices. When explaining their sorting, children sometimes provided accounts based on cultural tools (procedures, physical artefacts, contents). At other times, they based their accounts on the social valorisation of activities and roles. That is, sometimes they looked at one aspect of the representation, mathematical knowledge, and sometimes at the other side, the attached social value. Abreu's initial studies were conducted in places where some of the practices outside school still involved people who had very little schooling or were illiterate. These findings, however, have now been replicated in our studies in England. In order to illustrate the processes involved below, we summarise

**Table 13.1   Maths sorting tasks**

| Task | Aim: To investigate children's ... | Basic instructions | Examples of follow-up questions |
|------|-----------------------------------|--------------------|--------------------------------|
| 'Maths sort' | Understanding of situations in which people need to use mathematics | Now I would like you to separate the pictures. On one side of the table put the ones where you think people need to use mathematics, and on the other side the ones where you think people don't need mathematics | Why do you think people need to use mathematics in this group of pictures?<br><br>Why do they not need mathematics in this group? |
| 'Best–Worst Adults' | Beliefs about the links between 'success' and 'failure' in school mathematics and jobs | In these pictures here, who do you think was/is the best pupil in mathematics when they were at school? | Now tell me the reasons for thinking that |
| 'Best–Worst Children' | Beliefs about the links between 'success' and 'failure' in school mathematics and activities | Who do you think was/is the worst pupil in mathematics when they were at school? | |

**Table 13.2   Number of children who believed that the situation required the use of mathematics ($n = 24$)**

| Practices involving children | | Practices involving adults | |
|------------------------------|----|----------------------------|----|
| Two school girls operating a calculator | 23 | Shop assistant (food stall) | 16 |
| A boy measuring the length at home | 17 | Shop assistant (sweets stall) | 15 |
| Two school boys reading a book | 12 | Pharmacist measuring the volume | 13 |
| Young girl weighing sugar in the kitchen | 9 | Pharmacy assistant | 12 |
| Children playing hopscotch in the school playground | 3 | Office administrator | 11 |
| A boy and a girl playing computer games at home | 2 | Taxi driver | 2 |

some findings from Abreu et al. (1999). They were obtained from 24 children and included two ethnic groups (white-British versus Pakistani-British), different levels of school perform-ance in mathematics (high versus low achievement) and three levels of schooling (years 2, 4, 6; i.e. with children aged 7–11 years).

As illustrated in Table 13.2, the children seemed to believe that mathematics is needed more in some social practices than in others. School pupils using the calculator and shop assistants selling products in market stalls were more frequently chosen as people 'using mathematics'. In contrast, playing computer games at home and driving a taxi were less

**Table 13.3   Children's choices of best and worst pupils in school mathematics**

| Practices versus performance children | | | Practices versus performance adults | | |
|---|---|---|---|---|---|
| | **Best** | **Worst** | | **Best** | **Worst** |
| Young girl weighing sugar in the kitchen. | 3 | 14 | Taxi driver | 1 | 11 |
| A boy and a girl playing computer games at home. | 1 | 6 | Office administrator | 9 | 6 |
| Two school girls operating a calculator. | 6 | 2 | Shop assistant (sweets stall) | 6 | 4 |
| A boy measuring the length at home. | 8 | 1 | Shop assistant (food stall) | 3 | 2 |
| Children playing hopscotch in the school playground. | 1 | 1 | Pharmacy assistant | 0 | 1 |
| Two school boys reading a book. | 5 | 0 | Pharmacist measuring volume | 5 | 0 |

often viewed as practices that required the use of mathematics. This was an indication that these children had developed ways of categorising the practices as mathematical or less mathematical. However, it was evident that the criteria they used were not based only on actual use of mathematical knowledge. Otherwise, we could not explain why they thought that the taxi driver did not need mathematics. (The children knew that taxi drivers deal with money, which for them was seen in other contexts as requiring mathematics.) An alternative explanation was to review the children's basis for sorting in terms of their categorisation of groups of people in their social environment.

Table 13.3 summarises children's choices of pictures of the children/adults they thought would be the best and worst pupils in school mathematics. The boy measuring was often seen as the best and the young girl weighing sugar as the worst. For adults, the most popular choice for best was the office administrator (a white-collar profession) and for worst was the taxi driver (blue-collar). Our analysis was designed to examine what processes contributed to the formation of the social representation. The fact that children's choices of best adults tended to privilege white-collar jobs (14 out of 24) and vice versa for the worst (17 out of 24) seemed to be related to the process of social categorisation. For Tajfel (1978), social categorisations are distinct from physical categorisations because the former are often related to 'value differentials', or 'positive or negative evaluations of these categories'. Thus, to follow this line in the interpretation of the data one needs to make sure that children's performance in these tasks indeed involved more than their knowledge of mathematical content. If the categorisations were just based on this aspect, they could just follow the rules of the physical world. When they chose the youngest child in the set of photos as likely to be the worst in maths at school, that is presumably what was happening. The justifications children gave for other choices help to clarify that this was not always the case.

Some interesting evidence emerged in the analysis of children's justifications of their choices. First, children's justifications could be divided into two broad categories:

- related to the activity (mathematical content and artefacts present);
- related to the person in the picture.

Secondly, although both types of justifications were used for both adults and children, the key defining factor in the justifications relating to a person varied. When the actors were children, 'individual characteristics' were the main focus of children's justifications for their choices (e.g. bright, concentrating) and when the actor was an adult, they emphasised a social aspect (e.g. the status of the person's job).

As noted above, age was the main single criterion used in selecting the worst at maths among children. This suggests that children have a developmental theory regarding the acquisition of mathematical competence: an increase in age during childhood can affect mathematical performance. Although age is an individual characteristic, what one is expected to do at particular ages is also socially determined. So, in using the category children were also showing some understanding of these social expectations.

When the children were judging adults, age was no longer a salient feature. When they used it in this study, it still had a developmental dimension, but historical instead of maturational. The two children who used it referred to the resources available at a time when the adult in the photo was a child. More often, the social status of what someone did as a job was used by the children as a reference point when they speculated on school mathematical competence among adults. These observations reinforce the argument that the development of representations of mathematics is a social process, in which children come to understand social categories and the social valuing associated with them.

Table 13.4 summarises the frequency of use of each type of justification. It is clear that justifications that have as a reference point the person (a social category) were used as often as justifications based on the mathematical activity. There were 44 examples of each from the 24 children in the study. In our view, this supports the argument that representations of mathematical practices are based both on specific technological features of mathematics (nature of the activity, artefacts) and on the social value attached to these practices.

To conclude the analysis of how the sorting tasks helped us to understand the 'identification of the other', we introduce a short extract, from an interview with a Year-6 Pakistani boy:

*Interviewer*: Right. Why do you think then that he was the best at maths?
*Child:* Because look at him [office administrator], all wearing flashy clothes and like he looks like a rich … and he's got such a good job, and him, he's … nothing he has to do taxi. (…) Like if he's ain't good at something he'd have been like him [taxi driver], like he's probably not good at anything. (…) He's [taxi driver] probably came from Pakistan.

It is worth noting that in the town where the study took place a substantial proportion of taxi drivers, but by no means all, are from the Pakistani community. We selected this protocol because it seems to illustrate clearly what Tajfel referred to as the distinctive aspect of a social categorisation, that is the presence of 'value differentials' or 'positive or negative evaluations of these categories'; the way these values impact on the construction of social identities. Moscovici and Paicheler (1978) described the impact in the following terms: 'the process of social comparison enables us to understand and predict the existence, on the one hand, of a defensive distinctiveness and, on the other, of an assimilation towards someone who is superior or more legitimate. This assimilation can either imply a devaluation of oneself or it can become protective of one's inner security' (p. 254). In the above

**Table 13.4   Types of justifications for choices of best and worst performances in school mathematics**

| Focus | Type of justification | Task 2 Adult | | Task 3 Child | |
|---|---|---|---|---|---|
| | | Best | Worst | Best | Worst |
| Activity | Type 1: The activity the person is engaged in is seen as requiring or not requiring maths | 10 | 08 | 05 | 08 |
| | Type 2: Presence or absence of a 'mathematical tool' or 'object' (the computer, the taxi, the calculator) | 02 | 02 | 07 | 02 |
| Person (individual characteristic) | Type 3: Behaviour and psychological attributes of the person (e.g. concentrated; clever; knowledgeable; degree of independence) | | | 08 | 02 |
| | Type 4: Age of the children engaged in the activity (young, old, little, small) | | | 03 | 11 |
| Person (social actor) | Types 5: Reference to the importance of the job the person is engaged in (status of professions in the society – or 'social marking') | 08 | 10 | | |
| | Type 6: Age-related opportunities | 01 | 01 | | |
| Not possible to categorise | No clear explanation provided | 03 | 03 | 01 | 01 |

protocol we can see the devaluation of the child's own home background: 'He's probably from Pakistan'. In terms of the phenomenon of social valorisation this is very similar to Abreu's observations of Brazilian children placing a low value on farmers' knowledge. Within our framework the data presented above illustrate how individuals come to understand the social representations of identities associated with mathematics practices in their community. However, as already discussed, there is not a simple relationship between these identities and the specific trajectories of development in individuals. We will tackle this level in the next part of the chapter and will then attempt to address the re-construction of identity through participation in specific practices. We will, therefore, consider the two complementary processes of 'being identified' and 'self-identification'.

# 'Being identified': investigation of emerging identities associated with participation in home and school mathematical practices

In the same way that people give meaning to their social world by attributing social identities to the other, participation in social practices also helps them to develop an understanding of how they themselves are being identified. In practices where the person's participation is compulsory, developmental psychologists have suggested that being identified by the other may in fact be prior to self-identification (see Duveen, 2001). That is, first, the child internalises the community's identity, e.g. gender identity as given in the family, and only later is able to accept or reject this given identity. It is as if, in certain stages of personal development, social identities are extended to the developing person. We believe that we have identified evidence of this process in our interviews with the children. So, for example, since the criteria for success in schooled mathematics is externally given (e.g. by a teacher's judgement, by placing a child in ability groups, etc.), it seems that social identities in mathematics can be based on these external events. Thus, for instance, a pupil may first be identified as being 'good' in school mathematics, and only later come to accept or reject this given identity. The following extracts illustrate how one child understood identities extended to her by significant others. They were obtained in an interview with a 7-year-old girl from a Bangladeshi background. The reports issued by teachers and comparisons with her sister are the girl's basis for evolving a sense of identity in relation to school mathematics:

*I*: You know when you are at school, you know that some of the children are very good at Maths and others are not …
*C*: … my sister, my sister because she goes to Mrs … class for Maths and she doesn't really like Maths.
*I*: She likes it?
*C*: No she doesn't. Because why she doesn't like it, because she's good at English but she ain't good at Maths, and I'm good at Maths but I'm not good at English.
*I*: You're not as good at English?
*C*: Yes.
*I:* Maybe you are …
*C*: No I'm not.
*I*: Why do you think your sister is not good at Maths?
*C*: Because when the report came … it said that I have to try much more better at English and do spellings and everything. (..) When my sister's report came (..) it said on the report that she's not good at Maths because she has to try hard at Maths.

In the sequence of the interview, Sabina's narrative suggests that her father reinforces the identity the school extended to her by associating it with a projected professional identity. Thus, when the interviewer asked her whether difficulties in school mathematics would made a difference when a child grows up, she answered:

*C*: No … She can work in shops …
*I*: So, it does make a difference?

*C*: Yes. She must learn mathematics. This is why I come to school.

*I*: Why do you come to school?

*C*: Because my father says that I must be a doctor when I grow up. I am going to earn lots of money … And, I am also very good at sciences.

Sabina's father confirmed to the interviewer that he talks to her about being a medical doctor. What he seemed to be doing was trying to capitalise on her 'good' performance in school mathematics to start developing her awareness of possible links to future professional identities.

The teachers in the sample did not highlight the impact their reports on a child's achievements might have on the process of identity formation. Parents, however, gave us the impression that they were aware that these reports contribute to the child's understanding of how they are 'being identified'. Furthermore, parents also described explicit attempts to influence a child's awareness of identities that support success in schooled mathematics. For instance, the father of a Year-2 boy who was a low-achiever in maths commented that they have tried to place in his mind the idea 'that you are very clever at maths …' His mother also attempts to influence him by making clear the connection between failure in school mathematics and low-status jobs. So, she commented: 'He knows now, I have told him that if you don't study then you will become a refuse collector. Now he says: Mum, I won't pick rubbish will I? Can you see, I study every day'.

To sum up, we have analysed two sources for children's development of self-identification processes associated with mathematical practices. One source is their understanding of how others are identified, i.e. identities associated with particular communities of practice. The other source is their understanding of how they are being identified, i.e. how significant others (parents, teachers, peers) see their participation in a specific practice. Even from a perspective where social identities are not conceived as fixed, but as being continuously reassessed by the person facing new experiences, the fact that certain stages of development may be critically influenced by the way a person is 'being identified' is of considerable significance. What before was attributed to an innate ability to cope with mathematics can be reanalysed in terms of how certain forms of early identification by others can shape trajectories of learning and development. However, as Lloyd and Duveen have already demonstrated this social process does not necessarily match with the actual self-identifications, which are manifested in the person's preferences for forms of participation.

# Self-identification: the personal preferences

When external identifications are re-constructed by the developing individual in the course of their participation in social practices, they may be expressed through choices and the negotiation of forms of engagement in multiple communities. In our studies in England, we have examined the outcome of this process in terms of children's preferences for learning mathematics at home or at school. Among the 21 children (out of 24) who acknowledged having help with maths at home, 15 said it was different from the way their teachers taught them at school and articulated clear preferences between them. Four types of positioning emerged among the children: a declared preference for school; a declared preference for home; a flexible approach in which school was preferred sometimes and home sometimes; and an understanding of what Kelly (1995) would have called the specific 'range of convenience' of home and school mathematics. The most common type of positioning was a preference for school mathematics. This formation of identity is compatible with (and may perhaps be influenced by) a prevalent view within the school system that hardly acknowledges the distinct role that home mathematical practices can play in children's learning.

The main reasons children gave for their preferences for doing mathematics at home or at school covered cognitive aspects associated with specific properties of the mathematical tools and valorative/affective aspects based on social understandings. Thus, they referred to:

- *The specific mathematics that should be learned* – they expressed judgements about the mathematics they encountered at school and at home. These judgements could have a cognitive basis related to the identification of differences in strategies and methods and whether they were seen as facilitating learning, such as 'they are both right but it's easier to understand the way we do it at school'. Alternatively, they could have a social comparison basis in terms of how each type of knowledge was seen to be valued, such as 'Mum's methods are old-fashioned'.
- *The mediating role of others* – they analysed this role in cognitive terms (e.g. commenting on whose explanations they understood more – 'the more understandable way is probably my dad's way because it gets the same answers but its just easier to understand'), in affective terms (e.g. commenting on whom they felt more at ease asking for help – 'He is too busy [the teacher] he is like rushing around. She [the sister] is not in a rush'), or in social comparison terms (e.g. commenting on who was seen as owning knowledge or competence – ' Because teacher is important').
- *The mediating role of language* – this issue was treated by some Pakistani children at a cognitive level (e.g. commenting on whether they grasped mathematical concepts more easily in one language or other – 'I've learnt more words in English and less in Urdu'). For others, however, language preference had an affective-comparative basis (e.g. defined in terms of the language they felt more confident in – 'when you speak it (Urdu) you feel as if you're in Pakistan and it's got a better tune, and I can speak it well'.

To sum up, the child's preferences provided a window into experiences that were shaping forms of participation and, consequently, into the emergence of distinct trajectories of self-identification. We believe that the picture that emerged in our analysis of the child's preferences offers encouragement for further development of the approach outlined in this chapter. First, it was apparent that the child's preferences can be based both on the cultural nature of mathematics (the recognition that some tools may facilitate or support cognitive operations more effectively than others) and the social nature of mathematics (an understanding of the value-laden nature of the practices). Secondly, it was also apparent that the interpersonal nature of learning practices had an impact in terms of the recognition of the role played by others as mediators – a role that was experienced by learners in cognitive, affective and social comparison terms. Finally, learners also demonstrated the impact of learning practices at the personal level when they expressed personal preferences and showed an understanding of psychological aspects of learning.

# Conclusion

We argued in our introduction that due recognition of the cultural nature of schooled mathematics (and, indeed, any other type of mathematical practices) requires an analysis that locates these practices in their social-political context. Furthermore, we argued that the link between this dimension of the social plane and the personal development of the learner could be theorised in terms of links between social representations of mathematical practices and the development of social identities. The main reason for articulating such an approach is to take into account the social valorisation of mathematical practices, and its impact on the way knowledge is communicated, negotiated and appropriated. One of the interesting aspects of this analysis is that it enables us to explain the emergence of diversity among individuals who apparently participate in similar mathematical practices.

Similar social representations of a mathematical practice offer support for distinct social identities depending on the position that the participants in a practice assume toward it. Thus, for instance, immigrant parents who went to school in their country of origin may share their representations of schooled mathematical practices. For instance, they may share the knowledge of specific mathematical tools such as multiplication tables, they may share knowledge of the methods used in teaching and, finally, they may share an understanding of how these tools are valued in their country of origin in comparison with the host country. However, as research has indicated, the way parents in this situation organise mathematical practices for their children can vary. One of the key elements in explaining why they vary is not the representation in itself, but the position that they assume towards it. By accepting or rejecting a particular valorisation, parents attempt to create trajectories of development for their children. Views on the use of multiplication tables are a good example, because in spite of learning by rote being ostracised till recently in schooled mathematical practices in the United Kingdom, some South Asian parents continued to use it with their children. In conversations with parents, we learned that their adoption of this practice was very often based on comparisons they made with what members of their generation of the family were doing back home with their children. So, what at a surface level may seem no more than the negotiation of knowledge about a tool is, in fact, a complex process involving the negotiation of identities. Parents who follow this strategy indicated that they were, among other things, attempting to give their children the means of being included as participants in their home-culture mathematical practices.

What we have argued in this chapter is that both societal representations and the organisation of practices will provide resources for the personal development of social identities. They provide a framework for 'identifying the other' in relation to the position of various communities in society. So, from a very young age, children develop an understanding that certain mathematical practices are legitimised and others marginalised. Societal representations and the organisation of practices also provide the basis for understanding how one is 'being identified'.

Though we believe that understanding how learners construct their own identities as participants in mathematical practices could contribute to new developments in pedagogy, this research is still in its early days. The possibility that the process of being identified may be prior to self-identification, as illustrated in Sabina's case study, will need to be taken seriously. Among other things it could mean that common practices, such as setting children in 'ability' groups at a very young age, could be contributing to the development of trajectories of development that may exclude certain social identities.

# References

Abreu, G. de (1993) The Relationship Between Home and School Mathematics in a Farming Community in Rural Brazil. Doctoral Dissertation, University of Cambridge.

Abreu, G. de (1999) Learning Mathematics in and Outside School: two views on situated learning, in J. Bliss, R. Säljö & P. Light (Eds) *Learning Sites: social and technological resources for learning*. Oxford: Elsevier Science.

Abreu, G. de & Cline, T. (1998) Studying Social Representations of Mathematics Learning in Multiethnic Primary Schools: work in progress, *Papers on Social Representations*, 7(1–2), pp. 1–20.

Abreu, G. de, Cline, T. & Shamsi, T. (1999) *Mathematics Learning in Multiethnic Primary Schools*, ESRC – R000 222 381. Luton: Department of Psychology, Luton University.

Abreu, G. de, Cline, T. & Shamsi, T. (2002) Exploring Ways Parents Participate in their Children's School Mathematical Learning: case studies in multiethnic primary schools, in G. de Abreu, A. Bishop & N. Presmeg (Eds) *Transitions Between Contexts of Mathematical Practices*. Dordrecht: Kluwer.

Bishop, A. (1988) *Mathematical Enculturation: a cultural perspective on mathematics education*. Dordrecht: Kluwer.

Boaler, J., Wiliam, D. & Zevenbergen, R. (2000) The Construction of Identity in Secondary Mathematics Education, in J. F. Matos & M. Santos (Eds) *Mathematics Education and Society*. Montechoro, Portugal: Centro de Investigação em Educação da Faculdade de Ciências Universidade de Lisboa.

Cole, M. (1989) Cultural Psychology, in J. J. Berman (Ed.) *Cross-cultural Perspectives*, Nebraska Symposium on Motivation. Lincoln: University of Nebraska Press.

D'Ambrosio, U. (1985) *Socio-cultural Basis for Mathematics Education*. Campinas: Unicamp.

Duveen, G. (1997) Psychological Development as a Social Process, in L. Smith, P. Tomlinson & J. Dockerel (Eds) *Piaget, Vygotsky and Beyond*. London: Routledge.

Duveen, G. (2001) Representations, Identities, Resistance, in K. Deaux & G. Philogene (Eds) *Representations of the Social*. Oxford: Blackwell.

Forman, E. A., Minick, N. & Stone, C. A. (Eds) (1993) *Contexts for Learning*. Oxford: Oxford University Press.

Goodnow, J. (1993) Direction of Post-Vygotskian Research, in E. Forman, N. Minick & C. A. Stone (Eds) *Contexts for Learning*. Oxford: Oxford University Press.

Guberman, S. R. (1996) The Development of Everyday Mathematics in Brazilian Children with Limited Formal Education, *Child Development* 67, pp. 1609–1623.

Gulbrandsen, M. (2003) Peer Relations as Arenas for Gender Constructions Among Young Teenagers, *Pedagogy, Culture and Society* 11(1), pp. 113–132.

Ivinson, G. & Murphy, P. (2003) Boys Don't Write Romance: the construction of knowledge and social gender identities in English classrooms, *Pedagogy, Culture and Society* 11(1), pp. 89–111.

Kelly, G. (1995) *The Psychology of Personal Constructs*. New York: W. W. Norton.

Lave, J. (1988) *Cognition in Practice*. Cambridge: Cambridge University Press.

Lave, J. & Wenger, E. (1991) *Situated Learning: legitimate peripheral participation*. Cambridge: Cambridge University Press.

Lloyd, B. & Duveen, G. (1992) *Gender Identities and Education*. London: Harvester Wheatsheaf.

Moscovici, S. (1998) The History and Actuality of Social Representations, in U. Flick (Ed.) *The Psychology of the Social*. Cambridge: Cambridge University Press.

Moscovici, S. & Paicheler, G. (1978) Social Comparison and Social Recognition: two complementary processes of identification, in H. Tajfel (Ed.) *Differentiation Between Social Groups: studies in social psychology of intergroup relations*. London: Academic Press.

Nunes, T. (1992) Ethnomathematics and Everyday Cognition, in D. A. Grouws (Ed.) *Handbook of Research on Mathematics Teaching and Learning*. New York: Macmillan.

Nunes, T., Schliemann, A. & Carraher, D. (1993) *Street Mathematics and School Mathematics*. Cambridge: Cambridge University Press.

Pinxten, R. (1994) Anthropology in the Mathematics Classroom, in S. Lerman (Ed.) *Cultural Perspectives on Mathematics Classroom*. Dordrecht: Kluwer.

Restivo, S. (1998) *Mathematics, Mind and Society*, paper presented at the Mathematics Education and Society Conference, Nottingham, September.

Rogoff, B. (1995) Observing Sociocultural Activity on Three Planes: participatory appropriation, guided participation, and apprenticeship, in J. V. Wertsch, P. Del-Rlo, & A. Alvarez (Eds) *Sociocultural Studies of Mind*. Cambridge: Cambridge University Press.

Säljö, R. & Wyndhamn, J. (1993) Solving Everyday Problems in the Formal Setting: an empirical study of the school as context for thought, in S. Chaiklin & J. Lave (Eds) *Understanding Practice: perspectives on activity and context*. Cambridge: Cambridge University Press.

Saxe, G. B. (1982) Culture and the Development of Numerical Cognition: studies among the Oksapmin of Papua New Guinea, in C. G. Brainerd (Ed.) *Children's Logical and Mathematical Cognition*. New York: Springer Verlag.

Saxe, G. (1991) *Culture and Cognitive Development: studies in mathematical understanding*. Hillsdale, NJ: Lawrence Erlbaum.

Tajfel, H. (1978) Social Categorisation, Social Identity and Social Comparison, in H. Tajfel (Ed.) *Differentiation Between Social Groups: studies in social psychology of intergroup relations*. London: Academic Press.

Vygotsky, L. (1978) *Mind in Society: the development of higher psychological processes*. Cambridge: Harvard University Press.

Wenger, E. (1998) *Communities of Practice: learning, meaning and identity*. Cambridge: Cambridge University Press.

# Index

Page numbers followed by (Figure) or (Table) refer to Figures or Tables, e.g. Academic-Achievers, 154, 155–6 (Figure 11.1), 157, 159

Page numbers shown as roman numerals refer to the Introduction at the front of the book.